CW01347398

Jewish-Christian Dialogue and
the Life of Wisdom

Jewish-Christian Dialogue and the Life of Wisdom

Engagements with the Theology of David Novak

Matthew Levering

continuum

Continuum International Publishing Group
The Tower Building   80 Maiden Lane
11 York Road   Suite 704
London SE1 7NX   New York, NY 10038

© Matthew Levering, 2010

All rights reserved. No part of this publication may be reproduced or transmitted in any form or by any means, electronic or mechanical, including photocopying, recording, or any information storage or retrieval system, without prior permission in writing from the publishers.

British Library Cataloguing-in-Publication Data
A catalogue record for this book is available from the British Library.

ISBN: HB: 978-1-4411-3364-9

Library of Congress Cataloging-in-Publication Data
A catalog record for this book is available from the Library of Congress.

Typeset by Newgen Imaging Systems Pvt Ltd, Chennai, India
Printed in Great Britain by the MPG Books Group, Bodmin and King's Lynn

To Richard John Neuhaus

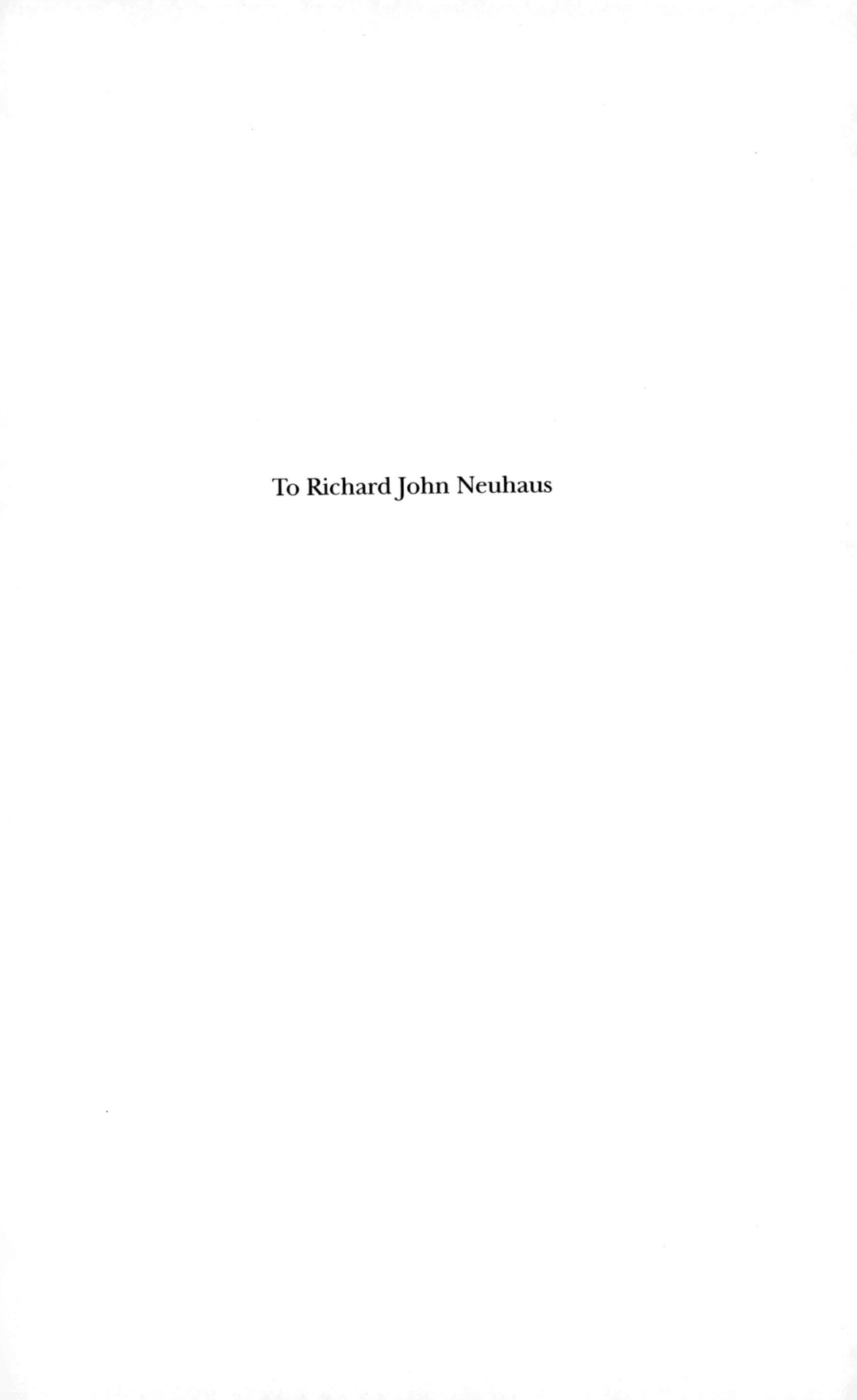

Contents

Foreword	ix
Acknowledgments	xiii
Introduction: In the Footsteps of Rosenzweig and Buber	1
Chapter 1 Supersessionism and Messianic Judaism	12
Chapter 2 Providence and Theonomy	47
Chapter 3 The Image of God	63
Chapter 4 Natural Law and Noahide Law	92
Chapter 5 Election and the Life of Wisdom	115
Conclusion	130
Notes	133
Bibliography	185
Index	195

Foreword

Of course, I am flattered by how deeply and how thoroughly Professor Matthew Levering has engaged my theology. Doesn't every thinker hope to be taken so seriously by another thinker, especially by a thinker from a religion other than one's own, by someone who could have easily said my religion is not his concern? Wouldn't Maimonides, for example, have been flattered to learn of how seriously he was taken by Thomas Aquinas? Yet more than flattered by Professor Levering's engagement of my theology, I very much respect it for its theological authenticity, because it is primarily his Christian theological reflection and only secondarily is it *about* my Jewish theology. It is his sincerely patient effort to learn something important *from* my work *for* his own theological purposes rather than trying to either judge my work *by* his own religious certitude or simply compare it *with* his own theology.

Theology is one's thoughtful reflection on the truth taught by the religion which is his or her own. When one's theology does engage another theology, especially a theology coming from another religion, his or her engagement of that other theology is either disputational or comparative or syncretistic or dialogical.

Any judgment of the theology of a thinker from one religion by a thinker from another religion—whether by a faithful Christian or by a faithful Jew—would have to be disputational, even when not totally dismissive of the religion of the other. Surely, one's faith commitment to his or her own religion requires one to assert the superiority of that religion's truth claims, whether when challenging someone else's religion or when being challenged by someone else's religion. But disputations are only significant events to be taken seriously when the challengers are coming from a position of political strength and those being challenged by them are coming from a position of political weakness. As such, those so offensively challenged can only fearfully defend themselves theologically against the stronger challengers pursuing them. Until recently, almost all Christian engagements of Judaism were disputational; and they were as theologically unsuccessful for the Christians as they were psychologically painful for the Jews. Only triumphalists or masochists could want the disputations as they really were in the past to be restored in the present. Accordingly, anyone who thinks the Jewish-Christian conversation can still be disputational, in the context of contemporary democratic political equality, that person is historically naïve, living in some sort of academic bubble. Happily, Professor Levering is not of their number.

To simply compare the insights of a thinker from one religion with those of a thinker from another religion does not require anyone doing that to have any faith commitment at all. Even if he or she does have any such faith commitment, it has to be suppressed by the comparative theologian for the sake of "objectivity." And, whereas much of the interest of Jews and Christians in each other's theology until recently was disputational, much of the interest of Jews and Christians in each other's theology has more recently been merely informational, employing the supposedly "value free" methods of the social sciences. Yet this type of theology is really "religious studies"; and when it claims to be theology proper, it is as philosophically naïve as any current revival of the old disputational type of theology is historically naïve. Furthermore, this comparative theology lacks the faithful attachment that at least makes the old type of disputational theology still have some vital interest, however misplaced. Happily, Professor Levering is not so theologically detached.

Professor Levering is quite persuasive in his rejection of the syncretistic Jewish-Christian theology of those Jewish converts to Christianity who call themselves "Messianic Jews," and who think they can be a true theological bridge between Christianity and Judaism. When reading his rejection of their arguments for a kind of Jewish-Christian syncretism—which are not really dialogical at all—I am reminded of Leo Strauss' wonderful quip about Spinoza: "He was both a Jew and a Christian and therefore neither." Happily, Professor Levering knows the difference of Christianity and Judaism from each other must be acknowledged for authentic dialogue between us to be possible, let alone sustainable.

In this book, Professor Levering is certainly engaged in authentic theological dialogue that is neither disputational nor comparative nor syncretistic. That is no small accomplishment. Thus, he is not trying to use my Jewish theology to make a case for why his Christian theology is truer or better. And he is not speaking as if there are no real differences between Judaism and Christianity, or that these differences are not about anything of ultimate concern. Instead, he is drawing upon my Jewish theology—and the Jewish tradition to which it is beholden—as a source for the ongoing work that is his by virtue of his being a theologian beholden to the Catholic tradition. Doing this he honors the Jewish tradition and me along with it, since he looks upon us as more than a historical source or influence to be overcome and thus left behind, and since he looks upon us as more than something only "interesting." Instead, we are taken to be important friends *for* him, who are neither a threat nor a curiosity. We are friends who are still here to be consulted in good faith.

Even though Matthew Levering is not Thomas Aquinas but only his posthumous disciple, and even though David Novak is not Maimonides but only his posthumous disciple, nonetheless, both Levering and Novak can look to Aquinas's engagement of Maimonides' theology as an exemplar to be emulated. What has always struck me about Aquinas' engagement of Maimonides in the *Summa Theologiae* is how dialogical it truly was, for Aquinas treated Maimonides' theology as one from which he could learn much rather than treating it as something superseded by his (or any) Christian theology, hence to be put down whenever he could. That does not mean there weren't disagreements between Aquinas and Maimonides, yet they are not different from the disagreements with those with whom Aquinas had theological commonality (like Anselm) or those with whom he had philosophical commonality (like Aristotle). And, when it came to Aquinas's engagement of Maimonides' theology of the Torah (for Aquinas, "the Old Law"), their agreements far outnumbered their disagreements. "Rabbi Moses," as Aquinas respectfully called him, was almost as much Aquinas' teacher (which is what a *rabbi* is) as was Augustine. Moreover, Maimonides himself, in a famous legal responsum, ruled that Jews may teach Torah to Christians, even with traditional Jewish interpretations, because Christians (like Jews, but unlike Muslims) accept the whole Torah as divine revelation. Or, as an old rabbinic legend had it: the representatives of non-Jewish communities are welcome to take home as much of the Torah as they want, since the Torah is not the hidden private possession of the Jews.

How Professor Levering engages my theology for his own theological agenda reminds me of how I have engaged Christian theologians like Thomas Aquinas and Karl Barth for my own theological agenda. I think that by so engaging them, rather than arguing against them or only noticing them, I have truly honored them, and in an authentically Jewish way. Maimonides and earlier Jewish teachers have taught us to learn truth from whoever has uncovered it, and to be explicitly grateful to them for it.

That God has enabled Matthew and me to engage each other's theology, both in writing and in face-to-face dialogue, for that I am profoundly grateful. That gratitude is like my gratitude for the similar dialogue I enjoyed for over 20 years with our mutual friend, the recently departed Father Richard John Neuhaus, to whose memory Matthew has dedicated this book. And I am most grateful for the way God has enabled Matthew and me, both separately and together, to seek the truth that belongs to neither of us nor to any other human being, truth that is still being revealed until the end of days to all who truly seek it here and now in this world.

David Novak

Acknowledgments

The opportunity to begin work on this book came about through the good offices of the Center for Ethics and Culture at the University of Notre Dame, which awarded me the Myser Fellowship for 2006–2007. I am grateful for David Solomon's encouragement, and also for conversations with my friends Michael Dauphinais, Barry David, and especially Rabbi David Dalin that led to the book. Kirsty Schaper, Tom Kraft, and Tom Crick at Continuum skillfully guided the manuscript to publication. Given my conviction that the wellbeing of Christian theology requires constant dialogue with Jewish exegesis, philosophy, and theology, I am grateful to have had the chance to discuss things that matter with David Novak. While at Ave Maria University I was able to host David for a conference in February 2006 and, 2 years later, for a few days in Naples where we enjoyed meals together and sketched a prospectus for future Jewish-Christian dialogue on a napkin—may God bring it to fruition! The book was much improved by corrections made by Daniel Keating, as well as by David Novak, who generously read the entire first draft. I wish to thank *The Thomist*, and especially its managing editor Gregory LaNave, for publishing a version of Chapter 3. For supporting a theological climate in which Jewish-Christian dialogue is valued, I am particularly indebted to Chuck Van Hof, Reinhard Hütter, Bruce Marshall, Richard Schenk, O.P., Thomas Joseph White, O.P., Russell Hittinger, Francis Martin, Gregory Reichberg, Gregory Vall, Francesca Murphy, Mary Healy, Michael Novak, Kendall Soulen, Markus Bockmuehl, Holly Taylor Coolman, Robert Louis Wilken, and many others whose labor has made a difference. My beloved Joy Levering made the work possible, and she put together the Bibliography with our newborn Lucy Joy Levering on her lap. In addition to my particular debt to David Novak, I am especially indebted, as regards the path that led me to this book, to Pope John Paul II's exemplary witness to Jewish-Christian dialogue and to Fr. Richard John Neuhaus, who for nearly 20 years led the monthly journal *First Things* and put Jewish-Christian dialogue at the forefront of his concerns. Between 2004 and 2008, I was able to come to know and love Father Neuhaus.

When he died in January 2009, the world lost a great light. I recall a conversation in which we discussed whether the bodily form that we have in this life will remain, recognizably, in heaven. Now he knows the answer. May he rejoice in the peace of the Lord!

Introduction: In the Footsteps of Rosenzweig and Buber

Writing to his friend Eduard Strauss in 1920, Franz Rosenzweig warned, "Jewish study and teaching, Jewish learning and education—they are dying out among us. . . . Since the time of Moses Mendelssohn and Leopold Zunz our Jewish learning no longer has the courage to be itself, but instead runs at a respectful distance behind the learning of the 'others.'"[1] What Rosenzweig sought was authentic Jewish discussion, rooted in shared desire to learn about what it means to be a Jew. His letters reveal his strenuous effort to open up such discussion with Martin Buber, with whom he collaborated on a German translation of the Hebrew Bible. For Buber "God is not a law-giver"; rather than observing Torah, therefore, Buber accepted "only what I think is being spoken to me."[2] In contrast with Rosenzweig's emphasis on the Jewish liturgy, Buber—whose teachings inspired a book-length study by Hans Urs von Balthasar[3]—famously located the meaning of Judaism in "Emunah," the faith or trust that flows from an I-Thou relationship with God.[4]

Not only did Rosenzweig and Buber succeed in sparking the Jewish discussion that Rosenzweig sought, but also their contributions bore fruit in the development of Jewish-Christian dialogue. In this regard, David Novak highlights three aspects of Buber's 40-year dialogue with the Protestant theologian Paul Tillich. First, Buber's and Tillich's dialogue "was not an 'argument' in the sense that one side was convinced that it had the truth and that all it had to do was break down the intellectual resistance of the other side."[5] Second, both thinkers accepted that the Bible speaks truth and that much biblical truth remains to be discovered by theological inquiry. Third, both thinkers embraced the tradition of philosophical investigation. Given these three aspects, Novak concludes that Buber and Tillich "vividly demonstrated that the most intellectually enriching Jewish-Christian dialogue may well be the open philosophical exegesis of Scripture, in which both Jews and Christians have—in one way or another—heard God's word."[6]

In dialogue with Novak's theology, I seek to undertake for our day just such "open philosophical exegesis of Scripture." Chapter 1 inquires into whether theological dialogue between Christians and Jews is in fact possible, not only in itself but also as regards the recent emergence of vibrant communities of Messianic Judaism. I explore these topics by examining David Novak's treatment of supersessionism and Messianic Judaism, in light of Mark Kinzer's recent proposal that Messianic Judaism opens a path beyond Christian supersessionism.

Regarding supersessionism itself, Kendall Soulen influentially distinguishes between the three kinds of "supersessionism," economic, punitive, and structural. Economic supersessionism holds that because Israel merely prefigures Christ, whereas the Church is fully the Body of Christ, "Everything that characterized the economy of salvation in its Israelite form becomes obsolete and is replaced by its ecclesial equivalent."[7] Punitive supersessionism adds to economic supersessionism the view that "God abrogates God's covenant with Israel (which is already in principle outmoded) on account of Israel's rejection of Christ and the gospel."[8] Structural supersessionism goes even further by reading Israel out of the Christian proclamation of the Gospel. Rather than attending to the history of Israel with YHWH, Christians jump from Adam directly to Christ, from the Creator to the Trinity, and so forth. Soulen comments, "Israel's history is portrayed as nothing more than *the economy of redemption in prefigurative form*. So construed, Israel's story contributes little or nothing to understanding how God's consummating and redemptive purposes engage human creation in universal and enduring ways."[9]

As a solution, Soulen suggests going back to the attitude of the "apostles and elders" (Acts 15.6) who debated Paul and Barnabas's view that circumcision is not necessary for the salvation of converted gentiles. Soulen argues that the apostles and elders "take it for granted that Jewish followers of Jesus remain obligated to the Torah; at the same time they rule that Gentile followers of Jesus are obligated to observe only the Noachide law. In back of this decision is the belief that what God has done in Jesus engages Jews as Jews and Gentiles as Gentiles."[10] This view is Mark Kinzer's as well, and it provides the foundation for Kinzer's proposal to overcome supersessionism through a bilateral *ekklesia*, Jewish and gentile, in which the Jewish believers in Jesus also affirm and practice Rabbinic Judaism (as Messianic Jewish congregations already do).[11] By contrast, indebted particularly to Novak,

I propose in Chapter 1 that Christian theological responses to supersessionism need to preserve both the Church's development of doctrine and Rabbinic Judaism's ability to define its own boundaries. Christian anti-supersessionism requires a deeper understanding of creation and providence, so that the covenantal relationship of Israel with YHWH is not negated by Messianic fulfillment but rather is all the more seen to participate in and embody divine wisdom.[12]

In accord with the first chapter's proposal for Jewish-Christian dialogue, I undertake constructive philosophical theology in dialogue with Novak in the middle three chapters. Jewish-Christian dialogue at its best will enrich the reflection of both Jews and Christians upon central biblical teachings. These chapters, therefore, address the biblical portrait of who we are and how we should live, under the rubrics of divine providence/theonomy, the image of God, and natural law. The chapters place Novak's broadly Maimonidean perspective in conversation with Thomas Aquinas. As in my earlier works of Thomistic theology, my purpose is not historical but contemporary: Novak exemplifies the path of theological *ressourcement* that illumines (in Randi Rashkover and Martin Kavka's words) "the correlation between a philosophy of human nature and a theology of covenantal life," and contemporary Christian theology should learn from Novak's path.[13] As David Burrell observes regarding faith in the free Creator: "absent such an operative belief, sustained by a community of faith, we lack a coherent account of the freedom we prize and require to sustain our human community."[14] This point takes on its full dimensions within the effort of these chapters to spell out what true freedom, in light of the relationship of creatures to the loving Creator, involves.

If these middle chapters advance Jewish-Christian dialogue on what it means to be creatures of the living God, Chapter 5 asks whether Christians and Jews would do better to bracket our covenantal commitments in pursuing such wisdom. I consider two (quite different) Jewish alternatives to Novak's approach: Harold Bloom's *Where Shall Wisdom Be Found?* and Leon Kass's *The Beginning of Wisdom*. Drawing upon Novak's work, I argue that in the face of suffering and death, God's covenantal election makes possible hope, lacking which the quest for wisdom runs aground. It follows that covenantal commitments stand at the center rather than the periphery of Jewish-Christian dialogue that seeks wisdom about the relationship of humankind, in history, to God. A theocentric doctrine of election, about which Novak has written profoundly, thus undergirds the work not only of this final chapter, but of the whole book.

The Goals of Jewish-Christian Dialogue

Even so, given that covenantal commitments divide (as well as unite) Christians and Jews, can the book's approach succeed?[15] Discussing Alasdair MacIntyre's account of how rival traditions of enquiry interact, Miroslav Volf remarks, "To earn one's bread by fine-tuning one's own tradition in constructive disagreement with other traditions is not the worst thing that can happen to you. But what do such fine-tuned, intelligent disagreements mean for warring people and the excluded needy? They may even make the ideological weapons of their destruction more deadly."[16] Volf suggests that a better path for dialogue consists in focusing not on the "coherence and comprehensiveness" of one's tradition, but rather on the "piecemeal convergences and agreements" that diverse traditions can attain.[17] He defends this position on the grounds that while Christianity is not amorphous, neither is it a "coherent tradition" in MacIntyre's sense: "The Scriptures come to us in the form of plural traditions. The texts and the underlying 'story of the history' which unites them . . . do not offer a coherent tradition. Instead, they demand a series of interrelated basic commitments—beliefs and practices. These commitments *can be developed* into traditions."[18] Without abandoning basic Christian commitments, then, the goal is to forge "hybrid traditions" that foster mutual enrichment.[19]

The separation that Volf makes between "beliefs and practices" and "traditions," however, poses difficulties not only for Christianity but also, I think, for Judaism. Granted that "beliefs and practices" develop over time, it does not follow that their development thereby *constitutes* "traditions." Put another way, why should "beliefs and practices" have priority over "traditions?" Admittedly, as Michael Fagenblat and Nathan Wolski point out, "Jewish life has accommodated a vast and contradictory set of interpretations while achieving unity through normative practices."[20] But these contradictory interpretations belong within an equally important set of affirmations about what traditionally counts as Jewish beliefs and practices. Augustine Di Noia's understanding of "traditions," drawn from George Lindbeck's approach, seems more descriptively adequate: "Each of the world's great religions seems to direct its adherents to some ultimate aim of life. . . . The traditions of religious communities are practical and comprehensive in this sense. They foster distinctive patterns of life to which their members strive . . . to conform, in view of some definition of the true aim of life."[21]

Here Franz Rosenzweig can also help. If for Buber philosophical exegesis is crucial, for Rosenzweig, as Novak notes, "Judaism alone saves Christianity from Gnosticism in all its guises,"[22] because of Judaism's emphasis on embodiedness and on the liturgy's role in the mediation of Jewish tradition. One thinks of the anti-Jewish theology of Friedrich Schleiermacher and Adolph von Harnack (although Rosenzweig recognizes that it is not only Christianity that needs saving from Gnostic elements).[23] As Peter Leithart observes with regard to Schleiermachian Christian theology: "Two of the key ingredients of theological liberalism were adherence to what Stephen Sykes has called the 'inwardness tradition' and a sharp, quasi-Marcionite separation of Christianity and the religion of the Old Testament."[24] The influence of this "inwardness tradition," found not only in Christianity but in varieties of Judaism, should inspire Christians and Jews to recover, in and through Jewish-Christian dialogue, a richer appreciation of revelation as the inbreaking of the living God.[25]

If Christian theology benefits from attention to theologies (such as Rosenzweig's) that arise from within postbiblical Judaism, however, is this different from the formation of a "hybrid tradition" that Volf urges? At issue is the nature of the "coherence and comprehensiveness" of traditions: are they open to the dialogic enrichment that Volf desires, without thereby becoming hybrids? I imagine that Volf would agree that the answer is yes, so long as no tradition imagines that "comprehensiveness" means having an exhaustive apprehension of truth. If both traditions understand their "comprehensiveness" to be open to enrichment, then mutual dialogic quest for truth enhances the peace that Volf seeks between competing traditions, without forming a "hybrid tradition." It is true, of course that the discovery of the coherence of another tradition can lead to conversion. The goal of dialogue is deeper appropriation of truth, not the conversion of one's dialogue partner, but true dialogue is not antithetical to conversion. Thus, while rejecting conversion as the *goal* of dialogue, Novak, like Maimonides, welcomes the conversion of Christians to Judaism.[26] Similarly, Joseph Ratzinger insists that dialogue "aims at conviction, at finding the truth; otherwise it is worthless," and so he denies that dialogue replaces missionary activity, as if conversion were obsolete.[27] In this light, focusing on attaining "piecemeal convergences and agreements" (as Volf recommends) does not lessen the theological character of the practice of Jewish-Christian dialogue.

Guided by theocentric "philosophical exegesis of Scripture," the practice of Jewish-Christian dialogue "relocates man within his genuine being: that is, his relationship to God" (to use Pierre Hadot's description of monastic spirituality).[28] But why is there a special need for Jews and Christians to undertake this "relocation" together? With this question in mind, Cardinal Walter Kasper eloquently states the principles that inform this book:

> Jews and Christians—for so long adversaries when not merely indifferent to each other—should strive to become allies. They have a great common heritage to watch over: the common image of the human person, its unique dignity and responsibility before God, the understanding of the world as creation, the concept of justice and peace, the worth of the family, and the hope of definitive salvation and fulfillment.[29]

Even so, why "Jews and Christians" rather than others? The experience of the Shoah privileges the practice of Jewish-Christian dialogue, despite the importance of other dialogues such as the "triadic context" (Jews, Christians, and Muslims) recommended by Reinhard Hütter and, in a series of studies, by David Burrell.[30] As Giuseppe Laras remarks, "Let us not forget that in the past century, in the heart of the European continent that some thought the most civilized, we witnessed the explosion of the Shoah, with its burden of suffering and death—and the idea of dialogue came as a consequence of the Shoah."[31]

For Christians, the practice of Jewish-Christian dialogue also affirms what John Paul II, commenting on the Second Vatican Council's *Nostra Aetate* (§4), said so well during his historic visit to the Synagogue of Rome (April 13, 1986): "the Church of Christ discovers her 'bond' with Judaism by 'searching into her own mystery.' The Jewish religion is not 'extrinsic' to us, but in a certain way is 'intrinsic' to our own religion. With Judaism, therefore, we have a relationship which we do not have with any other religion."[32] John Paul goes on to call Jews the "dearly beloved brothers" and "elder brothers" of Christians.[33] Interpreting John Paul's address to the Synagogue of Rome, Bruce Marshall remarks, "In this covenant with the God of Israel, the Church, to be sure, believes that she shares to the fullest possible degree—but not to the exclusion of the covenant's firstborn, the Jewish people. From this shared blessing of God's covenantal love arises, John Paul also suggests, the unique intimacy of the Church with the Jewish people."[34] This intimacy goes beyond what is possible for perspectives on Christianity and Judaism that see either (or both) as solely "politico-historical" realities.[35]

Speculative and Practical Theology

Since Novak does not separate his more speculative or theoretical discussions from practical implications,[36] let me conclude this Introduction by surveying ways a recent essay by Novak on the status of embryonic life displays the concerns of each of my book's five chapters. I first summarize Novak's essay and then briefly correlate its concerns with my chapters.

Novak treats the manufacture and destruction of embryonic stem cells from within the Jewish theological conception of Noahide law, which Novak considers under the rubric of natural law (see my Chapter 4 for a detailed discussion). Included within Noahide law is the prohibition "of shedding the blood of innocents (*shefikhut damim*)."[37] For a society to observe Noahide/natural law, the society must recognize "in its positive law and public policies that the human persons who live in that society or come into contact with it in any way have an essentially transcendent orientation that makes them inviolable."[38] Indeed, Noahide/natural law goes further: it is a duty, if possible ("short of sacrificing one's own life"), to rescue an innocent person from being killed.[39] For this reason Novak requires that "respect for the inherent dignity of all human life, at whatever stage of its development, be consistently affirmed and implemented."[40]

What about the Talmud's view that the embryo does not receive "form" until the 40th day of gestation? For the Talmud, prior to receiving form, the embryo lacks human status, because it is "'mere water.'"[41] Does this mean that abortion (or the killing of an embryo for research or other purposes) is acceptable prior to the 40th day of gestation? Novak first examines the contexts in which the great Talmudic commentator Rashi employs this understanding of the unformed embryo, and he finds that the cases apply to issues far removed from the actual killing of an embryo.[42] Indeed, he cites the medieval Jewish jurist and theologian Nahmanides as holding that "one should even violate the Sabbath or Yom Kippur to save a fetus that is less than forty days old"[43]: if this is the case, then surely the abortion of such a fetus would not be permitted. Furthermore, he argues that the status of the unformed embryo as "mere water" never takes on the role of a Talmudic principle, and thus seems to assume the Aristotelian biology of the era during which the Talmud was composed.[44] Since this biology has been shown to be in error, Jewish ethicists can no longer view the embryo as "mere water."[45] Instead, as Novak asks rhetorically to his fellow Jewish ethicists, "Does our reverence for human life as the image of God not require that we treat every human life, even the minuscule human life of the newly conceived embryo, with what the tradition calls 'human dignity' (*kvod ha-beriyot*)?"[46] Answering in the affirmative, he adds that this requirement can be known philosophically in addition to being confirmed by Jewish theology.

Even supposing that the status of the embryo as "mere water" meant that Jewish law permits abortion prior to 41 days of gestation, a position with which Novak disagrees, one could still identify other reasons for prohibiting it. Among these reasons is the devaluation of sexuality that occurs when men and women treat the embryo as property "which they may either keep or dispose of at will."[47] This view of the embryo as property ignores the fact that the free action of the man and the woman brought the embryo into being, and therefore the man and the woman have a responsibility to protect it from abuses of power. Novak identifies a rabbinic *responsum* by the seventeenth-century Jewish jurist Hayyim Yair Bachrach, who holds that the embryo's status as "mere water" stands as a legal reason in favor of abortion, but who nonetheless reaches the same conclusion as does Novak regarding abortion's impermissibility. Without ruling that abortion is contrary to Jewish law, Bachrach rules that abortion is not permissible, on the grounds that it fosters sexual immorality.[48]

As Novak points out, the clearest rabbinic prohibitions of abortion occur in the context of midrash of Gen. 9.6, "Whoever sheds the blood of man, by man shall his blood be shed; for God made man in his own image." For Novak this verse exemplifies what is meant by a Noahide law, since "[t]he prohibition of killing the innocent in Gen. 9.6 is presupposed rather than directly proscribed, and even the punishment set down for such killing is not a direct prescription."[49] For this reason, in the Mosaic law God repeats this Noahide law as the commandment "thou shalt not murder" (Exod. 20.13), thereby making the law into "a commandment (*mitsvah*) in the full covenantal sense for Jews."[50] When the rabbis interpreted this verse, they read "man by man" (*adam ba'adam*) as describing the unborn child in the womb: *adam ba'adam* "refers not to the human judges who are to execute murderers but to a human life that is still contained within another human life—that is, the body of his or her mother."[51] Novak thus arrives at his judgment that elective abortion is morally wrong on the basis not only of the written and oral Torah, including the commandment "thou shalt not murder," but also on the basis of Noahide or natural law, which can be apprehended (and debated) philosophically.

What about Exod. 21.22, "When men strive together, and hurt a woman with child, so that there is a miscarriage, and yet no harm follows, the one who hurt her shall be fined?" According to this precept, when the woman miscarries but does not herself suffer harm, the punishment for causing the miscarriage is a monetary fine rather than capital punishment, which is the punishment for murder (Lev. 24.17; cf. Exod. 21.23). Does this mean that the infant-in-the-womb is not considered a human being? As Novak remarks, when the Talmudic distinguishes between the punishment merited by killing an infant-in-the-womb and the punishment merited by killing an infant who has been born, the Talmud affirms "that abortion is not considered to be the equivalent of infanticide with regard to capital punishment."[52] But, Novak emphasizes, this leniency in punishment does not mean that the Talmud condones abortion.

Following rabbinic tradition, Novak holds that abortion to save the life of the mother is permissible. Even here, however, Novak observes that the rabbinic permission of abortion in this situation requires that the life of the mother truly be at stake, as it often used to be before the advent of Caesarian section surgery. He considers that "this kind of abortion has almost never been a moral option for at least the past fifty or more years in countries such as Canada and the United States,"[53] where doctors trained in Caesarian section surgery are easily available. But Novak agrees with the Talmud and with the great medieval commentator Rashi that a "fetus whose existence directly threatens the life of its mother" may rightly be killed in the womb, even though in no other case may the fetus be killed.[54]

How does this view not conflict with the fetus's possession, which Novak has already affirmed, of the "most basic human right: the right to life?"[55] If the fetus is a human being, would not killing of the fetus be forbidden by Gen. 9.6 and elsewhere, as well as by natural law? Returning to the Talmud, Novak finds that the rabbis appealed to the principle of self-defense, a principle that "is extended to a third party, who is required to save a would-be murder victim (*nirdaf*) from his or her assailant."[56] Killing the assailant is permitted if it is the only way to save the would-be victim. Obviously, as Novak says, "The question is whether the would-be murderer or pursuer (*rodef*) needs to be a person whose pursuit of the would-be victim or 'the pursued' (*nirdaf*) is acting out of free choice."[57] Can an infant-in-the-womb, who intends no harm, be treated as an assailant and justifiably killed? According to the Talmud, Novak states, the answer is yes: one must save the life of the would-be victim, no matter what the condition of the human being threatening the would-be victim's life. (The case is different, Novak adds, with "partial-birth" abortion. This is so because once the baby has partially emerged from the womb, the rescuer is equidistant from both the mother and the baby, and therefore cannot privilege one over the other.)

The life-of-the-mother exception to the prohibition of direct abortion, an exception that involves only a tiny number of cases, has also been advocated by many Protestant theologians, including Gilbert Meilaender and Kendall Soulen, who otherwise consider abortion illicit.[58] No matter how one weighs the competing claims of mother and baby, of course, abortion always is directed to killing the innocent. Can it be right to kill any innocent human being?[59] Rightly answering in the negative, John Paul II's encyclical *Evangelium Vitae* states, "All human beings, from their mothers' womb, belong to God who searches them and knows them, who forms them and knits them together with his own hands, who gazes on them when they are tiny shapeless embryos and already sees in them the adults of tomorrow whose days are numbered and whose vocation is even now written in the 'book of life' (cf. Ps. 139.1,13–16)."[60] Even a good purpose cannot justify abortion. Indeed, as Novak reminds us, "the covenant theologies of both Judaism and Christianity provide a more profound basis for the 'right to life' by emphasizing not only the immanent dignity of man, but even more, the transcendent sanctity of the human person, to whom, of all his creatures, God has chosen to reveal his presence. Even the unborn can be the subjects of revelation (Jer. 1.5; Ps. 139.13–16)."[61]

How are these practical reflections on embryonic life linked to my concerns in this book? Chapter 1 takes up the question of how Jews and Christians properly speak together despite our covenantal disagreements, thus making possible—as Novak shows—a shared testimony against contemporary abortion law. In light of the doctrine of divine providence, chapter 2 addresses the theme of theonomy, which grounds Novak's rejection of abortion law's autonomous ethics. Chapter 3 explores how to articulate what constitutes the "image of God"; recall Novak's appeal to "our reverence for life as the image of God." Given the significance of Noahide law for Novak's understanding of abortion, Chapter 4 engages the relationship of Noahide law, natural law, and Mosaic law. Chapter 5 returns from a different angle to the concerns raised in Chapter 1: Why should covenantal commitments, given their apparent divisiveness, guide the life of wisdom sought by Jews and Christians?

What is at stake in the present book is thus not only whether Novak's Jewish theology instructs Christians by its resources and conclusions, or whether Christians and Jews can dialogue constructively about the human creature's stance vis-à-vis the Creator. At stake also is whether any avowedly Jewish or Christian understanding of human life is worthy of public consideration. The biologist Richard Dawkins voices the suspicion of many contemporary academics: "I have yet to see any good reason to suppose that theology (as opposed to biblical history, literature, etc.) is a subject at all."[62] Insofar as theology—including philosophical theology—derives its principles from divine revelation, theology requires covenantal commitments. My engagement with Novak's work aims to make clear that theology is indeed a rational "subject," and thereby to strengthen Christian and Jewish public commitment to living as God's creatures destined for eternal life, rather than as autonomous selves destined for everlasting death.

Moreover, in seeking together to articulate what it means to be creatures of the Creator God who makes covenant, Christians and Jews gain a friendship rooted in shared affirmations about God and humans. In such friendships, as David Burrell says, believers find "the paradigm for sustaining a relationship beyond disagreements."[63] Such friendships bear fruit in this world by contributing to true human flourishing. May God complete them by making us perfectly his friends in everlasting life.

Chapter 1

Supersessionism and Messianic Judaism

Jewish-Christian dialogue begins with the question of "supersessionism," that is, what happens when Christian theologies leave no theological space for Judaism or Jewish theologies leave no theological space for Christianity—due to the Christian proclamation that Jesus of Nazareth is the Son of God incarnate who fulfills God's covenant with Israel and reconfigures Israel around himself. Recently, however, the emergence of numerous communities of "Messianic Jews" or "Jewish Christians" who profess faith in Jesus as Israel's Messiah and nonetheless continue to observe Torah has challenged the standard separations. Could Messianic Judaism be the path by which God wills to overcome supersessionism?

Although I think the answer is no, many Christian theologians disagree with me. George Lindbeck holds that "Jesus Christ fulfills, though he does not replace, the Torah as God's communally and universally normative self-revelation."[1] Surveying the history of supersessionism, Lindbeck highlights the importance of the decades after the destruction of the Temple in 70 AD, when "gentile Christians increasingly looked askance at the continued Torah observance of their Jewish fellow believers."[2] The result, he suggests, was a weakening of the "unity-and-community-building power" of the Holy Spirit through the Scriptures, since if God could annul his covenant with Israel he could also revoke the election of the gentiles. Lindbeck draws the conclusion that there is a "need for Torah-observant Jewish participation in the church if it is to be truly Israel in the new age."[3] As he is aware, this conclusion poses a challenge both to the Church and to Rabbinic Judaism:

> What the rabbis did to make the Jews in diaspora an interconnected people, the catholics did for the gentile Christians. Both went far beyond their common scripture, and they did so in different directions, one by means of the oral Torah, and the other through the New Testament. Yet each group lived in the world of Israel's story and of Israel's God and

claimed to be his chosen people. They thought their claims were mutually exclusive, but the Bible is a capacious instrument of God's Spirit: it bestowed its unity-and-community-building power on both.[4]

In other words, Lindbeck holds that the Church and Rabbinic Judaism should recognize that their claims regarding election and salvation are not "mutually exclusive": a deeper "unity-and-community," manifested by Torah-observant Jewish Christians within the Church, can arise from "the world of Israel's story."

Lindbeck's position is echoed by Markus Bockmuehl. Like Lindbeck, Bockmuehl points to the late first century and second century AD, when Christianity became a gentile reality rather than remaining within the domain of Judaism. By contrast to the Jewish Christians of the apostolic generation, who undertook "at great personal cost a Jewish welcome of Noahide Gentiles as Gentiles,"[5] later gentile Christians (exemplified, Bockmuehl finds, by anti-Jewish Church Fathers) refused to welcome Jews as Jews. In his view, modern Christians have the chance to reverse this error by welcoming Jews who, as in the apostolic generation, both observe Torah and acclaim Jesus as the Messiah. Aware of the difficulties posed for both Christians and Jews by Messianic Judaism, Bockmuehl argues that reflection on Messianic Judaism is "crucial for any further substantive progress in contemporary Christian-Jewish understanding."[6] Such reflection, he suggests, will enable Christians to recover the apostolic generation's memory of Jesus, who accomplishes the restoration of Israel and manifests God's fidelity to his covenant precisely as the Messiah and Lord of Israel. As Bockmuehl observes, what is distinctly Christian needs to be learned from within the Jewish context and therefore always in relationship to what is distinctly Jewish (no longer abrogated by supersessionism). On this view, Messianic Jews stand at the center of renewed Jewish-Christian dialogue: "Jewish believers in Jesus who remain faithful to their Jewish identity are in a unique position to attest, cement, and protect both what is shared and what is distinctive in this unique relationship."[7]

Does Messianic Judaism hold the key to a Jewish-Christian dialogue that is not undermined from the outset by Christian supersessionism? In this chapter, I first set forth David Novak's understanding of supersessionism and of the status of Torah-observant Jewish believers in Jesus. As a second step, I survey Mark Kinzer's proposal for a Messianic Judaism that would enable the Church to overcome supersessionism. Although I find Kinzer's work significant for dialogue among Christians, I argue that Jewish-Christian dialogue should instead follow Novak's evaluations of supersessionism and of Messianic Judaism. By exploring strategies for overcoming supersessionism, this chapter prepares the way for the book's constructive Jewish-Christian dialogue about the human person as created by God.

David Novak on Supersessionism

Edith Stein, Supersessionism, and Jewish-Christian Dialogue

Discussing the conversion (from the Jewish perspective, the apostasy) of Edith Stein from Judaism to Christianity, Novak observes that "[h]er logic was clearly supersessionist."[8] By supersessionism, Novak means the view that Christianity "solves the problems of Judaism better than Judaism can do without Christianity because Christianity provides the savior to whom Judaism has always looked."[9] Novak explains that through this savior, Jesus of Nazareth, Christians believe themselves to share in the fulfillment of God's covenants with Israel. Lacking the Messiah, Judaism can at best still look toward this fulfillment, despite its having (Christians believe) already arrived. Christianity thereby "supersedes" Judaism in the sense of going beyond it thanks to the Messiah. By recognizing Jesus as the Messiah and receiving the sacrament of baptism, Edith Stein affirmed Christianity's claims to go beyond Judaism as the messianic community, even if the fullness of this messianic community will be present only at the eschaton, the Second Coming of the Messiah.

To call Edith Stein a "supersessionist" is, as Novak recognizes, to make use of language that carries with it a highly negative connotation. Regarding supersessionism, Novak comments that "[m]any Jews have seen it as the core of Christian anti-Judaism."[10] Nor have only Jews taken offense at the concept. Christians too have seen in it a triumphalism that ill accords with the historical reality of the devastating persecution of Jews both by Christians and by nominal Christians. We should remark at once that Novak does not blame the Shoah on Christianity or on the Catholic Church. While noting that "Christian anti-Judaism was a contributing factor to Nazi ideology"—a fact that cannot be denied—Novak states that Christian anti-Judaism "was not the sufficient condition of that ideology at all. Nazism is not applied Christianity. Nazism is, rather, modern racism in extremis, which is the idolatry of the folk, the false gods of *Blut und Boden*."[11] Likewise, Novak rejects the view that Christians should not mourn Edith Stein as a Christian martyr of the Holocaust.

If Stein was a "supersessionist," however, did she thereby necessarily buy into the Christian anti-Judaism that without being determinative for Nazism, contributed to its rise? Novak's view is that Christian supersessionism need not be per se anti-Jewish or anti-Judaism. Rather, he compares Christian supersessionism with his Jewish view that Christianity, while "a valid gentile relationship with the Lord God, maker of heaven and earth, elector of Israel, giver of the Torah, and redeemer of the world,"[12] is in many ways a grave distortion of the Torah. Thus, he is happy to say "to a Christian wanting to convert to Judaism," such as Abraham Carmel (formerly Father Kenneth Cox), "You have made the best choice [as in the case of the pagan wanting to convert to Judaism], and Christianity has been an excellent preparation for that decision, having introduced you, however partially, to the Lord God of Israel."[13] Although Jews view Christianity as an acceptable form of worship for gentiles, for Jews Christianity is nonetheless a grave retrogression from Second Temple Judaism (from the Torah) and therefore Jews will welcome Christian converts to Judaism. Such converts have returned to a purer practice of Torah. Likewise, the Christian view that Christ fulfilled the Torah means that Christians will welcome converts from Judaism as having gone beyond Judaism and entered into the fulfillment of Torah in Christ and his Spirit.

Theologically, then, Christian supersessionism need not require condemnation of Judaism, no more than Judaism requires condemnation of Christianity—although on both sides there will be strong critiques. Stein's "supersessionist" logic is presented by Novak as an example of what Alasdair MacIntyre (quoted by Novak) calls "a judgment that by the standards of one's own tradition the standpoint of the other tradition offers superior resources for understanding the problems and issues which confront one's own tradition."[14] Such logic cannot be ruled out as invalid simply because it views one tradition as ultimately less rich than another.

But once one has become Christian, what can one make of Judaism—given that Judaism possesses Torah and the covenants and yet does not apprehend, from the Christian perspective, the Messiah who fulfills Torah and the covenants? Can Christians consider Jews to be what Jews consider themselves to be, the elect people of God who seek to practice fidelity to the God of Sinai? Or must Christians hold that Jews are no longer that people, and no longer (after the Messiah) have any claim to be practicing fidelity to the God of Sinai?

Novak holds that "Christian supersessionism need not denigrate Judaism."[15] On the contrary, Christian supersessionists such as Stein can still hold that Judaism, as practiced by living Jews, teaches Christians about the God of Israel and about the covenantal realities that the Messiah came to fulfill. Christians can still understand Jews as "elder brothers," because messianic fulfillment does not mean that God has "annulled His everlasting covenant with the Jewish people, neither past nor present nor future."[16] For Christians, the Messiah fulfills rather than negates (in the Hegelian sense of linear historical progression) the earlier covenants. The chosen people who, not recognizing the messianic fulfillment, continue in sincere obedience to practice the laws of Sinai do not thereby separate themselves from the covenantal God to whom they bear witness.[17]

Furthermore, Novak suggests that Christians cannot stop employing the supersessionist logic that he attributes to Stein, any more than Jews can stop viewing Christianity as a retrogression from the Torah. He argues that the affirmation that "God has not annulled his everlasting covenant with the Jewish people" suffices for Christians who seek to be sensitive to Jewish concerns as well as to the history of Christian anti-Judaism. As he puts it, "Jews cannot expect any more than that from Christians, and Christians cannot expect any more than that from yourselves."[18] This is so because Christians worship Jesus as the Messiah of Israel, and clearly this adds to and transforms Judaism. After all, Novak says, for those Christians who are embarrassed by Christianity's claims vis-à-vis the fulfillment of Israel, there is always the opportunity of conversion to Judaism. As he puts it, "If Christianity does not regard itself as going beyond Judaism, why should Christians not become Jews? It is always a ready possibility. Where else could you possibly find the Lord God of Israel?"[19] And if the answer to that last question is the divine Messiah of Israel, Jesus of Nazareth, then "conversely, any Jew who believes Christianity supersedes Judaism can only become a Christian in good faith—like Edith Stein."[20]

Does the fact that Christians are "supersessionist" in the sense of regarding Jesus as Israel's Messiah make dialogue between Christians and Jews impossible? So long as Christians grant that God's covenantal election of the Jews continues to possess positive meaning, Christians can respect Judaism. This respect ensures that dialogue is possible, even if the fundamental impasse cannot in this world be resolved.[21] For Jewish-Christian dialogue, in other words, supersessionism (or its Jewish counterpart regarding Christianity) is a problem only when the dialogue is inappropriately focused upon the impasse. Novak argues that Jews and Christians must consent to being "strangers" at the deepest theological level, that of the question of covenantal fulfillment of God's plan for the salvation of human beings. Such patience with each other, rather than trying to bridge all division, allows for fruitful dialogue about those elements of faith and reason that Jews and Christians share.

Judaism, Christianity, and the "Israel of God"

Novak also takes up the theme of supersessionism in two other recent essays, "Avoiding Charges of Legalism and Antinomianism in Jewish-Christian Dialogue" and "From Supersessionism to Parallelism in Jewish-Christian Dialogue." In the former essay, Novak reflects upon the fact that Jews and Christians as such cannot constitute a unified polity (whether in "Christendom" or in covenantal Israel). "From a Jewish perspective," he points out, "the only way Christians could live in a Jewish polity—governed by Jewish law, that is—would be in sort of resident alien status, a status held by one whom Scripture calls 'the sojourner in the city' (Exod. 20.10) and whom the Rabbis called the *ger toshav*."[22] Scripture and the Rabbis lay down clear guidelines for the place of such sojourners in Israel. Whether or not the positive law of a confessional Christian commonwealth could grant Jews full participation in the commonwealth, the fact remains that historically this was not the case. If this is so on both sides as regards the state, what about each side's claim to be the continuation of biblical Israel? For Judaism this claim follows as a matter of course: as Paul says of those Jews who did not accept Jesus as Messiah, "They are Israelites, and to them belong the sonship, the glory, the covenants, the giving of the law, the worship, and the promises; to them belong the patriarchs, and of their race, according to the flesh, is the Christ, who is God over all" (Rom. 9.4–5).

The claim to be the fullness of "Israel" might seem less requisite for Christianity, but in fact I think it is equally central. Christians understand themselves as "one body" *in* the Messiah of Israel (Rom. 12.5; cf. 1 Cor. 12.13, Eph. 1.23, Col. 2.17), as "the body of Christ" (1 Cor. 12.27). The messianic Davidic King has accomplished the promised "new covenant" (Heb. 8.10, quoting Jer. 31.31) and has united his kingdom to himself through his Spirit. This kingdom can be no other than "the Israel of God" (Gal. 6.16), which is in the Messiah's dispensation a "new creation" (Gal. 6.15). This kingdom includes both Jews and gentiles, both of whom now fulfill Torah in Christ. As Paul puts it, in an image cited by Novak, "But if some of the branches were broken off, and you [Gentiles], a wild olive shoot, were grafted in their place to share the richness of the olive tree [Israel], do not boast over the branches. If you do boast, remember it is not you that support the root, but the root that supports you" (Rom. 11.17–18).[23]

Commenting on Paul's image of the Church as an "olive tree" (Israel) with engrafted branches, Novak distinguishes between two kinds of supersessionism. The milder kind "does not reject the Jews from being forever *part of* Israel," but nonetheless affirms two points, neither of which Judaism can accept: "one, the Jews are no longer solely identical with Israel; two, the Church does have the more authentic definition of Israel than Judaism has."[24] Even if in this milder form of supersessionism Jews are not rejected as God's covenantal people, but rather remain God's covenantal people even while failing to recognize the Messiah, nonetheless they thereby forfeit their central covenantal place. As Novak says in response to this displacement (by Jesus) of Judaism's centrality in the world's salvation: "no Jew who is loyal to Judaism could possibly accept such a subordinate role for Judaism in good faith."[25] He goes on to explain that the second, "more radical" form of Christian supersessionism "has the Church replacing the Jewish people altogether in the covenant."[26] In this second view the Jewish people are no longer special people in the eyes of God; they lose their covenantal prerogatives altogether, and fall back to the status of all other peoples. Novak recognizes that the Catholic Church, among other Christian communities, has rejected this more radical supersessionism, and he notes that "that is all Jews can really ask Christians to do as Christians."[27]

In "From Supersessionism to Parallelism in Jewish-Christian Dialogue," Novak begins by comparing Christian supersessionists to Jewish "counter-supersessionists." Christian supersessionism here is the harsh form that teaches that God has absolutely no covenantal relationship with those Jews who do not affirm Jesus to be the Messiah; the earlier covenants are completely negated by Jesus. In such supersessionism Jews have no theological place other than a negative one, and it follows that such supersessionism rules out Jewish-Christian dialogue (as a theological dialogue). What then characterizes Jewish "counter-supersessionists?" Like Christians who hold the harsh form of supersessionism, Jewish counter-supersessionists grant absolutely no theological place to their (Christian) opposites. Novak explains,

> Jewish counter-supersessionists assert that Christians are a group of gentiles who erroneously—even arrogantly—think they are now God's people exclusively, having been first led to this position by a group of renegade Jews who removed themselves from Judaism. And the ultimate coup de grâce of the Jewish counter-supersessionists is to assert that Christians do not worship the Lord God of Israel as do the Jews but, rather, another god altogether.[28]

A believing Jew (or Christian) would be hard pressed to deny that St. Paul and other early Jewish proponents of Jesus as the divine Messiah "removed themselves from Judaism," at least in Novak's sense.[29] Indeed, first-century Jews, among them Saul prior to his fateful journey to Damascus, often responded in just this fashion. Where Jewish counter-supersessionists go further is in the insistence that this departure from Judaism was and is characterized fundamentally by idolatry. This view removes any theological ground from Christianity, and thus makes impossible Jewish-Christian theological dialogue.

Faced with worship of Jesus Christ and (correspondingly) the Trinity, those whom Novak calls counter-supersessionists conclude that Christians cannot, despite the Christian profession of faith, actually worship the one God of Israel. If Christians are not worshipping the one God of Israel, then Christian worship cannot be seen as other than idolatrous: either Christianity is worship of a mere man or it is worship of a triad (refined polytheism). This view that Christians do not worship the true God has parallels in Christian discourse about Jews, as Novak points out. Some Christians hold that since Jews do not worship the Trinity, Jews do not worship the true God; instead, Jews remain at the level of a fundamentally impersonal God, since to be Love, God must be interpersonal communion. On this view, the revelation of the Father, Son, and Holy Spirit so transforms the doctrine of God that Jewish worship hardly seems to rise above the level of the pagan philosophers. A similar conclusion is thereby reached by Christian supersessionism and Jewish counter-supersessionism: each holds the other (Jews or Christians) to be like pagans but worse, because the other should have known better. For supersessionism, by rejecting the Gospel, Jews lose any relationship with God; for counter-supersessionism, by rejecting the primacy of Torah, Christians lose any relationship with God.

In Novak's view, it is now clear that Christians have largely renounced the harsh form of supersessionism. As we have seen in his earlier essays, Novak does not draw from this fact a hope that the two religions will eventually come to agreement, which could only be possible were one or the other to reject its fundamental principles. On the contrary, he affirms that "the rival assertions of Judaism and Christianity . . . must remain with us until the end, when God will overcome all human rivalries."[30] What then is gained by the Christian rejection of harsh supersessionism? Following Karl Barth, Novak suggests that Christians thereby underscore the faithfulness of God, a faithfulness that Christians proclaim as fulfilled ultimately by Jesus (Rom. 3) and that does not depend upon human faithfulness.[31] Yet Jews are not mere signposts of God's faithfulness; since they are a living people, they can teach Christians about the God of Israel as known through Sinai. As Novak says, "Learning how God has not abandoned us to oblivion can greatly help you

[Christians] appreciate how God has not abandoned you to oblivion either."[32] He hopes that such learning will produce a Christian theology of Judaism that "can cogently recognize the continuing validity of Judaism and its commandments for Jews"[33]—or as I would put it, can recognize a theological ground distinct from the new covenant, without requiring that Christians deny that the new covenant in the Messiah fulfills and reconfigures Torah observance.

In turn, inspired by the Christian rejection of harsh supersessionism, Jews can abandon the counter-supersessionism that refuses to take at face value the Christian affirmation that Christians share fundamental beliefs with Jews, including (though not limited to) worship of the one God and commitment to basic moral precepts of the Torah (e.g., the Decalogue). As Novak points out, the abandonment of Jewish counter-supersessionism requires accepting that there are "cognitive bridges" between Jews and Christians that enable Christians to appreciate many aspects of "our [Jewish] public teaching of the Torah and our observance of its commandments."[34] He gives as an example the fact that Christians, more than others, can appreciate what it means for Jews to observe covenantal commandments such as circumcision. In light of challenges in Canadian courts to the practice of circumcision (as well as to the definition of marriage as between a man and a woman), he suggests that Jewish-Christian dialogue can foster a society that is more welcoming to Jewish observance of Torah.

Theology and Teleology

Exploring the theological deficiencies of harsh supersessionism, Novak also compares how Christians conceive of the relationship of the New Testament and Old Testament, to how Jews conceive of the relationship of the Oral Torah (Talmud) to the Written Torah (Scripture). In both cases, he suggests, the relationship between the two sources shows the error in supersessionist (or counter-supersessionist) mentality. He states that if the Old Testament relates to the New as a means to an end or as a cause to its effect (understood in the modern sense of causality, lacking "final causality"), then two alternatives follow.[35] Either the means/cause is no longer valuable once the end/effect has been attained (supersessionism), or else the means/cause is more valuable than the end/effect (counter-supersessionism). Novak observes, however, that the New Testament relates to the Old "neither as a replacement nor as an emergence."[36] Rather, for Christians the New Testament provides the perspective from which one can then understand the Old (just as for Jews the Oral Torah provides the perspective from which one can then understand the Written Torah). The Old Testament is not the means/cause of Christ and the Holy Spirit. Rather, the coming of Christ and his Spirit illumines the Old Testament so that the believer discovers the context in which salvation by Christ and his Spirit makes sense (just as the Oral Torah illumines the Written Torah so that the believer discovers the context in which the commandments make sense). As Novak puts it, for Christians "the 'Old Testament' is 'old' retrospectively, not as earlier 'potential' or as a prior 'cause.'"[37]

This "retrospective" illumination of the Old Testament involves what I would call a logic of fulfillment rather than of supersession. It is not the temporal sequence by itself that makes for "Old" and "New," but rather the fulfillment that suffuses the entire portrait. The Old Testament does not lose meaning when viewed "retrospectively" in light of the New (as if it could now be discarded), but rather gains its fullest positive meaning. Novak states, "Looking at the relation of Old and New Testaments in this way enables one to see 'old' as meaning neither 'passé' nor 'sufficient.'"[38] This description pinpoints the key problem with the harsh form of supersessionism (and counter-supersessionism). Namely, the historical past is never, for the believer, strictly or solely past; rather, the fulfillment of history governs and suffuses all history (because of the participation of time in the eternity of the providential Creator and Redeemer). This does not mean that the linear progression of history has no significance, but it does mean that earlier historical realities cannot be discarded once later historical realities have been unveiled.

When Novak rejects "teleological or causal logic" in the relationship of Israel's covenants (the Old Testament) and Christ (the New Testament), therefore, I take it that he means to exclude a mechanical teleology, stripped of real final causality, that treats biblical Israel as a mere mechanism by which God brings about Jesus, and which has no value once Jesus arrives.[39] Viewed in light of Christ, biblical Israel—and Judaism—find teleological fulfillment in Christ, but not the kind of fulfillment that can be seen to emerge necessarily from the operation of the mechanism, nor the kind of teleology that brings about its own fulfillment from within its own resources and that has value only in its end or goal. God's Word includes his good gifts to Israel. That these gifts are ordered to a further fulfillment is indeed teleological, but the gifts cannot be reduced to an immanent and mechanical teleology.

Yet once one allows for teleology, does one bring in supersessionism and counter-supersessionism through the back door? Assuming an appropriate time and setting, cannot Jews tell Christians to "come home" (and vice versa)? Yes, but neither Christians nor Jews can do so in a manner that denies or discards the realities that Christians and Jews affirm together. Sinai is not merely a trigger for something else, but rather proclaims realities that Christians and Jews both recognize as true. Sinai therefore cannot be solely claimed by either community. It follows that Christians can "hope that everyone will accept Christ" while engaging Jews as "elder brothers" rather than as adversaries.[40] Novak argues that the fact that the teleology is not mechanical in its causality, but leaves room for God's free action, means that neither community can claim demonstrable teleological superiority on immanent grounds. As Novak concludes, "That opens the ground for God to make the truly final demonstration of an end that will include us all"—which Christians believe God will do at the Second Coming, and Jews in the resurrection of the dead and World-to-Come—"making our present parallel lines converge in eternity."[41]

Novak's way of handling the loaded term of "supersessionism" thus identifies a path for Jewish-Christian dialogue that does not water down the claims of either Christianity or Judaism. With respect to his friendship with Robert Jenson, he remains able to affirm Judaism's claims: "The theological difference is that as a Christian and a Jew, Jens and I are existentially dedicated to faith assertions (i.e., willing to die for them if need be) about the truest relationship with God available in this world, which are undeniably not just distinctive but mutually exclusive head-on."[42] When viewed in their entirety, Judaism and Christianity are "mutually exclusive head-on," even if commonalities should also be affirmed due to shared roots in biblical Israel. Teleologically one can only ask, "Which is the best way to and from the Lord God of Israel: the Torah or Christ?"[43] The answer cannot be both. Judaism does not accept Jesus of Nazareth to be the Messiah, and Christians, who do accept Jesus as Messiah, believe that he has reconstituted the Torah around himself.

Novak on Jewish Christianity/Messianic Judaism

Convergence?

Could it be, however, that the rejection of harsh supersessionist and counter-supersessionist logic has opened the door to a new form of worship that would combine the practices of Rabbinic Judaism with the practices of Christianity? If Jews and Christians can move away from an adversarial relationship and take a true interest in each other, might not the lines regarding the "truest relationship with God available in this world" begin to converge now? What about combining Torah observance according to the practice of Judaism, with faith in Christ Jesus and the practice of the Christian sacraments?

In an essay titled "When Jews Are Christians," Novak rejects this possibility.[44] As we have seen, his theological work insists that Christians and Jews accord each other theological status. With gratitude he observes that after centuries of hostility, "some Jews and Christians are now able to engage in honest and fruitful dialogue and . . . are now able to recognize a number of overlapping interests."[45] But he warns that "a new type of Jewish convert to Christianity" poses a serious difficulty to Jewish-Christian dialogue.[46] Namely, this "new type of Jewish convert" accepts Jesus as Messiah without recognizing a need to cease practicing Rabbinic Judaism. How does their conversion, in their view, relate to their practice of Judaism? Does it make their Judaism more perfect qua Judaism? For some the answer is yes, whereas others argue simply "that they are practicing *a* true Judaism."[47] Granted Novak's opposition to supersessionism and counter-supersessionism, why does he not affirm that these Jewish converts to Christianity have done what scholars were unable to do, namely effectively putting together the two religions in a way that does not deny the specific claims of either religion?

The emergence of forms of Messianic Judaism merits discussion in any treatment of the problem of "supersessionism." Historically, Novak points out, Jews who converted Christianity accepted both their lack of a distinctive place in the Church—"there is neither Jew nor Greek . . . in Christ Jesus" (Gal. 3.28)—and their status as apostates according to Jewish authorities. The recent development of Jewish converts to Christianity who continue to desire to be practicing Jews therefore calls into question the traditional view of such converts. Could it be that such Jewish Christians are in fact not apostates from Judaism? Should Jewish Christians have a distinctive place in the Church, one that marks them as "a kind of personal link between the now gentile Church and its Jewish origins?"[48]

From a Jewish perspective, Novak answers by emphasizing the doctrines of the Incarnation and the Trinity. The issue of Messiahhood, he grants, caused the original division between Jews (and thus between Jews and Christians). At the outset "Jews and Christians were members of the same religio-political community and spoke the same conceptual language."[49] They could at that time argue about what constituted Messiahhood and whether Jesus was the "Messiah." For Second Temple Jews the central question regarding the Messiah was not whether or not he would be divine, but what he would accomplish as regards Israel. Recall the question posed by the disciples to Jesus after his Resurrection: "Lord, will you at this time restore the kingdom to Israel?" (Acts 1.6). Thus, from a contemporary Jewish perspective, Novak limits Messiahhood to "a political designation for a divinely restored (or, at least, divinely sanctioned) Jewish king in Jerusalem, who will gather in the exiles, establish a state governed by the Torah, and rebuild the Temple."[50] The key question for Judaism is whether Jesus has done what the Messiah politically must do.

As N.T. Wright and others have argued, Jesus did so but in a way that transformed every aspect of the Messianic expectation. Novak does not adequately describe Christian belief when he states that Jesus' "messiahhood, for Christians, has now been postponed to the Second Coming, when Christians believe he will rule on earth as Christ the King (see Jn 18.36)."[51] Christians do not believe that Jesus' Messianic kingship has been postponed; the kingdom of God is present here and now. Paul knew the reasons for holding that Jesus "was not the Messiah precisely because he did not bring about the full restoration of the Jewish people to the Land of Israel and God's universal reign of peace,"[52] but nonetheless Paul still appealed to his Jewish brethren to accept Jesus as the divine Messiah. Nor can I agree with Novak's position that "neither Jews nor gentiles relate to Jesus as the Messiah now."[53] Yet Novak's key claim—that the context for discussion of Jesus' messianic status has changed due to the Church's Christological and Trinitarian doctrinal development—seems incontrovertible as a historical point. As Novak comments, everything that has occurred since Jesus' time "has made any simple division between messianic and non-messianic Jews inappropriate"; Jews cannot simply take up the first-century debate again as it then stood.[54] In hearing the Gospel, Jews now also have to deal directly with the theology of the Incarnation and Trinity, cast in language that does not arise, as Paul's, Peter's, and Stephen's did, from training in Torah and within the context of debates between Jews who at least at the outset shared "the same religio-political community." This is true even if one supposes, as I do, that the key question remains whether Jesus (crucified and risen) is the Messiah of Israel.

From the perspective of "normative Judaism," then, the discussion that arises from the existence of Jewish Christianity is not first a debate about whether Jesus was the Messiah. Rather, the discussion within living Judaism involves first and foremost what it means for Jews to profess faith in the Incarnation of the Son of God, the second Person of the Trinity, and to participate in the sacraments of faith. Certainly, from the perspective of Judaism, such Jews remain Jews: their membership in the elect people of God cannot be lost.[55] Yet those who speak authoritatively within Judaism can rule upon when Jews have sinned and broken covenant. In the case of

Messianic Jews, those who speak authoritatively within living Judaism have ruled that no Jew can affirm the Incarnation and the Trinity, and practice the sacraments, without sinning. As Novak puts it, "the Christhood (incarnational/trinitarian status) of Jesus of Nazareth is not an option within God's everlasting Covenant with the people of Israel. Jewish Christians are still Jews, but they are no longer practicing a religion Jews regard as part of Judaism."[56] They have become apostates, and thus it falls to "the authorities of the Jewish community" to exclude them "from communion with the normative Jewish community (*keneset yisrael*)."[57]

Messianic Judaism, Judaism, and Christianity

Describing the Church as "reconfigured Israel," John McCade observes that "[i]ts basis, accessible to all through faith, is a *halakah* of Torah-observance, conducted through Christian discipleship and a sacramental sharing in Christ's passion."[58] In addition to this observance of Torah in Christ, Jewish Christianity or Messianic Judaism suggests that Jewish Christians retain a covenantal responsibility to observe Torah as Jews. If, in response to Messianic Judaism, all Christians were to conclude that Christian practice can include Jewish Torah observance, one question would be whether Christians can allow Jews to decide what "Judaism" requires. If Rabbinic Judaism rules that "Judaism" cannot include believing that Jesus is divine and celebrating Christian sacraments, what happens if Christians overrule the decision that Rabbinic Judaism has made about itself?

It seems to me that Christians would thereby be proclaiming that living Judaism has no say over what counts as Judaism. Rabbinic Judaism would simply be ruled out of court. In other words, ignoring the rabbinic authorities' decision over what counts as Judaism would be even more accurately described as supersessionism than the action that generated the problem of supersessionism in the first place, namely Paul's and others' disagreement with other Jews over what constituted the Messianic fulfillment. Debating the claim that the Messiah has definitively fulfilled and reconfigured Torah is one thing; denying that Rabbinic Judaism can define what counts as the practice of Rabbinic Judaism is another.

When Christians accept Messianic Judaism, then, Rabbinic Jews wonder whether they have been superseded *as Jews* so as to be replaced by a better set of Jews. How could Christians continue to dialogue respectfully with Jews whom Christians deny can even be trusted to understand what belongs to Rabbinic Judaism qua Rabbinic Judaism? Novak remarks in this respect that the acceptance of Messianic Judaism by some Christians "strongly suggests to many Jews—very much including those most favorably disposed to the new Jewish-Christian relationship—that the Jewish Christians are being held up to the rest of the Jews as exemplars."[59] Once Messianic Judaism is accepted, the key issue in the dialogue must inevitably become Christian understanding of Judaism qua Judaism, versus Jewish understanding of Judaism qua Judaism. Christians would be saying that Christians not only understand Israel's Messiah better—mild supersessionism—but also that Christians better understand Rabbinic Judaism as such. If so, what further need for dialogue? Living Judaism would have been thoroughly superseded. Novak argues that any dialogue under such conditions would be reducible to Christian proselytism. He concludes that "Christian acceptance of the self-proclaimed Judaism of the new Jewish Christians, as opposed to accepting them simply as *any* converts are accepted, can only undermine the position of the pro-dialogue and cooperation party within the Jewish community."[60]

Are Christians, then, to reject the desire of Messianic Jews to accept the Gospel? By failing to encourage Messianic Jewish communities, would Christians be suggesting that Christians no longer desire Jews to believe in Jesus as the Messiah?

My view is that the invitation to Jews—and to all who do not believe in Jesus—to receive Jesus as Messiah can and should still be made in appropriate modes and contexts.[61] But this invitation cannot be made under the presumption that Christians understand Rabbinic Judaism qua Rabbinic Judaism better than does the historical body of Rabbinic Jews. As Novak says, had the Church "chosen what might be called the 'halakhic' Christianity of the 'pharisaic Christians' mentioned in Acts 15.5, it is conceivable that the whole Jewish-Christian relationship might well have developed altogether differently,"[62] in which case Christians would have more claim to make decisions about what constitutes Rabbinic Judaism. As it stands historically, however, Christians do not possess such a claim. Because ongoing Rabbinic Judaism has developed without Christian participation, Christians cannot legitimately "supersede" Rabbinic Judaism by approving as "Judaism" a Judaism practiced within Christian communities.

What if Rabbinic Judaism eventually changes its view of Messianic Judaism, and affirms Messianic Judaism as a legitimate form of Judaism? It seems to me that this possibility, which Novak does not consider, would require at least two steps. First, Rabbinic Judaism would need to grant that worshipping Jesus Christ does not contradict Rabbinic Judaism's understanding of the first commandment of the Decalogue. This seems unlikely. Second, Messianic Judaism would need to affirm that Torah observance remains covenantally obligatory, rather than simply fitting, for Messianic

Jews. This would mean that Christ does not fulfill and transform Torah for Jews, a claim that Rabbinic Judaism requires but that would be problematic, to say the least, from a Christian perspective.

Beyond the question of Rabbinic Judaism's view of Messianic Judaism, Novak mentions another theological difficulty that Messianic Judaism poses for Christianity: "it would seem that any formal conferral of a unique status upon them would mark the acceptance of a permanent division of Christians *de jure* into a Jewish and a gentile branch."[63] In other words, what does Torah observance and being a member of the people of Israel add to being Christian? Has Christ "broken down the dividing wall" (Eph. 2.14) between Jew and gentile by fulfilling God's covenants with Israel and bringing the nations into this fulfillment, or has Christ not done so? Can Christians truly be divided in the Church according to Jew and gentile, if Christians are united in Christ's definitive worship through his Cross?

Mark S. Kinzer's Postmissionary Messianic Judaism

In light of the above concerns, we need to explore Mark Kinzer's view that Messianic Judaism overcomes the legacy of Christian supersessionism. In his book, published 14 years after Novak's "When Jews Are Christians" first appeared, Kinzer does not take up Novak's work directly. Even so, he raises (from a perspective opposite to that of Novak) a number of the same issues, which merit a detailed exposition.[64]

Postmissionary Messianic Judaism and Non-Supersessionist Ecclesiology

In his Introduction to *Postmissionary Messianic Judaism*, under the subheading "Postmissionary Messianic Judaism and Non-Supersessionist Ecclesiology," Kinzer briefly summarizes his understanding of Christianity and his account of what Messianic Judaism should be. Christianity, he holds, possesses two basic principles or "critical convictions": "(1) the mediation of Yeshua [Jesus] in all of God's creative, revelatory, reconciling, and redemptive activity, and (2) the church's participation through Yeshua in Israel's covenantal privileges."[65]

One should ask whether this is a sufficient description of Christianity's "critical convictions." Does the Church simply participate through Jesus/Yeshua in the covenantal privileges of Israel? Or does Jesus bring these covenantal privileges to a transcendent fulfillment, so that Christians receive a "new covenant" (Heb. 12.24) in which we "become partakers of the divine nature" (2 Pet. 1.4) and share in "the whole fullness of the deity" (Col. 2.9) as "heirs of God and fellow heirs with Christ" (Rom. 8.17)?[66] Does the Church simply affirm "the mediation of Yeshua" in all God's activity, or is it necessary to say clearly that "the Word was God" (Jn. 1.1) and not merely mediator of God?

Certainly Kinzer does not deny that Jesus is divine (at least he goes on to refer to Jesus' "divine mediation"[67]), but his way of putting it does not sufficiently expose how Jesus differs radically from any mediator whose mediation could fit within Israel's covenantal privileges. But as Kinzer notes, even his relatively weak way of phrasing the two convictions makes supersessionism difficult to avoid. According to Kinzer, the only way for the Church to avoid supersessionism, as it now wishes to do, is to add to these two critical convictions "a postmissionary form of Messianic Judaism."[68]

What are the constitutive elements of postmissionary Messianic Judaism? First, it requires Jewish believers in Jewish "to live an observant Jewish life as an act of covenant fidelity rather than missionary expediency."[69] Here Kinzer seeks to counter the view that Messianic Jews aim at proselytizing other Jews by separating them from Torah observance. Messianic Jews, qua Jews, seek to be just like other observant Jews. By seeking to observe Torah in fidelity to God's election of them as Jews, they are "postmissionary," not a proselytizing movement but a movement that seeks to enable Jews to be faithful to God's election while at the same time being faithful to the Messiah.

Second, while remaining sensitive to the concerns of Jews such as Novak, postmissionary Messianic Judaism is "Judaism." As Kinzer puts it, "postmissionary Messianic Judaism embraces the Jewish people and its religious tradition, and discovers God and Messiah in the midst of Israel."[70] In this sense, postmissionary Messianic Jews move in two directions. On the one hand, they inevitably "bear witness" to other Jews, and do so as "a visible sign of this hidden messianic presence."[71] On the other hand, they find this Messiah within Judaism. They are "at home in the Jewish world," because they honor "*postbiblical* Jewish history, customs, and institutions."[72] They do not represent a different Judaism, because they argue that the Torah observance of Rabbinic Judaism need not be superseded by belief in the Messiah. Both can go together. As Kinzer insists, "Messianic Judaism can perform its necessary ecclesiological role only if it is an embodiment of Jewish covenant fidelity at home in the Jewish world."[73]

Third, they are "Messianic." Kinzer sees this third aspect as Messianic Judaism's most significant contribution to (gentile) Christianity. Unlike the gentiles, Jews have an intrinsic connection with the people of the Messiah, because they are "the physical decendents of Abraham, Isaac, and Jacob."[74] They can thereby make manifest that the Church is none other than "a multinational extension of the people of Israel."[75] Thus, within Judaism (Messianic Judaism's "inner mission") they are a sign of the Messiah, and within Christianity (their "outer mission") they are a sign of the people of Israel, of "God's enduring love for the family chosen in the beginning to be God's covenant partner."[76] They bring to Christianity a vision of the Church that emphasizes the Church's identity as "a multinational extension of the Jewish people and its messianically renewed covenantal relationship with God."[77] Without Messianic Judaism, the (gentile) Church—what Kinzer calls "the church of the nations"—cannot sufficiently claim its identity as "an extension of Israel."[78]

Kinzer argues that these three markers—"postmissionary," "Judaism," and "Messianic"—result in the overcoming of Christian supersessionism. He states that in partnership with Messianic Judaism,

> the Christian church can affirm Yeshua's universal mediation in a non-supersessionist manner, since its postmissionary Messianic Jewish partner enables it to recognize Yeshua's mysterious presence throughout Jewish history. Israel's covenant endures, the church draws nourishment from its Jewish root, yet Yeshua remains the Messiah and Lord for both Jews and Gentiles. The Christian church can now affirm its own identity as an extension of Israel in a non-supersessionist manner, since its connection to the Jewish heritage has become a concrete sociological reality rather than a spiritual abstraction.[79]

The benefits for Christians are evident. Christians gain a connection with the rich spiritual heritage and ongoing Torah observance of Judaism, which fits with Christians' sense that the spiritual and intellectual depth of observant Jews is not foreign to Christianity.[80] Christians gain a way of bridging the sad divides described in the book of Acts (as well as, indeed, throughout the New Testament). Perhaps most importantly, Christians renew themselves, as many Christians have sought to do over the centuries, by returning to the time of the earliest Church and theologically rethinking the Church and Christianity in Jewish terms, in accord with Second-Temple understandings of the Messianic restoration of Israel.

The benefits for Jews also seem clear. In predominantly Christian societies, Jews and Jewish Torah observance would no longer be marginalized. So long as Messianic Judaism remains "postmissionary" and does not seek to be a new Judaism, furthermore, other Jews would not be pressured to be anything but Rabbinic Jews. Both Jews and Christians would also benefit from knowing how to respond to the existence of communities of Messianic Jews. For both Jews and Christians, welcoming Messianic Jews—rather than being placed in the awkward position of (for Jews) rejecting them as Jews or (for Christians) rejecting them as Christians—would have tangible benefits on a number of levels.

Problems

Before reviewing the arguments that Kinzer develops in the chapters of his book, however, I should point out two problems raised by the three elements that Kinzer defines as integral to "the type of Messianic Judaism that is needed for the emergence of an integrated, faithful, non-supersessionist ecclesiology."[81] The first problem, as our reading of Novak will have made clear, is Kinzer's understanding of "covenant fidelity." Certainly, Torah observance is a complex enough matter that it is not easy to define "covenant fidelity." But for the observant Jew, "covenant fidelity" occurs from within Rabbinic Judaism. If living Rabbinic Judaism repudiates the practices of Messianic Judaism, can Messianic Judaism be Judaism in a condition of "covenant fidelity" (and thus be "postmissionary")?

The second problem, which should also already be evident, has to do with the term "Messianic." Recall Kinzer's definition of the Church as "a multinational extension of the Jewish people and its messianically renewed covenantal relationship with God."[82] Can "extension" suffice for the Church's understanding of the transcendent fulfillment and reconfiguration around himself that Jesus accomplishes as the divine Messiah? Can "renewal" ("messianically renewed") suffice for the Church's understanding of the *new* covenant in the Messiah—one which certainly fulfills all God's covenants with Israel but, as Christians have understood it, does more than "renew" them? Does not the advent of the Messiah, and our participation in his saving death and Resurrection, require a new worship? Furthermore, can Kinzer's understanding of "Messianic," which leads him to make a strong distinction between the gentile Church or "church of the nations" and the Jewish Church, suffice to characterize the unity that the Messiah brings? Again, does Kinzer's understanding of "Messianic" give due weight to the Church's historical development, and particularly to the community of the apostles who gave shape, guided by Christ and the Holy Spirit, to Christian faith and practice? Are *these* Jewish roots, whose reality concretely ties the living Church to Jesus and to the Jews who witnessed the Messiah, to be superseded by the development of a Jewish *ekklesia* and a gentile *ekklesia*?[83]

These problems illumine the difficulty with Kinzer's claim that postmissionary Messianic Judaism overcomes Christian supersessionism by unifying Christian faith and practice with that of Rabbinic Judaism. The difficulty consists in whether Kinzer's approach actually negates or supersedes both the historical and living form of rabbinic Judaism, and the historical and living form of the Christian Church.

Kinzer is aware of this difficulty, and the arguments of his chapters seek to defuse it. He has particularly in view the concerns of Rabbinic Judaism. As he notes, "I would have preferred to address this book to the Jewish community—explaining the new form of Messianic Judaism that is gradually emerging, and providing reasons for why we deserve a place within Jewish communal life."[84] Instead, he directed the book toward a Christian audience on the grounds that his Jewish audience would ultimately be more persuaded by an exemplification of the "postmissionary" task "of representing and defending the Jewish people and the Jewish tradition before the multinational ekklesia."[85] In order to evaluate Kinzer's proposal, it is necessary to set forth his understanding of the New Testament, the development of Christianity, and Rabbinic Judaism.[86]

Kinzer on the New Testament

Kinzer begins by observing that most scholars consider the New Testament texts on Jews and Judaism to be in tension with each other.[87] In his view, however, scholarly perspective has been distorted by employing "the anachronistic terms 'Christian' and 'Christianity'" to the disciples/apostles, which suppresses the difference in "social location" between the earliest followers of Jesus and modern-day Christians.[88] Methodologically, he proposes that attending to the historical developments of the past two millennia, including the negative developments, assists interpreters in understanding the truth that the divine Author intends.[89]

Kinzer applies these insights to New Testament texts that pose difficulties to his view of the compatibility of Torah observance and Christianity. Discussing Mk 7.19 ("Thus he [Jesus] declared all foods clean") in light of fifth-century midrash, he argues that the text does not necessarily "imply that Jewish Yeshua-believers are now free to eat what is permitted to non-Jews."[90] The text may simply be instruction for Mark's gentile audience. Likewise, he argues that the book of Acts consistently reflects "Luke's expectation that Jewish Yeshua-believers will live according to Jewish practice."[91] In this vein, he notes how Paul "purified himself" and "went into the temple, to give notice when the days of purification would be fulfilled and the offering presented" (Acts 21.26). He reads Peter's vision (Acts 10), in which God commands Peter to eat food that Peter recognizes as unclean according to the Torah, as having to do *not* with the actual eating of food, but "as symbolizing Jews and Gentiles," who henceforth must associate with each other.[92] He interprets Paul's statement that "neither circumcision counts for anything nor uncircumcision, but keeping the commandments of God" (1 Cor. 7.19) to mean simply that "circumcision and Jewish identity do not elevate the Jew above the Gentile before God."[93]

With respect to Paul's remark that "I know and am persuaded in the Lord Jesus that nothing is unclean in itself; but it is unclean for any one who thinks it unclean" (Rom. 14.14) and other similar comments in Rom. 14–15, Kinzer suggests that the "weak in faith" (Rom. 14.1) are not fellow believers in Jesus, but Jews who do not believe in Jesus. Thus Paul, far from holding that Jewish believers in Jesus need no longer obey the food laws, is urging the gentile believers not to scandalize nonbelieving Jews.[94] Regarding Gal. 2.12, where Paul notes that Peter at first ate with gentiles and then wrongly "drew back," Kinzer argues that the text does not mean that Peter ate nonkosher food, nor does it mean that "Peter and Paul no longer order their lives according to Jewish practice."[95] When Paul says that "to those under the law [*hupo nomon*] I became as one under the law—though not being myself under the law" (1 Cor. 9.20), Kinzer suggests that Paul means that he would not "act in a way that implied the inferior status of Yeshua-believing Gentiles."[96]

Kinzer reads other texts in John and Hebrews in a similar fashion, and likewise he interprets the New Testament texts on the Jewish people as showing that for the New Testament authors, despite their general dismay regarding the Jewish leaders of the day, "the Jewish people as a whole remain 'the children' to whom God shows special regard."[97] He observes that while the New Testament authors hold that "Jerusalem and Israel must face judgment before receiving national redemption"[98] because of the rejection of the Messiah (a judgment that takes place with the destruction of Jerusalem), it is the national redemption that has the greater theological place.[99] This national redemption, on which the ultimate redemption of the world hinges, requires an ongoing "distinctive Jewish communal presence"[100] which the New Testament authors expect to be that of the community of Jews who do not believe in Jesus.

Critique of Kinzer on Paul

Especially as regards Torah observance for Jewish followers of Jesus, I do not agree with Kinzer's exegesis. This is particularly true for Paul's writings.

Consider, for example, the Letter to the Galatians.[101] Paul recalls, "I said to Cephas before them all, 'If you, though a Jew, live like a Gentile and not like a Jew, how can you compel the Gentiles to live like Jews?'" (Gal. 2.14). Is it plausible that Paul could charge Peter with living "like a Gentile" and not intend this to refer to Torah observance? Further, Torah observance has its purpose within the covenantal relationship with God, but Paul seems to suggest that the Messiah now mediates the covenantal relationship. Paul argues, "We ourselves, who are Jews by birth and not Gentile sinners, yet who know that a man is not justified by works of the law but through faith in Jesus Christ, even we have believed in Christ Jesus, in order to be justified by faith in Christ, and not by works of the law, because by works of the law shall no one be justified" (Gal. 3.15–16). If "works of the law" do not justify, and if Paul approves of Peter living "like a Gentile," could it truly follow that Paul wishes to require Torah observance on the part of Jewish believers in Christ?

As Paul develops his argument in Galatians, this question becomes even more difficult to answer in the affirmative. Paul conceives of the Torah as a "custodian" that gives way when the Messiah comes. He states, "Now before faith came, we were confined under the law, kept under restraint until faith should be revealed. So that the law was our custodian until Christ came, that we might be justified by faith. But now that faith has come, we are no longer under a custodian; for in Christ Jesus you are all sons of God, through faith" (Gal. 3.23–26). If Paul thinks that Jewish Christians must continue to observe Torah, why does Paul state that he, a Jewish Christian, is no longer under the "custodian" of the Torah? It is in this sense—"no longer under a custodian"—that Paul holds that "[t]here is neither Jew nor Greek . . . for you are all one in Christ Jesus" (Gal. 3.28).

Did the Messiah then negate the Torah, so that we are stuck with the alternative of harsh supersessionism? Jesus did not negate the Torah, but rather fulfilled it and reconfigured it around himself through his Spirit. As Paul puts it, "when the time had fully come, God sent forth his Son, born of woman, born under the law, to redeem those who were under the law, so that we might receive adoption as sons. And because you are sons, God has sent the Spirit of his Son into our hearts, crying, 'Abba! Father!'" (Gal. 4.4–6). Paul points out that were he in fact still preaching Torah observance, then his fellow Jews would not "persecute" him: "But if I, brethren, still preach circumcision, why am I still persecuted? In that case the stumbling block of the cross has been removed. I wish those who unsettle you would mutilate themselves!" (Gal. 5.11–12). Could this be the man who requires his fellow Jews to observe Torah?

In addition, now that the communion with God promised by the Torah has been fulfilled for both Jews and gentiles by the Messiah, Paul warns against any return by believers to Torah observance as a covenantal obligation: "Now I, Paul, say to you that if you receive circumcision, Christ will be of no advantage to you. I testify again to every man who receives circumcision that he is bound to keep the whole law. You are severed from Christ, you who would be justified by the law; you have fallen away from grace" (Gal. 5.2–4). If believers in Christ observe Torah as a covenantal obligation, they have not yet understood what Christ has accomplished. As Paul states, "For neither circumcision counts for anything, nor uncircumcision, but a new creation. Peace and mercy be upon all who walk by this rule, upon the Israel of God" (Gal. 6.15–16). The "Israel of God" now observes the "rule" of the "new creation" in Christ and the Spirit, rather than observing Torah outside of Christ's fulfillment of it.

Kinzer briefly comments on these passages from Galatians by connecting them with 1 Cor. 7.17–20, which reads,

> Only, let every one lead the life which the Lord has assigned to him, and in which God has called him. This is my rule in all the churches. Was any one at the time of his call already circumcised? Let him not seek to remove the marks of circumcision. Was any one at the time of his call uncircumcised? Let him not seek circumcision. For neither circumcision counts for anything nor uncircumcision, but keeping the commandments of God. Every one should remain in the state in which he was called.

On the basis of this text and Gal. 5.3, Kinzer argues that the "necessary conclusion" is that "[a]ll those who are born as Jews are obligated to live as Jews."[102] But is this a "necessary conclusion?" Gal. 5.3 is much more of a warning than Kinzer grants, and 1 Cor. 7.17–20 denies that "circumcision counts for anything." In Kinzer's view, once his "necessary conclusion" is in place, "the third text [Gal. 5.11] makes sense. 'Paul was accused by . . . other missionaries of being inconsistent: that although he preached a circumcision-free gospel to the Galatians, he continued to "preach circumcision" among Jews.'"[103] For Kinzer this set of texts means that "Paul urged Jewish Yeshua-believers to live as faithful Jews and Gentile Yeshua-believers to remain as non-Jews. His early Jewish opponents found this twofold message inconsistent and untenable. His later Christian adherents found it incomprehensible."[104]

Is Kinzer's interpretation adequate? As we noted above, in Gal. 5.11–12 Paul remarks, "But if I, brethren, still preach circumcision, why am I still persecuted? In that case the stumbling block of the cross has been removed. I wish those who unsettle you would mutilate themselves!" It would seem that Paul's meaning is that he does not "still preach circumcision," which explains why he is "still persecuted." If he were still preaching circumcision, he suggests that he would be removing "the stumbling block of the cross." This is so far from the case that Paul concludes with a curse: he wishes that his opponents on this point—those who preach circumcision and thereby remove for their Jewish auditors "the stumbling block of the cross" (Gal. 5.11; cf. 1 Cor. 1.23)—would castrate themselves.[105]

What does Paul mean by "the stumbling block of the cross?" Christ institutes a new worship that fulfills and transforms Torah observance. More than a mere addition to or extension of the Torah, this new worship is a covenantal sharing in the Paschal sacrifice of the Messiah that fulfills Torah and thereby brings about the reconciliation manifested on Pentecost.[106] Paul testifies to this new covenant: "For I received from the Lord what I also delivered to you, that the Lord Jesus on the night when he was betrayed took bread, and when he had given thanks, he broke it, and said, 'This is my body which is for you. Do this in remembrance of me'" (1 Cor. 10.23–24). Likewise Jesus commands his disciples/apostles to baptize, "Go therefore and make disciples of all nations, baptizing them in the name of the Father and of the Son and of the Holy Spirit" (Mt. 28.19). Paul notes that "[t]here is one body and one Spirit, just as you were called to the one hope that belongs to your call, one Lord, one faith, one baptism, one God and Father of us all" (Eph. 4.4–6). It is difficult to imagine that the author of this text means to require Jewish believers in Christ to observe Torah outside of practicing the worship that fulfills and transforms Torah observance.

As the fulfillment of God's covenantal promises to Israel, the relationship of Christ and the Church is like a marital union, the marriage of God and humankind (cf. Hos. 2.16,19–20). Paul takes up this theme with reference to Gen. 2: "'For this reason a man shall leave his father and mother and be joined to his wife, and the two shall become one.' This is a great mystery, and I mean in reference to Christ and the church" (Eph. 5.31–32). Kinzer points out in this regard that Luke Timothy Johnson connects the relationship between Jew and gentile in Eph. 2 to the relationship of husband and wife described in Eph. 5.32: both are relationships of "unity in plurality." For Kinzer, this means that "the unity of Jew and Gentile does not imply the elimination of all distinction between the two, any more than the unity of husband and wife eliminates all gender differentiation. Instead, the unity envisioned is one of mutual 'respect and love and service.'"[107] The Church, however, is one bride of Christ. If this bride is twofold (Israel and the Church rather than Israel fulfilled), then does not the image of the marriage of Christ and the Church break down?

Consider also Paul's description of the bridegroom, Christ. Paul states that "now in Christ Jesus you who once were far off have been brought near in the blood of Christ. For he is our peace, who has made us [Jews and Gentiles] both one, and has broken down the diving wall of hostility, by abolishing in his flesh the law of commandments and ordinances, that he might create in himself one new man in place of the two" (Eph. 2.13–15). It would be difficult to read this passage as suggesting that Christ Jesus abolished "in his flesh the law of commandments and ordinances" solely for gentiles. Since Gentiles had never been under the Torah, it seems most reasonable to interpret Paul's words as referring to Christ's fulfillment of the Torah for Jewish believers through Christ's establishment of the messianic unity "in one body through the cross" (Eph. 2.16).[108] In other words, Jesus accomplishes more than a linear renewal and extension of the existing covenant.

Kinzer is obviously correct that in the earliest Church, there was a "circumcision party" (Tit. 1.10), a significant group of believers who argued that Torah observance remained not only permissible in certain circumstances (as Paul clearly thought) but also covenantally necessary for Jewish believers and even quite possibly also for gentile believers. Since this party was a significant portion of the earliest believers, it is in this context that one should read such texts as Mk 7.19, "Thus he [Jesus] declared all foods clean." Mark's parenthetical remark seems meant as instruction not about the ontological status of all foods—as Kinzer rather implausibly argues[109]—but about Jesus' intention regarding the ceremonial status of foods. The Church's practice on a controversial issue was at stake.

Similar considerations bear upon Paul's injunction in Rom. 14.1, "As for the man who is weak in faith, welcome him, but not for disputes over opinions." Kinzer supposes that this person who is "weak in faith" is a Jew who does not believe in Christ Jesus. Not only does this reading go against Paul's understanding of "faith," but it also neglects the context that Kinzer otherwise emphasizes, namely the dispute between believers who held that Torah observance remains necessary for Jewish believers and those who held that Torah observance no longer remains necessary. In the context of this dispute, Paul states, "I know and am persuaded in the Lord Jesus that nothing is unclean in itself; but it is unclean for any one who thinks it unclean" (Rom. 14.14). He then advocates tolerance: "Do not let what you eat cause the ruin of one for whom Christ died" (Rom. 14.15).

Paul's practice of such tolerance is well known. As he says, "To the Jews I became as a Jew, in order to win Jews; to those under the law I became as one under the law—though not being myself under the law—that I might win those under the law. To those outside the law I became as one outside the law—not being without law toward God but under the law of Christ—that I might win those outside the law" (1 Cor. 9.20–21). But Kinzer reads Paul's statement that he is within "the law of Christ" as a statement of his Torah observance. Such an interpretation both turns on its head Paul's statement that he is not "under the law" and lacks a sense for Paul's theology of fulfillment. Why can Paul participate without hypocrisy in Torah observance, as he clearly often does? Because he is "free" (1 Cor. 9.1). Yet he is free in a manner ordered by charity. As he says when discussion whether Christians should partake in food that has been offered in pagan sacrifices, "'All things are lawful,' but not all things are helpful. 'All things are lawful,' but not all things build up. Let no one seek his own good, but the good of his neighbor" (1 Cor. 10.23–24).[110] Paul grants that Jewish believers in Jesus can in certain circumstances observe Torah, but he does not suggest that they must do so or that they can do so as a covenantal obligation, now that they fulfill the covenant "in one body through the cross."

Similarly, the evangelist John depicts Jesus' encounter with the Samaritan woman as an announcement of the Messianic fulfillment of God's covenant: "Jesus said to her, 'Woman, believe me, the hour is coming when neither on this mountain nor in Jerusalem will you worship the Father. You worship what you do not know; we worship what we know, for salvation is from the Jews. But the hour is coming, and now is, when the true worshipers will worship the Father in spirit and truth'" (Jn 4.21–23).[111] John presents this worship "in spirit and truth" as belonging to the accomplishment of the long-promised marriage of God and his people: "Every man serves the good wine first; and when men have drunk freely, then the poor wine; but you have kept the good wine until now" (Jn 2.10).

The key New Testament text with regard to the ongoing Jewish people is Rom. 9–11. In light of this text, Kinzer explains the failure of the second generation of the Church's leaders as a providentially willed parallel to the temporary hardening (Rom. 11.7) of the Jews who did not acknowledge Jesus as Messiah. For Kinzer, God allowed these Jews to undergo a "partial hardening"[112] in order to preserve Torah observance in the world. Kinzer thinks that God also allowed the gentile Church to stumble, and thus he hopes that his work, and that of Messianic Judaism, is the harbinger of the eschatological fulfillment of both Rabbinic Judaism and the gentile Christian Church. As Paul says regarding the Jews who did not accept Jesus as Messiah, "So I ask, have they stumbled so as to fall? By no means! But through their trespass salvation has come to the Gentiles, so as to make Israel jealous. Now if their trespass means riches for the world, and if their failure means riches for the Gentiles, how much more will their full inclusion mean!" (Rom. 11.11–12). Was this "full inclusion" present in Paul's day, as Kinzer suggests, with Torah-observant Jewish followers of Jesus combining in the Church with non-Torah-observant gentile followers of Jesus? This does not seem to be what Paul has in view.

Kinzer on the Development of Christianity

In light of the ongoing controversy that also characterized Paul's day, Ignatius of Antioch remarks, "It is monstrous to talk of Jesus Christ and practice Judaism."[113] In the decades after Paul, there was clearly an escalation in polemical language. Yet what Kinzer sees as a tragic falling away from Paul's message in Galatians and elsewhere, seems to me to be its theological continuation.[114] The salient issues can be seen in the debate between Augustine and Jerome over whether Paul truly observed Torah. Even while holding that Paul did so, Augustine rejects Torah observance for any Christian believer of his own generation. Thomas Aquinas, agreeing with Augustine, holds that Torah observance by a Christian would be a "mortal sin" since it would signify liturgically that Christ has not yet fulfilled Torah (and thus that Christians do not fulfill Torah in a transcendent mode in Christ by his Spirit).[115]

Kinzer approvingly quotes in this regard the challenge that the Jewish theologian Michael Wyschogrod poses to Aquinas:

> For even if there is, from the point of view of Christian faith, a large element of prefigurement of Christ in the Old Testament, does it have to follow that someone who refrains from eating pork or who fasts on the Day of Atonement is committing a mortal sin? Must his actions be interpreted as saying that "Christ was to be born" (103, 4 Reply) rather than that he had been born, thereby denying Christ? Could adherence to the Mosaic Law not be interpreted much more benevolently, as love of God and his commandments, as fidelity to a holy way of life out of which—for Christian faith—the Redeemer was born? If the commandments before Christ predicted him, could they not after Christ celebrate the prediction that came true and point to the final fulfillment that both Jews and Christians await? In short, the argument that the Mosaic commandments predict Christ and that to adhere to them after Christ is a mortal sin because one is denying that he has come by so doing is a rather thin reed on which to hang the case for the ceremonial commandments turning into mortal sin after Christ.[116]

Is there any answer to Wyschogrod's challenge, especially to his basic point that Torah observance among Jewish Christians could "be interpreted much more benevolently?" Like Augustine, Aquinas understands worship, including Israel's ceremonial commandments, in terms of "signs."[117] Bodily signs express and foster spiritual worship. For Aquinas, the sacramental "signs" of the New Testament should be understood in terms of the transformative fulfillment of Torah and Temple accomplished by Christ Jesus. For a contemporary believer in Jesus to observe, as a covenantal obligation, both biblical Israel's signs and the New Testament's signs would indicate that the believer misunderstands what Christ Jesus has accomplished: not an extension or renewal of Israel's signs, but an internal reconfiguration of those signs around himself. In this sense, the believer would be signifying that the covenantal responsibility of Jews is not fulfilled through sacramental participation in Christ. Objectively (though not necessarily subjectively) this misunderstanding would separate the believer from the reality of Jesus' Pasch.

By contrast, Kinzer argues that in light of the presence of Torah-observant Jews in the early Church, "Only a preexisting theological commitment to supersessionism could lead one to be satisfied with the explanation of the relevant biblical texts offered by Augustine and accepted by Aquinas."[118] This charge follows only if one accepts Kinzer's New Testament exegesis. It seems to me, on the contrary, that Augustine and Aquinas express the New Testament theology of Christ Jesus as the one who fulfills Torah and Temple from within and thereby reconfigures them around himself for those who share in his body by his Spirit. Kinzer's conclusion therefore misses the mark: "The eventual consensus position of the Gentile ekklesia makes Justin [Martyr] look like a paragon of toleration. This is a church that has no place for Judaism and no place for Jews. It has retained the Jewish Bible and believed in the Jewish Messiah, but it has said no to the Jewish people and its ancestral way of life."[119] Rather, the Church has taken its bearings from Paul's statement, "For all the promises of God find their Yes in him" (2 Cor. 1.20).

This fulfillment theology does not entail the negation of Judaism, as if Judaism and Jews had "no place." God gave his covenantal people the Torah as the "place" in which they would be formed in true worship of the one God, and Judaism and Jews continue to possess this covenantal "place" even as Christians invite the Jewish people to discover the messianic fulfillment of this "place." The fact that in the new covenant Jews fulfill their covenantal obligations (Torah observance) *sacramentally*, in union with gentiles in the Body of the Messiah, does not take away the "place" of Judaism and Jews, because this "place" participates in the saving work of the Messiah.[120]

Bilateral Ecclesiology and Christian Ecclesiology

Recall that Novak holds that theological necessities within Christianity require a mild form of supersessionism (since for Christians the "Messiah" must be the Davidic king of the Jews, and his covenant fulfillment not solely for gentiles) even while Novak rightly rejects the harsh supersessionism that denies Judaism and Jews any theological ground. For Kinzer, however, the overcoming of anti-Jewish supersessionism requires that "traditional ecclesiology, in which a Gentile church stands over against the Jewish people, must give way to a bilateral ecclesiology in solidarity with Israel."[121] Agreeing with Novak, I have argued that even though gentiles have been "grafted in" (Rom. 11.19), the Church is not simply an extension/renewal of Israel's covenants. The Church is rather the fulfillment of Israel in "one body in Christ" (Rom. 12.5) whose many members are united in and through the sacramental worship and discipleship that they offer in Christ by the Spirit to the Father.

Kinzer accepts much of the historical (gentile) Church. He observes that "we must avoid the temptation to see church history in purely negative terms. The Gentile ekklesia preserved the essential message entrusted to it."[122] In describing this "essential message," Kinzer does not name the Trinity and the Incarnation, or the doctrine of the Church as one, holy, catholic, and apostolic and as constituted sacramentally in Christ.[123] Instead, for Kinzer the "Gentile ekklesia preserved the essential message" because "[i]t continued to proclaim Israel's risen Messiah. It rejected Marcionism and accepted the Jewish Bible as inspired, authoritative, and canonical. It collected the books of the New Testament and arranged them in a manner that further countered Marcionite anti-Judaism."[124] But can the Church accept these elements as defining the "essential message" of Christianity?

Kinzer adds some caveats that cause further concern. He states, "In forbidding rather than requiring Torah observance from its Jewish members, the ekklesia annulled its right to claim continuity with biblical Israel."[125] Is the contemporary Church then not the "Israel of God" that Paul envisions? If the contemporary Church is not the messianic community, then could Christ Jesus have willed the Church and truly bestowed his Spirit upon it? As we noted, Kinzer also proposes that from the first century onwards, there has been "an internal schism *within* the Messianic ekklesia—between the Gentile ekklesia and its Jewish counterpart."[126] The Church has not been "bilateral" as Jesus (followed by the apostles), in Kinzer's view, intended it to be.

In a deep sense, then, the Church has neither been "one," nor "catholic," nor, above all, "apostolic." The Spirit whom Jesus promised would descend upon the apostolic community, and who did so at Pentecost, remained (it seems) largely extrinsic even to the apostolic community, which was already (even if unconsciously) in the process of abandoning the "Jewish ekklesia" and thereby any claim to a link with Israel.

Lumen Gentium, the Second Vatican Council's Dogmatic Constitution on the Church, teaches that "the new Israel, while journeying through this present world in search of a permanent city which lies in the future (see Heb. 13.14), is also called the church of Christ (see Mt. 16.18), since he has acquired it by his own blood (see Acts 20.28), has filled it with his Spirit and set it up with means suitable for visible and social unity" (§9).[127] Could Kinzer accept this account of the Messianic "new Israel" that since Christ's Resurrection has been "the visible sacrament of this saving unity?" It seems incompatible with Kinzer's views that "the ekklesia annulled its right to claim continuity with biblical Israel,"[128] that since the first century there has been "a schism in the heart of the people of God,"[129] and that "the ekklesia can claim to be (part of) Israel only if it contains within it 'Torah-observant' Jews."[130] If the (gentile) Church grossly misunderstood itself from the beginnings of the patristic period, can we trust that the (gentile) Church rightly understood Israel's Messiah and Israel's God, especially when it comes to doctrinal development?

Kinzer argues that the (gentile) Church, in order to return to the true (bilateral) Church of Acts 15, must "assert that Jewish Yeshua-believers are not only free to live as Jews, but obligated to do so."[131] Having taught authoritatively the opposite (on the grounds of Christ's Paschal mystery), with what authority could the Church now teach Jews who have faith in the Messiah that they are "obligated" to follow the Torah observance of Judaism? For Kinzer, however, the bilateral ecclesiology he proposes is ultimately not an academic issue but an existing reality that may foreshadow the coming eschaton:

> The first great wave of Jewish immigration to the land began in the same year that [Joseph] Rabinowitz stood on the Mount of Olives and concluded that Yeshua was Israel's Messiah. Messianic Judaism originated in the years immediately following the reunification of the city of David. Many today see these events as "signs of the times" that point to a new and decisive stage in God's dealings with Israel, the church, and the world. The restoration of a *bilateral ekklesia in solidarity with Israel that affirms Israel's covenant, Torah, and religious tradition* would certainly confirm such a perspective.[132]

Kinzer does not hinge his proposal for a bilateral ecclesiology on this eschatological vision. Rather, he holds that the (gentile) Church lost its true unity and catholicity in the mid to late first century, and now has the opportunity, if it enters into conversation with Messianic Judaism, to "come home to Israel" and to "rediscover its own catholicity" by reuniting with the other part—the Jews—of the extended "one Body of the Messiah."[133] But this union must be guided by the Jewish ekklesia, not the gentile one: for Kinzer the development of the Jewish ekklesia should be the work of Jews, not a work internal to particular Christian churches.[134]

Were one to accept Kinzer's New Testament exegesis, theology of history, and ecclesiology, one point seems certain: the Church as lived out for centuries by Catholics, Orthodox, and most Protestants—and as dogmatically defined for Catholics in *Lumen Gentium*—would be superseded. The Jewish Church and the gentile Church of the future would have to negotiate (without a clear source of authority) an entirely new understanding of the Church and its doctrines, beginning with the affirmation that Jesus was the Messiah, and sifting through twenty centuries of history. The (gentile) Church would retain some theological ground due to its preservation of faith in the Messiah, but it is unclear how this theological ground would suffice for remaking itself entirely. How would one know that the bilateral Church was now getting it right?

Postmissionary Messianic Judaism and Judaism

In "When Jews Are Christians," David Novak states, "To see them [Messianic Jews] as a unique link between the Jewish people and the Church, and to expect faithful Jews to concur in that judgment, asks too much of us."[135] Would Kinzer's account of his practice of Judaism relieve Novak's fears regarding the Judaism of Jewish Christians, and thereby would take away the charge of having superseded Judaism so far as the evaluation of what counts as Judaism is concerned?

Kinzer first points out that "John Howard Yoder has argued that neither the Jewish people as a whole nor Judaism as a religion ever 'rejected Jesus,'"[136] because by the time that a separate "Christianity" and "Judaism" emerged, "the 'Christ' to whom [Judaism] said no was thoroughly dejudaized."[137] If Judaism has only apparently and not in fact said "no" to Jesus as Messiah— having never been presented with Jesus in a context sufficiently Jewish— then "Judaism" is not intrinsically connected to a rejection of Jesus as Messiah. Accepting the theological legitimacy of Rabbinic Judaism, Kinzer argues that "Judaism is not a religious artifact from biblical times but a dynamic way of life embodied in and transmitted by a living community. The abstract affirmation of Judaism has no meaning unless it is expressed as a practical affirmation of the actual religious tradition of the Jewish people."[138]

Novak's concern, however, is that Jewish Christianity or Messianic Judaism cannot enter into the "dynamic way of life embodied in and transmitted by a living community," because Rabbinic Judaism is this "living community" and as a community it has rejected the view that Rabbinic Jews can practice Judaism faithfully and affirm Jesus as Messiah at the same time. For Novak, Messianic Judaism, having been rejected by living Rabbinic Judaism, can at best attach itself to an "abstract" portrait of Rabbinic Judaism. Against the supposition that Judaism could never have rejected Jesus as Messiah because by the time "Judaism" emerged Jesus had been already hellenized, Novak argues that it is not possible to leap over past centuries so as to repristinate the pre-hellenized (pre-second Person of the Trinity) Jesus. Living Rabbinic Judaism has never been able to affirm that the Jesus that it knows about is the Messiah, and there is no way of returning to the first century to take up anew the original intra-Jewish debate.

By contrast, Kinzer notes that the Gospels envision Jesus as "the representative and individual embodiment of Israel,"[139] and if so, the restoration accomplished by Jesus cannot be separated from the restoration of Israel. As Kendall Soulen puts it, the risen Jesus is the "first fruits of God's eschatological vindication of Israel's body."[140] If the risen Jesus is so closely connected with Israel's eschatological vindication, then Jesus may be God's yes to the Jewish people even if the Jewish people have said no to him.[141] Similarly, the Jewish "no" may actually be, in the post-first century context, a participation in Jesus' "yes"—especially when Jews were martyred for their refusal to convert to Christianity. As Kinzer remarks of Jews martyred by Christians, "For one who believes in Yeshua, all true martyrdom—faithful witness to the God of Israel at the cost of one's life—involves participation in the suffering and death of the ultimate 'faithful witness' (*ho martys ho pistos*). In this case, saying no to the Yeshua proclaimed by the church became a way of sharing in his perfect yes to God."[142] Kinzer notes also that Edith Stein described the Jewish people's suffering at the hands of the Nazis as a sharing in the suffering in Jesus.[143]

In short, according to Kinzer the Jewish people not only have not been able since the first century to say "no" to the true Messiah, but also their innocent sufferings at the hands of Christians since the first century have been a participation in the innocent sufferings of the Messiah. Likewise, because the God who is embodied in Jesus' Jewish flesh is the God who elects Israel, Christians cannot separate from the Jewish people. Thus the inseparable connection cuts both ways: "The (apparent) Jewish no to Yeshua has not expelled his Messianic presence from Israel, and the (actual) Christian no to the Jewish people and Judaism has not expelled Israel's presence from the church's inner sanctum."[144]

Leaving aside the ordering that will be fully revealed at end of time, where as Novak says of Jews and Christians "we all hope to be the lasting friends of God and thus lasting friends of each other,"[145] the question remains, however, whether it is accurate to say that living Rabbinic Judaism can only *apparently* say "no" to Jesus. It seems reasonable to suppose that just as communities of Christians can decide that they should not observe Torah, so also communities of Rabbinic Jews can decide that they do not wish to have faith in Jesus as the divine Messiah or to practice the Christian sacraments. Just as the Christians' decision has meaning for their relationship with living Rabbinic Judaism, so also, it would seem, the Jews' decision has meaning for their relationship with the Church.

In neither case does this earthly relationship necessarily define the eschatological relationship with God that the communities or individuals involved will enjoy. As Kinzer emphasizes, at the eschatological level, it may well be that the refusal turns out to have been only an apparent one. Although we cannot in this world make such an eschatological judgment one way or the other—since the judgment belongs to God—it does seem, however, that we can say that if living Rabbinic Judaism (or the living Church) denies that a particular affirmation or practice is consistent with Judaism (or with Christianity), then one cannot hold to that affirmation or practice while remaining within living Judaism (or living Christianity). The question then is not whether one can give an account of Rabbinic Judaism that shows why, in fact, its refusal of Jesus may turn out to be implicit affirmation of and participation in Jesus as Messiah. Without doubt, such an account can be given, as can an account of Christianity that shows why Christians' failure to observe Torah may turn out to be implicit affirmation of Torah observance. Rather, what is at issue, as we have already discussed, is whether Kinzer's desire to speak to (gentile) Christians from the side of living Rabbinic Judaism is possible if living Rabbinic Judaism refuses to grant that his beliefs and practices, taken as a whole, conform to faithful Judaism.

Concluding Reflections

As Kinzer shows, some eminent Christian theologians have seen in Messianic Judaism a way to reformulate Christian faith so as to affirm

Judaism by affirming the ongoing Torah observance of Jews in the Christian community, thereby rectifying a mistake made by the first-century Church. The growth of Messianic Judaism seems to some Christian theologians to be a ready-made path for overcoming both supersessionism and the anti-Jewish attitudes that have plagued the Church. In this context, Novak's nuanced account of supersessionism offers guidelines for Christian dialogue with Rabbinic Judaism. In his essays that touch upon Christian and Jewish supersessionism, Novak demonstrates appreciation of the historical development of Judaism and Christianity, awareness of what divides and what unites Jews and Christians, and understanding of (even if disagreement with) messianic fulfillment theology.

For Novak—and I agree with him—Christian proclamation of Jesus as the Messiah mandates a form of supersession, but one that does not "denigrate Judaism."[146] Believing they have found the Messiah of Israel who has established the kingdom of God by his Pasch, Christians must hold that "the Church does have the more authentic definition of Israel than Judaism has."[147] Recognizing that the Church could not claim to be the community of the Messiah without making at least the claim that "Christianity provides the savior to whom Judaism has always looked,"[148] Novak observes that "all Jews can really ask Christians to do as Christians" is to affirm that the Jews and Judaism have not lost their covenants with God, and thus that Jews and Judaism retain a theological place.[149] This perspective exhibits his appreciation for the communal character of both Christianity and Judaism. As he says, "To look at Judaism and Christianity as covenantal religions is to see that the relationship with God of the individual Jew and the individual Christian is always within *covenanted community*."[150] Novak thereby allows Christian theologians, within Jewish-Christian dialogue, to affirm that believers' participation through the Holy Spirit in Christ's life, death, and Resurrection means that believers have become "God's temple" (1 Cor. 3.16), "the Israel of God" (Gal. 6.16).

This approach informs Novak's practical concern that "Christian acceptance of the self-proclaimed Judaism of the new Jewish Christians, as opposed to accepting them simply as *any* converts are accepted, can only undermine the position of the pro-dialogue and cooperation party within the Jewish community."[151] This is so because Messianic Judaism seems plagued by supersessionism. Ongoing Rabbinic Judaism involves authoritative rabbis on whom Rabbinic Jews depend to determine the boundaries of Jewish belief and practice. Although Rabbinic Judaism recognizes Messianic Jews as Jews, nonetheless Rabbinic Judaism rejects the "Judaism" of Messianic Judaism.[152] The only option for Messianic Judaism qua Judaism is thus to assume that Rabbinic Judaism has misunderstood itself (its "no" is really a "yes"), and on this basis to declare itself to be a true form of Rabbinic Judaism. But for Christians to accept this claim *in Jewish-Christian dialogue* (rather than to engage Messianic Judaism within ecumenical dialogue) would require Christians to assume that Rabbinic Judaism has no authority to define itself. Ongoing Rabbinic Judaism would thereby become invisible, for practical purposes, to Christians. Furthermore, since Messianic Judaism supposes that Christianity has also misunderstood itself, the Church would also need to be superseded by a "bilateral *ekklesia.*"

Guided by Novak and sharpened by engagement with Kinzer's vision of Messianic Judaism, this chapter identifies parameters for Jewish-Christian theological dialogue. Jews and Christians agree that history does not stand outside the wisdom and power of God: "The earth is the Lord's and the fulness thereof, the world and those who dwell therein" (Ps. 24.1); "before him [God] no creature is hidden, but all are open and laid bare to the eyes of him with whom we have to do" (Heb. 5.13). It follows that God is a provident God, and that human action is theonomous rather than autonomous (Chapter 2). In order to understand human participation in God's providence, Jews and Christians turn to the doctrine that human beings are the image of God (Chapter 3) and to theories of natural or Noahide law, understood within the context of God's election of Israel for the redemption of the world (Chapter 4).

In taking up these questions in dialogue with David Novak, I draw not only upon his erudition but also upon his awareness that theology speaks to basic human concerns: Does God care for us? What makes human life worth living and worth preserving? How should we live? Novak's work is responsive to what Nicholas Boyle diagnoses as the widespread "feeling that individually and collectively we no longer know who we are."[153] For Novak, the nexus of election, theonomy, the image of God, and natural law offers a persuasive portrait of "who we are." As Novak recognizes, the rejection of harsh supersessionism opens the door for constructive dialogue about "who we are" as rational creatures in search of God and for whom the electing God searches. Without minimizing differences between Jews and Christians, let us inquire into the ways in which Jews and Christians share, and might better proclaim, "the hope of Israel" (Acts 28.20).

Chapter 2

Providence and Theonomy

Since Jews and Christians worship "the everlasting God, the Creator of the ends of the earth" (Isa. 40.28), providence and theonomy should be central themes of constructive Jewish-Christian dialogue. As a starting place for constructive dialogue on providence and theonomy, this chapter takes up Karol Wojtyla/Pope John Paul II's poetic evocation of the Holy Land as a sign of providence—a sign that culminates in Christ Jesus.[1] On this basis, I explore David Novak's groundbreaking book *Jewish-Christian Dialogue*, which aims to foster shared Jewish and Christian witness to "theonomous morality."[2] In light of Novak's insights, I then return to providence through the perspective of Moses Maimonides. As I hope to make clear, it is the doctrine of providence that grounds Novak's "theonomous morality," and so the emphases of Novak and Wojtyla/John Paul II support and enrich each other.

John Paul II and the Holy Land

Pope John Paul II was particularly concerned about the loss of the sense of theonomy and providence in post-Enlightenment cultures. In what is arguably his most important encyclical, *Veritatis Splendor*, John Paul II observes that "obedience to God is not, as some would believe, a *heteronomy*, as if the moral life were subject to the will of something all-powerful, absolute, extraneous to man and intolerant of his freedom" (§41). Since obedience to God fulfills human freedom, he states that "[o]thers speak, and rightly so, of *theonomy*, or *participated theonomy*, since man's free obedience to God's law effectively implies that human reason and human will participate in God's wisdom and providence" (§41). In his last book, *Memory and Identity*, John Paul describes the worldviews of Communism, Nazism, and the culture of death as linked by their rejection of such providential theonomy:

> What is the root of these post-Enlightenment ideologies? The answer is simple: it happens because of the rejection of God *qua* Creator, and

consequently *qua* source determining what is good and what is evil. It happens because of the rejection of what ultimately constitutes us as human beings, that is, the notion of human nature as a "given reality"; its place has been taken by a "product of thought" freely formed and freely changeable according to circumstances.[3]

One of John Paul's most acute commentators, Russell Hittinger, has similarly contrasted the pre-Enlightenment view of the human creature as "located in an order of divine providence" with modern Enlightenment accounts of human nature in which "natural law came to mean the position of the human mind just insofar as it is left to itself, prior to authority and law."[4]

In his cycle of poems "Journey to the Holy Places," published in 1965 under the pen name Andrzej Jawien, Karol Wojtyla connects the Holy Land first of all with the person of Abraham. As a wanderer, Abraham embodies the journey of each person toward God: "A whole people must repeat and repeat again the wanderings of Abraham."[5] Abraham is "a man of the great encounter."[6] This great encounter with God requires that humans learn to journey in complete trust of God's plan. It requires also that, in their outward wanderings, humans train themselves for the journey inward to God in their soul. Yet Wojtyla suggests that modern conveniences have left us unprepared for such difficult journeys, for the wandering that is trusting in God. He asks, "Have we distanced ourselves from the hardship of wanderings, transferring the barrenness of old earth to the wide open spaces?"[7] Even though it seems we are more settled, we are less so. In modern civilization, we must return again and again to Abraham's wandering, so as to apprehend how our lives together have meaning. This meaning is found only in journeying in the presence of God.

The same theme of divine providence marks Wojtyla's poetic reflections on why this particular land is "holy." The Holy Land, for Wojtyla the pilgrim, draws us into its providential meaning. Pilgrimage to the Holy Land indicates one's desire to share more deeply in how God has known and loved human beings in the earthly place of the Holy Land. The earthly place thereby becomes also an interior place: God's providential plan, enacted in the Holy Land, is enacted in the heart of the believing pilgrim. Wojtyla writes,

> Oh, corner of the earth, place in the holy land—what kind of place are you in me? My steps cannot tread on you; I must kneel. Thus I confirm today you were indeed a place of meeting. Kneeling down I imprint a seal

on you. You will remain here with my seal—you will remain—and I will take you and transform you within me into the place of new testimony. I walk away as a witness who testifies across the millennia.[8]

He thus can rejoice at seeing a well in the Holy Land both because it reminds him of the wells built by the patriarchs and the meeting of Jesus with the Samaritan woman at the well, and because he himself encounters God at the well. By seeing the visible Holy Land around him, he finds himself more attentive to the reality that he, too, is an actor in God's providential plan. He explains, "I am on a pilgrimage to identity. . . . This is the identity of finding one's own self in landscape. Here I come on a pilgrimage. And this place is holy."[9] The landscape is the view from Mount Tabor, the sights of Galilee, Lake Genezareth, and so forth; but it is also one's interior landscape in which one's pilgrimage to the Holy Land becomes a more conscious entering into God's providential plan as realized in these very places. In turn, the pilgrim becomes increasingly able to share the Holy Land with others. As Wojtyla puts it, "Oh, place, you have to be carried to many, so many places."[10] He knows well that "since those times the sand has run interminably through over and over again. Not a grain is left."[11] Nonetheless carrying stones from the Holy Land is, he recognizes, a way to share his faith in God: he tells of carrying some stones from the shore of Lake Genezareth back to Poland and putting them "in the hardworking hand of a fisherman by the Notec River."[12]

A connection with the earthly place of the Holy Land enables us to recognize more deeply how God gives us a place in his providential plan. In Wojtyla's words, "A place, the place is important, the place is holy." He explains that pilgrims do not fill the Holy Land with their own personalities, but rather pilgrims are marked and filled by the identity of the Holy Land as the earthly expression of God's providence for creation. As Wojtyla says in another poem about the desert of Judea: "Land of meeting, the one and only land, through which all earth became this land, as everything became that which it is through Him Who Is."[13] All comes into being through the Creator; all receives its full identity in and through the deeds accomplished in the Holy Land. The Holy Land is the place where God fulfills his providential plan for union with humankind. It follows that the Holy Land is not solely an earthly place (marked by violence), but also a place that serves as a sign of the truth about creation, namely, God's care for his creatures. Speaking to God, Wojtyla remarks, "You chose this place centuries ago—the place in which You give Yourself and accept me."[14] Or as he says in the same vein in the first poem of this cycle: "And today, why do

I come? Don't be surprised. Here for nineteen hundred years each gaze passes into that one gaze which never alters."[15]

In 2003, Wojtyla, as Pope John Paul II, published a final set of poems, titled *Roman Triptych: Meditations*. The first poem of the triptych places John Paul in his beloved mountains where he contemplates how the created order both discloses and hides God. The second poem places him in the Sistine Chapel meditating upon the book of Genesis, upon the human being as the image of God capable of self-giving love, and upon his own death and the selection of the new successor to the Apostle Peter. Finally, the third poem places him on pilgrimage in the land of Abraham. In these three poems John Paul moves from the wonder of the philosopher, to the revelation that human life is in the divine image of God the Creator, to the revelation of God's plan for the community of Jesus' disciples.

The third poem carries forward his earlier poetic meditations on the Holy Land and his experience of pilgrimage. He writes, "If today we go to these places whence, long ago, Abraham set out, where he heard the Voice, where the promise was fulfilled, we do so in order to stand at the threshold—to go back to the beginning of the Covenant."[16] The threshold, for John Paul, is the place of hope for the fulfillment of the promise, of trust that God will accomplish his plan. Each human being must stand at this place. As a place on earth, the Holy Land inspires each human being to trust God's providence.

John Paul focuses our attention upon the land of Moriah where God commanded Abraham to sacrifice Isaac, his beloved son and the son of the promise. It would appear that the Holy Land is a place of terrifying and unintelligible renunciation. Yet in the land of Moriah, Abraham finds the meaning of the Holy Land: a complete reliance on God to accomplish his plan for us. Abraham's hopes center upon the continuance of his line in Isaac, and yet Abraham finds fulfillment by his willingness to relinquish these hopes and to trust God. Abraham learns in the land of Moriah "what it means for a father to sacrifice his own son—a sacrificial death."[17] The beloved Son's free offering of himself, out of love for us, stands at the heart of God's providential plan in which human beings are transformed from self-centered to self-giving.

For Karol Wojtyla/John Paul II, therefore, the fact that a particular land on earth is called "holy" indicates that humans, in our brief sojourns on Earth, have a "place" where our lives are measured and valued not by time but by God's eternal presence. In order to find this "place," each person must learn, like Abraham, to entrust his or her "wanderings" to God, to enter upon a life that is sacrificial. To meditate upon and make pilgrimage to the Holy Land is to allow oneself to be filled by the guidance of God's providence and to find a "place" within God's plan, rather than vainly seeking to establish a permanent place in the world on one's own. In short, understanding what it means to be human requires recovering a God-centered account of human life, marked by trust in providence. Secular modernity, Wojtyla/John Paul suggests, will find this renewal of meaning and purpose by walking in the footsteps of Abraham (whose footsteps lead to Christ).

Wojtyla/John Paul, however, does not envision divine providence outside its Christological fulfillment. Does providence then in fact belong among what David Novak calls the "points of true commonality"[18] between Jews and Christians?

David Novak on Jewish-Christian Dialogue and Theonomous Morality

Points of True Commonality: Between Syncretism and Triumphalism

Novak certainly does not think that the footsteps of Abraham lead to Jesus of Nazareth as the Messiah. As Novak points out, Jews and Christians have already made their positions in this regard sufficiently clear: "Christians asserted that the covenant that began with Abraham was fulfilled in Jesus. Their basic accusation against the Jews was that the Jews were fixated at a stage of the covenant's incomplete development. . . . Jews, though, saw Christianity as a distortion of the original covenant, a covenant that Israel alone had preserved in faithfulness to God."[19] Indeed, as we saw in Chapter 1, Novak permits Jews to affirm that Christianity is (in a certain sense) "a distortion of the original covenant" and also permits Christians to affirm that Judaism is (in a certain sense) "the covenant's incomplete development." In this vein Novak raises serious concerns about interfaith worship services where "Jews avoid mentioning the doctrine of the chosenness of Israel, and Christians avoid mentioning Christ."[20] As he says, "Such services seem to be the devotions of Jews who have bracketed Sinai and Christians who have bracketed Calvary."[21]

For Novak, then, Jews could not have a doctrine of providence that excludes the primacy of Sinai, and Christians could not have a doctrine of providence that excludes the fulfillment of God's covenantal relationship with Israel by Christ Jesus. He rightly observes: "For Jews and Christians, respectively, the events of Sinai and Calvary are total and irreversible. Even though God can be affirmed as creator before these events, and by those who never experienced them, the affirmation of creation by Jews and Christians is mediated by revelation."[22] But if this is so, what kind of dialogue about divine providence and theonomy can take place between Jews and Christians?

While insisting upon the covenantal particularity of Jews and Christians, Novak requires the abandonment of what he calls "spiritual triumphalism."[23] As he says, "There can be no real dialogue if each side's view of the other is essentially a view of a phantom of its own projection."[24] Jewish theologians construct such a "phantom" when they suppose that "whatever legitimacy Christianity has, it is because of Judaism. As such, Christianity must be ultimately interpreted by Jews."[25] Christian theologians construct such a phantom when they propose that "Christians are now to be considered the people of God in the fullest sense, but Jews have not been totally removed from that status, for Christian hope for the ultimate conversion of the Jews cannot be based on the denigration of Judaism as spiritually corrupt."[26]

Yet are not these "phantoms" required by the implications of both Jewish and Christian covenantal theology? Novak remarks approvingly that "Judaism and Christianity base themselves on their election to receive unique revelation from God. The very logic of that revelation requires that the community receiving it take an absolute stance toward it in distinction from the revelation claimed by any other community."[27] But Christians understand Jesus to be the Messiah of Israel, the transformative fulfillment of Sinai, from which it follows that "Israel failed to obtain what was sought. The elect obtained it, but the rest were hardened" (Rom. 11.7).[28] Jesus makes present in Israel the full meaning of Sinai. This is the broad import of Paul's comment that "to this day whenever Moses is read a veil lies over their minds; but when a man turns to the Lord the veil is removed" (2 Cor. 3.14–16).[29]

If this is the Christian perspective, what about the Jewish perspective? Novak, I think, would agree with Jacob Neusner's remark: "Jews believe in the Torah of Moses and form on earth and in their own flesh God's kingdom of priests and the holy people. And that belief requires faithful Jews to enter a dissent at the teachings of Jesus, on the grounds that those teachings at important points contradict the Torah."[30] On this view, Paul's understanding of Jesus is simply mistaken and so, despite Novak's warning against triumphalism, it would follow that "Christianity must be ultimately interpreted by Jews."[31] How can we get beyond this impasse? Paul suggests that God's judgments and ways are "unsearchable" and "inscrutable" (Rom. 11.33), and it seems to me that this concern that God alone be judge also stands at the heart of Novak's rejection of "spiritual triumphalism" or "phantoms." Although Jews and

Christians each believe their own community to be "*uniquely related*"[32] to divine truth, Jews and Christians can dialogue "in such a way that . . . . [t]he other one standing before me must be discovered with his or her phenomenological integrity."[33]

Novak certainly does not aim to make Jewish-Christian dialogue "nonreligious."[34] Jews and Christians, he observes, do not have the freedom to negotiate on this basis, because "[t]he schema of sacred events—creation, election, revelation, judgment, and redemption—which is essential to both Judaism and Christianity, is seen by Jews and Christians as being prior to any interhuman agreement."[35] Dialogue between Jews and Christians cannot proceed on the humanly constructed basis of a secular "social contract," because Judaism and Christianity can have only one foundation: God's action, which requires "human action to be faithfully responsive rather than autonomously initiatory."[36] Jewish-Christian dialogue on providence and theonomy must itself belong to this "faithfully responsive" action. But how can this take place if Judaism and Christianity differ with respect to the content of faithful response? Novak here notes that secular modernity generally supposes that belief in God, and especially covenantal monotheism, is "immediately and ultimately divisive"[37] and cannot account for the true common good of humankind. According to Novak, then, dialogue should take as its starting point the reasons Jews and Christians can give each other regarding why justice and peace are better pursued in Judaism and Christianity than, for example, by means of "the tolerance of polytheism or the ahistoricity of the Eastern religions."[38]

At this stage, recall the key images that we identified from Karol Wojtyla/John Paul's poetic depictions of the Holy Land: "a pilgrimage to identity," "land of meeting," "each gaze passes into the one gaze," "the threshold . . . the beginning of the Covenant."[39] At the "threshold" or "beginning of the covenant" in Abraham, Wojtyla/John Paul finds the willingness to renounce oneself that characterizes self-giving love. When based upon the free gift of the provident God, the formation of one's identity does not require conflict with others.

Commonality and Duality

Yet, does not revelation sharply divide those communities that have received revelation from those that have not, thereby making theonomy/providence a sectarian doctrine? This question demands a carefully nuanced answer. In the concluding chapter of *Jewish-Christian Dialogue*, Novak observes that Jews are related to other Jews in a "singular" or intimate fashion, as members of a shared historical community or family, whereas Jews are related to non-Jews in a "general" fashion.[40] In order to understand the "singularity" of one's relationship with one's family members, one must learn how to distinguish one's family members from other human beings. Novak explains in this regard that "one's own covenantal relationship calls for the constitution of the more general background of the human world that is not part of one's own covenant. This is how Jews can intelligently constitute the role of Christians for themselves and how Christians can do likewise for Jews."[41]

Novak describes three kinds of views on the relationship of the "singular" to the "general." In the first, rejected by Novak, the "singular" tolerates and governs the "general" and provides a rationale for its existence. In the second, the "singular" is seen as "that which leads toward the general," as for instance in Alexander the Great's efforts to constitute a universal world civilization out of Hellenic culture.[42] Singularity here finds its full expression by either sublating the "general" culture into itself, or else (what is perhaps the same) being sublated into the general culture. As Novak points out, however, "the metaphysical priority assigned to the general over the singular is inconsistent with the theological primacy of the singular road from Sinai to the Messianic Jerusalem. For Christians, the road from Calvary to the Parousia is just as singular."[43]

The third view of the relationship of the singular to the general sees the latter as developing, by means of its intrinsic resources, into the singular. Novak ascribes this teleological view to Aristotle, and among Jewish theologians, to Maimonides: "Maimonides saw the more general Noahide law as the preparation for the full Torah revealed to Moses. In his words, the Noahide law was 'completed' (*ve-nishlamah*) by the Mosaic Torah. . . . Maimonides uses the complete Torah to mean the actualization of the potential Torah of the Noahides."[44] For Maimonides Christians misinterpreted the Torah and thereby fell back into the "general," but nonetheless they have the potential to relearn Torah aright under the guidance of Jewish teachers, and furthermore their monotheism will ultimately contribute to the Messianic completion of Judaism on earth.[45] Novak sees this view as embodied by Jewish-Christian dialogue that possesses the implicit goal of proselytizing, whereas he holds that actual "dialogue presupposes a true mutuality based on a duality that is not to be overcome in the process of the dialogue itself."[46]

Let us pause very briefly on this point before moving on to Novak's fourth and final way of relating the singular to the general. Certainly, Christians cannot envision Jews as unrelated to the Messiah. Can Christians, then, grant that there is a "duality that is not to be overcome in the process of the dialogue itself?"

I suggest a threefold answer. First, even if, as the *Catechism of the Catholic Church* states, "the New Testament lies hidden in the Old and the Old is unveiled in the New" (§129), nonetheless the Incarnation of the Son of God and the grace of the Holy Spirit are far more than the actualization of potencies. For this reason, God's action in Christ Jesus fulfills God's earlier action in Israel without negating the significance of the revelation to Israel. The latter is not a pure potency whose value ends at the moment of full actualization. As the *Catechism* says, "the Old Covenant has never been revoked" (§121) and "the Old Testament retains its own intrinsic value as Revelation reaffirmed by our Lord himself" (§129).[47] Second, since for Christians the Torah has a "literal" as well as a "figurative" sense, Christians do not need to envision their Jewish dialogue partners strictly as "potential Christians," as if Jews had no theologically recognizable identity in their own right. Third, questions regarding the relationship of the covenants need not constitute the material for the formal dialogue.[48] As we will see, the doctrine of theonomy/providence in Jewish-Christian dialogue exemplifies dialogue construed along these lines.

Turning to Novak's fourth and final way of understanding the relationship of the singular to the general, Novak begins with revelation, with "the singularity of God's election of Israel and his giving the Torah to them."[49] Having placed God's action at the center, he then interprets the "general" as the "background of possibility" into which God's action comes.[50] While elsewhere Novak criticizes Maimonides for relying too heavily on "potency-act" teleology, here Novak praises Maimonides's "possibility-realization logic."[51] Maimonides argues that only God can make someone a prophet: the merely human actualization of potencies is not enough. Human beings have a "possibility," not a "potency," to be prophets. If God's action in revelation answers to a possibility rather than a potency in the prophet, then, Novak reasons, there is no "one outcome" that is the necessary result of the realization of the possibility, in contrast to the actualization of a potency, and so no one revelation exhausts the entire "background of possibility."[52] Other revelations will realize aspects of the "background of possibility," and in so doing will reveal the "preconditions" that Jews share with those who have not received or have not understood the Torah. Novak concludes that "from its singularity Judaism relates to the general world as a realm of possibility; namely, with what it sees out there as its own preconditions it can converse."[53]

Christian theologians, I think, should disagree with Novak's denial that the content of other revelations "can be ultimately understood only within the context of the one, true, actual revelation, of which their revelation is at best the potential."[54] On this issue, where Novak disagrees with Maimonides, Christian theologians need to agree with Maimonides. However, Christian theologians can join with Novak in seeking to avoid what Novak fears will follow from Maimonides's position. He fears that "potency-act" logic will both immanentize the covenant and make it impossible for dialogue to "be constituted in such a way that each side can recognize itself in it" with its "phenomenological integrity."[55] Christians too must avoid positing that covenantal fulfillment is the actualization of resources intrinsic to human beings, and Christians should likewise recognize that God's covenant with the Jews is not solely potency. Aquinas emphasizes this by identifying not only "figurative" (potency-act) but also "literal" reasons for each of the commandments of Sinai.

Novak observes that "Revelation's most evident precondition is morality,"[56] and it is upon this "realm of possibility" that Novak suggests Jewish-Christian dialogue should focus. Here we find the grounds for Jewish-Christian dialogue that takes up Wojtyla/John Paul's "pilgrimage to identity."

Theonomous Morality

Novak identifies four points that together constitute "theonomous morality." These points are as follows: (1) God created the human person primarily for relationship with God; (2) this relationship is primarily enacted in human response to God's commandments; (3) as social creatures, human beings can only enter into covenant with God from within a covenantal community that presupposes both "a general morality of socially pertinent standards" and "specific intercovenantal norms"; (4) human fulfillment (individual and collective) "lies in a future and universal redemptive act by God, one as yet on the unattainable historical horizon."[57] All law, including the covenant-specific commandments, pertains to the accomplishment of God's providential plan for bringing human beings into a relationship of holiness with him (in and through his covenantal community): as Aquinas puts it, "every law aims at establishing friendship,"[58] and "the end of the divine law is to bring man to that end which is everlasting happiness."[59]

Explaining the importance of theonomy, Novak emphasizes that "[t]o make any other voice [than God's] the *Grundnorm* is an idolatrous rejection of God the creator."[60] Is theonomy compatible with personal freedom? Novak suggests that for external authority to be acceptable to humans, we must hear that authority as a voice that affirms and secures our personhood, as a command that calls us into personal fulfillment in the future.

If we cannot trust that God by his providence draws us toward the goal for which he created us, then God's voice will seem false: "A voice calls one from the present and promises a future if one will act toward it."[61] As Novak observes, theonomy includes this future dimension, so that obedience means life with God: "One is commanded toward the future; the future itself does not command. Nevertheless . . . God's creative thrust is present, leading into a mutual future all those who hearken to God's commandments and do them as best they can here and now: 'There is hope for your future [*tiqvah l'ahareetekh*], says the Lord' (Jer. 31.16)."[62] What at first might seem a loss of human values (autonomy and heteronomy) is in fact, as Wojtyla/John Paul says, the "land of meeting."

Does the affirmation of theonomous morality have anything to say to the rise of nonbelief in God in Western cultures over the past two centuries? Novak's answer is a mystical one: nonbelievers should be invited to wait in the openness of silence for the voice of the Lord, and Jews and Christians can join such nonbelievers in solidarity, because "we who have heard it must be silent with them, for we need to hear it once again."[63] This silent waiting characterizes the stance of the believer, since for both Jews and Christians, hope depends on active waiting on God's providence. Yet this "silence" and "waiting" cannot be passive, unengaged with the world. Rigorous Jewish-Christian dialogue need not cede the rational ground to views that, as John Paul II observes, emerge from "the rejection of God *qua* Creator, and consequently *qua* source determining what is good and what is evil."[64]

If theonomy is necessary for contemporary "pilgrimage to identity," a pilgrimage that should characterize Jewish-Christian dialogue, then the retrieval of earlier theological resources belongs at the heart of the active "waiting" to which Jews and Christians are called in the contemporary world. It is no accident that Novak's writings engage continually with the Rabbinic tradition and medieval Jewish thinkers such as Saadiah and Maimonides. The final section of this chapter therefore takes up Moses Maimonides's theology of providence as a testament, despite certain weaknesses, to the necessity that theonomy be supported by a strong doctrine of providence. In this way I aim to underscore the unity of the concerns of Novak and Wojtyla/John Paul.

Maimonides on Providence

How can "theonomous morality" (Novak), as central to our providential "pilgrimage to identity" rooted in the "land of meeting" (Wojtyla/

John Paul), handle the problem of the suffering of the just? This problem stands at the heart of Maimonides's theology of providence.[65] As Maimonides observes, the ancient philosophers reasoned that if the good suffer and the wicked flourish, either God is ignorant, or else he knows; and if the latter, either he knows and arranges matters perfectly, or he knows but is powerless, or he knows but despite sufficient power does not care to help.[66] Of these three alternatives, says Maimonides, the last two are clearly unworthy of God; and so it comes down to either God knows and arranges matters perfectly, or else God is ignorant. The ancient philosophers who pondered this problem and found that human affairs do not seem to be well arranged, concluded that God is ignorant of human affairs.

In response to the ancient philosophers' view, Maimonides argues that they fell "into something worse than that which they tried to avoid" because "in trying to avoid imputing negligence to God, they decided that He is ignorant and that everything that is in this lowly world is hidden from Him, and He does not apprehend it."[67] Maimonides grants that they base their judgment about God's lack of knowledge on philosophically sophisticated claims: they argue that God, since his knowledge does not depend upon the senses, can know only the species, not individuals (differentiated by matter). Similarly, they argue that because God's knowledge, like his being, is one, he can know only himself rather than many things. Yet for Maimonides they err not only philosophically, by implying imperfection in God, but also by differing with the teaching of Scripture.

Maimonides proceeds to set forth briefly four ancient philosophical theories of providence. The first theory, credited to Epicurus, is that there is no providence, but rather there is solely chance; Maimonides relies upon Aristotle in rejecting this view. The second theory Maimonides attributes to Aristotle. On this view the unchanging spheres, the unchanging species, and the natural inclinations of individuals are governed by divine providence, but other movements of individuals belong strictly to chance and are not governed by providence. Maimonides argues that Aristotle's position on providence is shared by Jews who reject Torah: "Those who, deviating from our Law, believed in this opinion were those who said: *The Lord hath forsaken the earth* [Ezek. 9.9]."[68] It hardly needs saying that Maimonides repudiates this position.

The third and fourth theories belong to distinct groups of Muslim thinkers, the Ashariyah and the Mu'tazila, respectively. According to the Ashariyah, Maimonides says, God causes everything, including all natural processes and all sufferings.[69] Everything that happens is ultimately necessary, even if it appears, from the human perspective, that there are multiple possibilities. Maimonides holds that this view not only takes away the truth of free will, but also thereby leaves God fully responsible for all injustice. This aspect makes the theory intolerable for Maimonides. The fourth theory affirms human free will, God's supreme justice, and God's providence over all things. Maimonides wonders, however, whether one can really succeed in accounting for physical defect, illness, and death as being only apparently evil for the human being who endures them (but who actually, according to the Mu'tazila, benefits from them). Likewise, he questions whether it makes sense to hold that God's providence extends to nonhuman creatures. Can the slaughtering of a sheep, for example, be viewed in terms of providential punishment and reward? For the Mu'tazila, "Even when a flea and a louse are killed, it is necessary that they have a compensation for them from God. They say in the same way that if this mouse, which has not sinned, is devoured by a cat or a hawk, His wisdom has required this with regard to the mouse and that the latter will receive compensation in the other world."[70] It seems absurd to suggest that God permits the destruction of an irrational animal with an eternal reward in view.

Nonetheless, Maimonides does admire elements of each of the last three theories. From Aristotle, he takes the view that God's providence does not include plants or nonrational animals; from the Ashariyah, the affirmation of God's omniscience; and from the Mu'tazilites, the affirmation of God's justice.[71] In proposing his own theory of providence, Maimonides argues that "In this lowly world—I mean that which is beneath the sphere of the moon—divine providence watches only over the individuals belonging to the human species and that in this species alone all the circumstances of the individuals and the good and evil that befall them are consequent upon the deserts, just as it says: *For all His ways are judgment* [Deut. 32.4]."[72] For Maimonides, Scripture requires the affirmation of God's universal providence over human beings as well as God's perfect justice in this regard.[73] Similarly, he argues that the entire histories of Abraham, Isaac, and Jacob confirm God's perfect providence over human beings. Regarding the perfect justice of God's providence over human beings, he appeals to texts from the Torah that describe God's promise to judge human sins: see Exod. 32.33–34 and Lev. 20.6, 23.30, and 26.16.[74] To this degree, then, the Ashariyah and the Mu'tazilites are correct.

By means of Scripture and Aristotle, however, Maimonides seeks to leave room for free will and for the disordered state of the world. In this regard his key scriptural passages come from the Psalms: "What is man, that thou takest knowledge of him?" (Ps. 144.3) and "What is man, that thou art mindful of him" (Ps. 8.8). These psalms suggest that while human beings are (however undeservedly) fully known by God, other less important things need not be fully known and happen by chance. Likewise, the prophet Habakkuk observes that it might appear that God, by allowing the idolatrous Chaldeans to destroy the righteous among the people of God, is making "men like the fish of the sea, like crawling things that have no ruler" (Hab. 1.14) and that are indiscriminately killed by fisherman. Habakkuk goes on to state that in fact God is using the Chaldeans as instruments of punishing justly the sins of his people. For Maimonides, the point is that while fish do not have a providential "ruler," human beings do. For this reason, although many events occur by chance, the involvement of human beings in these events always introduces the aspect of providence. Thus a shipwreck, Maimonides says, may be the product of a chance weather pattern, but the deaths of particular human beings on that ship belong firmly to the governance of providence.[75]

Why does Maimonides give human beings this special prerogative? In addition to the warrant of Scripture, Maimonides draws upon Avicenna's view that there is only one "active intellect" (in which each human being participates through the "passive intellect"). As the divine intellectual "overflow," the active intellect provides the conduit for God's providence.[76] As Maimonides remarks, "Accordingly everyone with whom something of this overflow is united, will be reached by providence to the extent to which he is reached by the intellect."[77] God providentially rewards and punishes each person, even persons who do not know Torah, because every human being possesses an "inborn disposition" that is "the prohibition against wrongdoing and injustice."[78] Indeed, Maimonides explains all intellectual and moral virtue, including almost all prophecy, in terms of the human participation in the divine overflow.[79] Good human beings receive and nourish God's intellectual influence; bad human beings ignore and neglect it. The latter degenerate to the level of animals, and, in their wickedness, can be justifiably killed.[80] As examples of those who live according to the influence of the divine intellectual overflow and are thereby blessed by divine providence, Maimonides cites not only the patriarchs but also the ancient Greek philosophers.[81] On this basis, Maimonides considers that real suffering in this life manifests a lack of conformity to divine providence; he remarks that "[w]ith regard to providence watching over excellent men and neglecting the ignorant, it is said: *He will keep the feet of his holy ones, but the wicked shall be put to silence in darkness; for not by strength shall man prevail* [1 Sam. 2.9]."[82]

However, if "providence" means simply that humans participate (or fail to participate) in the divine intellectual overflow, what does the Torah add?

As Novak recognizes, Maimonides's approach tends toward rationalism.[83] One can thus appreciate why Novak emphasizes obedience to God's voice in depicting the structure of theonomous morality.[84] Maimonides's reliance in his doctrine of providence upon an Avicennan view of the active intellect also calls into question whether the Holy Land constitutes a "land of meeting" (Wojtyla/John Paul) any more than Athens does. It is correct to distinguish between God's providence for rational and nonrational creatures and to hold that virtuous persons participate more deeply in God's providence, but one need not account for God's providence solely in terms of the emanation of the divine intellect.[85] Since creatures are finite created participations in being, providence is the ordering to the end that God gives to his entire creation.

Both in its strengths and in its weaknesses, Maimonides's treatment of providence assists contemporary Jewish and Christian investigation of providence and theonomy. Over against the ancient philosophers, whose position is echoed by secular thinkers today, Maimonides's insistence upon providence affirms that cosmic disorder does not negate the possibility of theonomy. At the same time, Novak's emphasis on theonomy avoids an overly human-centered (rather than God-centered) account of providence.

Conclusion

In an essay comparing Maimonides and Aquinas on natural law, Novak remarks: "How fortunate for himself and for posterity that Aquinas's engagement with Judaism was located in his engagement with the thinker whom no subsequent Jewish thinker can ever really leave behind when thinking about Judaism."[86] Novak holds that Maimonides influences Aquinas's account of practical reason even more significantly than he does Aquinas's metaphysics. Discussing the two thinkers' theologies of law, Novak observes that "each theologian had to deal with the question of the natural preconditions for revelation."[87] This question provides them with points of "true commonality" that foster the most constructive kind of conversations between Jews and Christians.

In this tradition of Jewish-Christian dialogue, this chapter draws together providence and theonomy. As Wojtyla/John Paul suggests, the true "pilgrimage to identity" reveals that it is God who provides us with permanence and hope; it is God who grounds our personhood and our dignity. Providential theonomy thus accords not only with revelation of moral law but also with the "background of possibility" to covenantal revelation supplied by the created order. Recall Wojtyla/John Paul's words: "I come across these places which You [God] have filled with Yourself once and for all. I do not come to fill them with my own self, but to be filled. Oh, place, you have to be carried to many, so many places."[88] Dialogue regarding providence and theonomy enables Jews and Christians to share more fully in the transmission of this "land of meeting"[89] that the world needs.

Chapter 3

The Image of God

At the root of all Jewish and Christian understandings of human nature are God's words in the first chapter of the Bible:

> Then God said, "Let us make man in our image, after our likeness; and let them have dominion over the fish of the sea, and over the birds of the air, and over the cattle, and over all the earth, and over every creeping thing that creeps upon the earth." So God created man in his own image, in the image of God he created him; male and female he created them. (Gen. 1.26–27)

The doctrine of the image of God constitutes the bridge between God's providence and human participation in providence by means of God's law.[1] Like many contemporary Christian thinkers, however, David Novak has concerns about the traditional account of the image of God as human rationality.[2] Focusing in particular upon Novak's *Natural Law in Judaism* and *Covenantal Rights*, this chapter explores how Novak interprets Genesis's teaching that the human being is the image of God. In light of Novak's position, and with particular attention to his concerns about the traditional account, I then examine Thomas Aquinas's theology of the image of God. By means of this Jewish-Christian dialogue, I hope to enhance the contemporary discussion of how human nature is relationally receptive to providential theonomy via the *imago dei*. This chapter thus links Chapter 2 with Chapter 4.

The Image of God according to David Novak

Human Nature and Divine Power: Creation and Covenant

Novak argues against the view, held by Aristotle as well as by Jewish thinkers such as Maimonides, that the human relationship with God is part of a cosmic teleology. For Novak, such a view undermines the priority and gratuity of the covenantal relationship of human beings with God.[3] Although for Maimonides the eschatological "world-to-come" will include only persons "whose moral conduct is oriented in the context of a relationship with God,"[4] he reaches this conclusion primarily on the basis of the doctrine of creation rather than that of covenant. As Novak says regarding Maimonides's teleology, "the whole orientation of the human person is to be related with God; that relationship is the telos for which human nature is ordered at creation."[5]

Novak insists upon the priority of covenant. Even so, he underscores the importance of a philosophical "theory of human nature, one that recognizes a basis of concern with one's fellows."[6] As examples of nonteleological theories of human nature, he cites those of Immanuel Kant and Martin Buber. Such theories help "explain the rules that structure the relationship between humans in society and even the supreme relationship with God."[7] Novak suggests that Jews and Christians can contribute to such theorizing about human nature by working within their covenantal commitments. On the basis of the Hebrew Bible/Old Testament, Jews and Christians affirm that God creates human beings to be related to him.[8] Novak distinguishes here between philosophical and theological thinking on the part of Jewish and Christian scholars: "By philosophical grounds, I mean theories about human nature and its capacity for concern with fellow humans, its sociality. By theological grounds, I mean theories about the human capacity for a relationship with God."[9]

Against any hint of human autonomy, Novak holds that the human being "has no ontological foundation upon which any basic moral claim must ultimately rest."[10] Not even the created order circumscribes God's absolute power; God may do anything he wishes to creatures. Merely as created, human beings have no claim in justice upon the transcendent God: "At this level, they have not yet been given any ground from God. Here we are painfully aware of the edges of our mortality, where we have no power at all."[11] As Novak puts it elsewhere, "God creates everything, even justice itself, and nothing in the world can stand over God as judge."[12] Related to Novak's emphasis on God's absolute power is his insistence that "[t]he primary response of humans to the power of God is terror (*pahad*)."[13] He cites Deut. 32.39, "See now that I, I am He and there is no power (*elohim*) along with me. I kill and I give life; there is no one who can escape my hand." Before the living God, human beings cannot but feel their tremendous weakness, ignorance, and dependence.

Although Novak regards the movement from terror to fear as "a concession to us by God" in which "God limits the full range of his power," nonetheless Novak also appreciates God's wisdom: "our terror of God's power is mostly sublimated into our reverence for God's wisdom."[14] Yet in light of the unity of wisdom and will in God, do rational creatures in fact have a "moral claim" upon God—not a moral claim that proceeds primarily from the creature, but a moral claim that expresses what God owes to himself as the wise Creator who orders his creatures to an end that he knows from all eternity? In this light, the word "terror" would mistakenly suggest an arbitrary God. Even if "terror" does not accurately describe the human position, nonetheless, as Novak emphasizes, in the presence of the living God we experience "fear," since we are not autonomous self-creators. Novak observes that when applied to ethics, "fear of God" means refusing to violate the moral "order that God has enabled humans to know through their very nature."[15] Thus, Novak affirms that there exists a "natural law" that is "the law of God by which the universe is run."[16] God gives this law an "ontological foundation" in the created order so that it "is universally intelligible to all humankind."[17] Natural law guards human beings against the encroachment of positive law that claims to be autonomous.

Although Novak does not locate the relationship of justice between human beings and God in the order of creation, therefore, he does locate in the order of creation the relationship of justice between humans. He also recognizes the importance of affirming that rational creatures have some "ground under them upon which to stand up before God."[18] He argues that God freely gives this ground by relinquishing some of his own power. In order for human beings to have a relationship with God, "God must relinquish some of his own space, as it were, to allow his human creatures a place on which to stand before him—but never successfully against him."[19] He relinquishes "some of his own space" by inviting human beings into a relationship of mutuality (even if not equality) with him. How does God relinquish "some of his own space?" Following Genesis, Novak states that

> humans, the only beings whom we know to be addressed by God, are granted a special status at the time of their creation. "And God created humans (*adam*) in his image, in the image of God (*be-tselem elohim*) He made him: male and female He created them" (Gen. 1.27). And when humans leave the otherworldly haven of the Garden of Eden to take their place in this world, God says: "Now humans (*ha'adam*) are one like Us, knowing good and bad." (Gen. 3.22)[20]

Humans receive the "special status" of being "in the image of God" (Gen. 1.27).

Novak suggests that the special status is confirmed "when humans leave the otherworldly haven of the Garden of Eden to take their place in this world," because it is only then that "God says: 'Now humans (*ha'adam*) are one like Us, knowing good and bad' (Gen. 3.22)." Does Adam and Eve's disobedience, then, receive a reward rather than a punishment? Certainly, Novak by no means approves of Adam and Eve's actions. On the contrary, he rejects the "frequently uttered modern liberal Jewish notion" that "Judaism has no doctrine of original sin, that Christianity teaches that humans are evil by nature whereas Judaism teaches that they are good by nature."[21] But Novak does distinguish sharply between the "eating of the forbidden fruit in the Garden of Eden" and the "subsequent human attempt to see this act as making humans God's equals, thus making God no longer God."[22] Only the latter, Novak thinks, is sinful and merits punishment.

Novak explains that God's commandment regarding the tree of the knowledge of good and evil intends only "to present a conditional offer rather than a categorical imperative: If you want to experience good and bad—that is, to be part of the world—then you must accept your own mortality in the bargain."[23] Seen in this light, Adam and Eve's eating from the tree is not an act of disobedience. Rather, as a free acceptance of mortality, their eating from the forbidden tree inaugurates their entrance into full personhood and full dialogue with God. According to Novak, then, humans receive our dialogic status vis-à-vis God by stepping forward to "experience good and bad—that is, to be part of the world." God relinquishes "some of his own space" in order to make this human experience possible. The fact that they can now either obey or disobey God's commandments indicates that God has given them "some power as persons."[24]

Novak notes that "no orthodox Christian exegete could possibly interpret the text in this way in good faith."[25] This is true, first and foremost, because of the interpretation that St. Paul gives to Gen. 2–3. Paul states, "Therefore as sin came into the world through one man and death through sin, and so death spread to all men because all men sinned" (Rom. 5.12); to which he adds that "the wages of sin is death" (Rom. 6.23). But even employing only the texts of Genesis, one wonders whether Novak's reading is plausible. The Lord explicitly commands that "of the tree of the knowledge of good and evil you shall not eat" (Gen. 2.17). Having issued this command—"you shall not"—the Lord describes what will happen if Adam and Eve disobey his command: "you shall die" (Gen. 2.17). Tempted by the serpent, Adam and Eve disobey the Lord's command. Why would their disobedience not be sinful? Indeed, in his list of specific punishments for Adam and Eve's disobedience, the Lord includes death: "you are dust, and to dust you shall return" (Gen. 3.19).[26] From this perspective, the exile of humans from Eden is not the culmination of the human initiation into freedom/power, as Novak thinks, but rather a reduction of true human power.

Whether or not Novak's particular interpretation of Gen. 2.16–17 can stand, Novak's fundamental point is that God freely grants dialogic status to human beings. As we have already intimated, Novak holds that since "God's power is inherently infinite," it follows that "the consistent execution of justice is actually God's own limitation of that infinite power for the sake of covenantal relationality with the world."[27] For Novak, this accentuates God's free gift of mercy and justice; God accedes to Abraham's plea that the Lord not destroy Sodom if even ten righteous men reside there (Gen. 18.22–32). As Novak understands this passage, Abraham argues with God that "if you choose to be involved in the world with your human creatures, especially as their judge, then you must function as the archetype and model of justice."[28] By choosing to enter history, God enters into the moral context of the world (even if the world as created, "prior" to God's covenantal entrance, can make no claim upon God). Yet the covenant does not determine God's justice or limit his freedom; rather he freely determines covenantal justice.

For this reason, Novak emphasizes that divine justice in history, the ground upon which Abraham successfully argues with God, does not impinge upon divine freedom. He states, "When he [God] chooses Israel, he owes them nothing, just as when he creates the world, he owes it nothing. All obligations on God's part are subsequently self-imposed."[29] To imagine otherwise, in Novak's view, would be to fall into anthropocentrism ("liberal theology").[30] Comparing human freedom to God's freedom, he observes that for human beings, justice comes before freedom, because we humans find ourselves located in a moral context (the world) not of our own choosing. By contrast, "With God, however, freedom is entirely creative. According to Scripture, only God has autonomy; only God can make laws that are not derivative from something else in the world. 'Justice is God's' (Deut. 1.17) . . . .. God's freedom, then, comes before justice."[31] Although God "invokes the natural created order to 'testify' against Israel" when Israel violates "natural justice"—as God does with respect to Sodom and Gomorrah—this "natural created order" does not bind God himself, because "when he creates the world, he owes it nothing."[32] When he chooses to enter into a relationship of justice with his creatures, he imposes justice upon himself "subsequently" to his creative action.

We find a similar emphasis on God's freedom in Novak's understanding of divine transcendence. As we have seen, Novak insists that God is "the free creator of the world and everything in it" and that God is not determined by anything created.[33] Novak remarks, "God has the freedom either to make or not to make a covenant with anyone, which is like his freedom to create nature or not."[34] Thus, God radically transcends history. Yet when confronted with the metaphysically "unchanging" God of Maimonides, Novak fears that such a God cannot truly enter into history. He remarks that in Maimonides's understanding of the relationship of humans to God, "All concern is in one direction: from man to God. Maimonides in no way ever attempts to constitute a truly responsive role for God. There is no real reciprocity here. But the covenant is surely characterized by constant transaction between God and Israel, with that activity being mutual."[35]

The question is how God can be responsive if his action is transhistorical, that is, if he creates and redeems without moving from potency to act (in accord with Aristotle's understanding of Pure Act). If God's action is so different from ours as to involve no "change" on his part and thereby to take place on an entirely different metaphysical level, how can God respond historically to the actions of his covenantal people? Moreover, if God is the fullness of being, lacking nothing and therefore absolutely transcendent, what does God gain from his covenantal relationship with Israel? Novak comments in this vein that "the relationship Maimonides constitutes is more than anything else a relation *to* a God who seems to closely resemble the God of Aristotle. It is a relation where only God and not man is the object of love."[36] In Novak's view, Maimonides cannot account for the intimacy between Israel and God, an intimacy inseparable from the human status as the "image of God," in which Israel truly acts *with* and even *for* God rather than simply worshipping God from afar. In short, Maimonides accounts for God's transcendence but not for God's immanence, and thereby gives Israel no real, active "participation in her salvation."[37] As Novak remarks, "Pascal was right at this point: the God of Abraham, Isaac, and Jacob is not the God of the philosophers, certainly not the God of Plato and all whom he influenced."[38]

In short, Novak strongly affirms divine transcendence as regards God's freedom, even though he fears that divine transcendence, at least as depicted in Aristotelian terms by Maimonides, undermines God's freedom to engage in a true, reciprocal covenantal relationship with Israel in history. So far as I know, Novak does not pursue this metaphysical tangle further. He insists upon God's absolute freedom in both contexts, without seeking to reconcile the metaphysical issues involved.

The Image of God as Relationship

With these metaphysical preliminaries, we are now ready to focus on how Novak's emphasis on divine freedom and agency shapes his discussion of the image of God, which he depicts in light of the interpersonal relationship of God and Israel. Crucially, he argues that "the problem with seeing the image of God in substantial terms, as some inherent property of human nature, is that such a characteristic can be constituted phenomenologically without reference to God."[39] Once one makes the image of God an "inherent property," how can one uphold the view that the image of God involves a relationship with God? After all, an ontological relationship need not be characterized by the (phenomenological) mutual responsiveness that we normally associate with interpersonal relationships. An ontological relationship can exist without any mutual responsiveness at all; human beings need not even be aware of it. As Novak observes, if "the image of God is a transfer of some divine power, be it reason or will, to a special creature," then this creature can exercise this power (reason or will) without any reference to the God whom the power images.[40] The image of God then denotes simply a power that human beings can and do experience as exercised autonomously from God, indeed as having nothing to do with God.

If the image of God does not constitute an identifiable and concrete relationship with God, however, then the phrase "image of God" loses the promise contained by the notion of being God's very image. As Novak asks rhetorically, "What does saying 'humans *receive* their reason or their will from God' add to the meaning of the proposition 'humans are rational or willful'?"[41] How can it add something if the affirmation that "humans are rational and willful" remains true in the very same way even without any mention of God? Even if the rational and volitional powers were God-like, the lack of a need to mention God would suggest that the human person can be God-like in an autonomous fashion. Novak thus finds that those who wish to locate the image of God in a human attribute (reason and/or will) make of God merely the extrinsic cause of the attribute in which is supposed to reside the divine "image." Surely for humans to be the "image" of God means something richer than that a human power, with God as its extrinsic cause, enables human beings to experience themselves as autonomously God-like.

Having offered this critique of accounts of the image of God that envision it as "some inherent property of human nature," Novak argues that what is needed is more attention to the phenomenological dimensions of God's richly evocative words, "Let us make man in our image, after our likeness"

(Gen. 1.26). These words, Novak observes, suggest that God intends to have a relationship with human beings that goes beyond the ontological relationship that he has with the other creatures he has made. The fact that human beings are made in God's "image" is thus not primarily an ontological statement, but rather primarily a statement about the kind of relationship God the Creator wills to have with the human creature. God's words express the establishment of a common bond between God and the human creature, so that God and the human creature will be able to relate personally to each other. As Novak puts it, God's words promise "the intimacy of a relationship *between* God and humans," the "intimacy of a relationship *with* God."[42]

What is required for a relationship to be both intimate and mutual ("*between* God and humans")? The activity in the relationship cannot all be on the side of the "image"; God too must be active in the relationship. This mutually active relationship must occur on the level of history, and so in order to describe the intimate mutual relationship between God and the human creature, a relationship worthy of God's "image," Novak suggests that we look not to human ontology or "some property of human nature," but to human history. He states, "The only way one can constitute the intimacy of the relationship *with* God, which Scripture suggests is a possibility *for* humans from the very beginning and continually thereafter, is to see the 'image of God' as that which God *and* humans share in what they do *together*."[43] Far from being an inherent ontological property that precedes human intentionality (and phenomenologically does not require divine intentionality), "The image of God is the active mutuality possible only between God and humans."[44]

What kind of "active mutuality," then, defines the image of God? Novak's understanding of the image of God is guided by the "active mutuality" that is the covenantal relationship of God and Israel, constituted preeminently by the observance of Torah. Through this relationship, Israel shares in "the creative word of God" and co-constitutes with God a "covenantal world."[45] Novak observes that this is so because Israel's human intentionality unites with God's intentionality: "Essential human action, which is the practice of the commandments of God, is unlike all other things that are made *by* the creator. Instead, it is done *along with* the creator. In rabbinic teaching, even God himself is imagined to observe the positive commandments of the Torah in order to share with his people the basic reality of *their* active life together."[46]

Although Israel's Torah observance makes especially manifest for the world the true content of the image of God, Novak does not limit the image of God solely to the people of Israel in relation to their God. On the contrary, "all human beings are either the subjects or the objects of God's commandments."[47] Universalized, the image of God consists in "the normative relationship when humans recognize that the moral law, which is consistent with their nature, is rooted in the commandment of God."[48] This recognition does not require revelation, let alone being part of the Torah-observant people of Israel. In Novak's view, "Any inkling of the presence of God, however mediated by nature or tradition, always calls forth a dutiful response or a rebellious refusal on the part of any human."[49] As the image of God rather than autonomous self-creators, all humans find ourselves in the presence of the God whose creative word requires obedience. Drawing upon the biblical portrait of God's creating by speaking a word, Novak notes that the proper human response to God's creative word is to ensure that "our words correspond to God's word."[50] Humans accomplish this correspondence by acknowledging that the moral law is God's commandment and should be obeyed as such.

Put another way, in order for our words to "correspond to God's word," we must accept that we are subject to norms that do not originate with us. In order to co-speak with God rather than to descend into babble, we must accept the primacy of God speaking. When we do so, we make possible the human flourishing that follows from correspondence to God's creative word. As Novak states, "Being commanded, however we hear that commandment, is something that enables us to do well in the world. Without that sense of being commanded, when our own practical power becomes the measure of all things, we destroy ourselves and our world."[51] Outside of the relationship of "active mutuality" in which "God is for us through his commandments" and "we are for God through our obedience,"[52] we obscure the image of God in us by our pride. Such pride spurs us to reject any created order and to suppose that we can construct human happiness out of human resources alone. The result is violence, as the biblical account of Cain and Abel makes clear. Commenting on Cain's murder of Abel, Novak elsewhere states that "the original sin of humankind, namely, that which is repeated by everyone at one time or another, is twofold: the temptation to see oneself as God's equal, and as the absolute superior of one's fellow humans. Idolatry thus breeds violence."[53]

Novak adds a further argument in favor of his view of the image of God as "the active mutuality possible only between God and humans." Namely, if the image of God is human rationality, what about people who are unable to exercise reason? Would not such a doctrine of the image of God validate the denial of the humanity of such individuals as "the unborn, the permanently and severely retarded, the irrevocably comatose?"[54] Since for Jews (and Christians) "all those born of human parents" must be humans made in the image of God, the exercise of rationality cannot be constitutive for the image of God.[55] Prior to recent decades, biblically influenced societies had not challenged the humanity of "all those born of human parents." By contrast, societies now routinely deny the humanity of those unable to exercise reason.[56] For Novak, to suppose that the image of God is human rationality now means to condone the killing of the innocent, which is the primal consequence of the distortion of the image of God by idolatry.

The Image of God as Shadow

In addition to the proposal that the image of God is the active mutuality of God and humans, exercised in the relationship of commanding and being commanded, Novak offers another approach in order to facilitate discourse that takes place outside the covenantal commitments of Jews and Christians.[57] He suggests that the image of God can be defined "negatively," according to a *via negativa*, which "helps us to determine what humankind is not, thereby preparing us to know what humankind is."[58] Since the knowledge of "what humankind is" comes ultimately through Revelation, however, does biblical Revelation warrant the idea that the image of God is a "negative" concept?

By means of an etymology of the Hebrew phrase translated as "image of God," *tselem elohim*, Novak seeks to show that the answer is yes. He argues that "[a] plausible etymology of the word *tselem* is that it might come from the noun *tsel*, which means a 'shadow.'"[59] By contrast to an image, which has a positive content, a shadow has only the outlines. A shadow "simply tells us that something is there (*Dasein*), but not what it is."[60] When one sees a shadow, one knows that something is producing the shadow, but one often does not know more than that as regards what stands behind the shadow.

Novak emphasizes the interpretative and theological potential of this etymology on the grounds that it radically undercuts the temptation to posit human autonomy. If the image of God is considered a substantial attribute of the human person, then the image will soon seem to be an autonomous attribute. As Novak puts it, "What does saying 'humans *receive* their reason or their will from God' add to the meaning of the proposition 'humans are rational or willful'?"[61] When one says that humans are the image of God because of rationality, "image of God" comes to seem a mere ornamental phrase. We experience ourselves as exercising rationality autonomously, without the assistance of God. By contrast, the focus on shadow "prevents us from assuming that what is there comes from ourselves. It thus reminds us that everything we can possibly say about the shadow is only tentative until the real presence behind it makes itself known."[62] A shadow does not possess substantial attributes that can be mistaken for autonomous powers; rather a shadow always points to the mysterious reality of which it is merely the shadow. Instead of allowing one to rest content in what one sees, a shadow makes one desirous of coming to know the reality so as to understand the shadow.

In other words, if human beings are "shadows," we cannot construct a doctrine of human nature that can stand on its own. The goal is to avoid positing human autonomy, since autonomy would be the very opposite of the God's intention in making human beings in his image. Novak states, "The shadow itself is *nothing* without its connection to what lies behind it. As a shadow of something *else*, it limits what use we can make of the space that it occupies. One can thus see the relation of the shadow to its source as limiting our pretension, both theoretical and practical."[63] Our knowledge of human nature becomes clearly dependent upon what stands behind the shadow; we can truly know what is human only by coming to know what stands behind the shadow.[64] Thus, unlike subhuman natures in the world, human nature can be known only at the *personal* level, as pointing toward the transcendent. In a significant sense, the *humanum* is a mystery waiting to be unlocked by divine revelation, because "the human person cannot be definitively categorized by any category by which we determine the nature of the things of the world. Any such categorization, including the category of *animal rationale*, reduces the human person to a merely worldly entity."[65]

Why would the definition of human nature as "rational animal" reduce "the human person to a merely worldly entity?" It would seem that rationality need hardly be restricted to the status of "a merely worldly entity." After all, God does not lack rationality, even if he utterly transcends our finite apprehension of that perfection. We can understand Novak's negative view of "rational animal" by returning to his critique of the traditional connection of rationality with the image of God. He summarizes this traditional connection: "Just as God is the rational power in the macrocosmos, so man is the rational power in the microcosmos. Creation in the image of God means, then, that reason is what distinguishes humans from the rest of creation by enabling humans to have something substantial in common with God."[66] When described in this manner, the connection gives rise to a twofold problem. First, since the spheres governed by divine rationality and by human rationality are quite distinct, human beings appear to have autonomy in their sphere ("the microcosmos"). Second, rationality is presented as a substantial property shared by God and humans, which seems to undercut (through univocity) the transcendence of divine rationality. If God and humans have rationality "in common," then such rationality must be simply the rationality that we observe in this world. In short, rationality belongs firmly to the sphere of this world, and therefore this categorization "reduces the human person to a merely worldly entity."

In Novak's view, therefore, the identification of human beings as "rational animals" cedes ground that must not be given up, even if human beings are the only creatures in this category. Rationality is a capacity that we experience as an autonomous possession, no matter how much one might insist that it is a gift of God. Thus the notion of rational animal seems to give human beings, rather than God, charge over the worldly sphere. Indeed, Russell Hittinger, surveying the development of Catholic moral theology over the past 40 years, concludes that many Catholic theologians have treated the natural law in exactly the manner feared by Novak. Taking the influential moral theologian Josef Fuchs as an example, Hittinger notes that for Fuchs, "the notion that the human person 'is illuminated by a light that comes, not from one's own reason . . . but from the wisdom of God in whom everything is created . . . cannot stand up to an objective analysis nor prove helpful in the vocabulary of Christian believers.'"[67] In the same vein, comparing Fuchs's position on natural law (as a participation in the eternal law) to that of Augustine and Aquinas, Hittinger observes,

> For the older tradition, there is a clear distinction between the mind's *discovering* or discerning a norm and the being or *cause* of the norm. The human mind can go on to make new rules because it is first ruled. This, in essence, is the doctrine of participation as applied to natural law. Natural law designates for Fuchs, however, the human power to make moral judgments, not any moral norm regulating that power—at least no norm extrinsic to the operations of the mind.[68]

The question however is whether Novak's answer, namely his emphasis that human beings "are always *in* the world, but never truly *of* it,"[69] suffices. On the one hand, it seems that Novak's answer does suffice. If human beings are never *of* the world, then human identity, human nature, comes from a transcendent source and is intelligible only in relationship to this source ("active mutuality"). It follows that human life must be given value no matter what attributes the particular human being does or does not possess. As God tells Cain, "The voice of your brother's blood is crying to me from the ground" (Gen. 4.10).

On the other hand, the price of claiming that human beings are "never truly *of*" the world is a steep one. By placing human freedom and identity far above this-worldly human characteristics, one leaves the latter open to dehumanization. The strong separation between personhood and nature, with the latter pertaining to the this-worldly realm, tends toward the denigration of what is "natural" in the human, with the result that human flourishing seems to depend solely upon the workings of human freedom. As Hittinger shows, this is the result that Enlightenment philosophers sought in their efforts "to tame the biblical myth, and to render it 'speculatively' amenable to the notion that man causes himself to be distinct from his zoological fundaments."[70] Hittinger describes the Enlightenment account of human freedom over against human bodiliness: "Like the animals that serve man, the protohuman must be tamed, shaped, and humanized. Of course, the protohuman is knowable in terms of physical and psychosomatic structures; in another, and more important sense, however, it is not knowable as specifically or normatively human. The latter knowledge is a function of freedom and culture."[71]

Novak, however, seeks to take in another direction the dictum that humans "are always *in* the world, but never truly *of* it." As we have seen, he argues that "negative anthropology," which refuses to determine what human nature is, "prevents us from appropriating the shadow into any of our own schemes."[72] This is so because negative anthropology glimpses, without being able to apprehend, the transcendent source toward which the *humanum* points. Novak says in this regard that "even before revelation, humans have some inchoate notion of their special status, and that it is beyond anything one could get from the world."[73] This "inchoate notion" can be misused by those who wish to proclaim Adam's autonomous rule over himself and over all things. Such thinkers see only the "special status" without attending to the fact that it implies a transcendent source. Yet the very claim of such thinkers to *autonomous* human transcendence over nature reveals the contradiction. How could transcendence be the accomplishment of one who is fundamentally "*in* the world?" As Novak says, "Our existence intends more transcendence than our action does or could do. That is so whether our action be thought or deed."[74] Transcendence is something that we strive for, that we desire. It is not something that we autonomously give ourselves. We cannot accomplish what we seek.

For Novak, then, it is our desire that gives the lie to any claim to autonomy, and that is the mark of our "special status" and our transcendence of the categories of this world: "Without that desire, I am something much less, a disposable thing of the world."[75] We are not *of* the world because we desire to be known by our transcendent source. This desire is both what separates us from any purely worldly reality, and what exposes our neediness, our lack of autonomy. Novak remarks that "one can take this essential limitation of human pretense as knowledge that can well inform human action. Only when human finitude has been properly accepted can God's light shine through into the world."[76] Despite views to the contrary, our rationality does not give us dominion over ourselves, because our rationality cannot enable us even to know ourselves. Our rationality can only teach us inchoately that our fulfillment—and therefore the answer to the question, "what is human nature?"—utterly transcends the worldly realm compassed by our finite powers. It is only in this transcendent realm, the realm not of our dominion but of the Lord's, that we can find out who we are. Novak's separation of human personhood from every "worldly category" thus stands at the service not of elevating human freedom to de facto autonomy over every natural order, but of deflating every human pretense to autonomous self-fulfillment in this world.

In short, unlike other creatures, which fit worldly categories, humans are like a "shadow" because we are "*nothing*" without our connection to our transcendent source. Only in this source does our life make sense, and so human dignity (far from being autonomously constituted) derives from this source: "Ultimately, we affirm the worth of every human person because we believe somehow or other that we are all the objects of God's concern. To apprehend that concern and Who is so concerned for us is the desire of all desires."[77] On this basis, Novak argues that the separation of what is human from everything this-worldly, to the point of rejecting the definition "rational animal," does not increase violence against human beings, but rather stands firmly against such violence.

Recall Hittinger's point that the separation of freedom from nature results in the postulate of a "proto-human" realm of "physical and psycho-somatic structures" that is "not knowable as specifically or normatively human," and that therefore opens the entire human being to degradation by unmoored human freedom.[78] Novak, by contrast, rejects the definition "rational animal" (in which the terms are both categories of this world) so as to affirm that human beings cannot define ourselves but instead point beyond this world. If we cannot define ourselves in this-worldly terms, he suggests, then the ground of our value and dignity must also be located beyond this world.

According to Novak, humans thereby make clear that we can only be understood as the object of a transcendent subjective concern (he thinks that whether or not this transcendent subjective concern actually exists cannot be answered outside of divine revelation[79]). He notes that "to regard any human person as anything less than the object of God's concern is to fundamentally deny the true intention of his or her existence—and our own, even if the goal of that intention is only to be found in our desire of it."[80] All humans, no matter whether capable of exercising rationality or not, possess this claim to "God's concern." Each human thus owes every other human the treatment owed to God's beloved. Quoting Prov. 17.5, "Whoever belittles (*lo'eg*) the poorest one blasphemes his Maker," Novak remarks that "[n]o one can desire God's concern for himself or herself alone without denying the very meaning of that concern. Its very operation can only be apprehended as being for more than one existence."[81] Whereas the "image of God," when viewed as reason, can be distorted both in the direction of substantial autonomy and in the direction of supposing that only those who exercise rationality are in the image of God, the image of God under the rubric of "shadow" underscores the finitude of human beings and our utter dependence on the transcendent source toward whom each and every one of us is oriented.

Novak's Position vis-à-vis the Traditional View

Like Hittinger, Novak argues against the notion that humans must "humanize" ourselves in order to achieve our proper dignity. As Novak states, "human beings *are* more than they can ever *do* or *make* of themselves."[82] Because Novak consistently affirms God's dominion, he would not agree with the claim (in Hittinger's words) that "the human body is raw material to be shaped according to a mandate of dominion."[83] Similarly, Hittinger, following Karol Wojtyła/John Paul II, is open to the kind of phenomenological analysis by which Novak defines the image of God. Hittinger notes appreciatively that in his book *The Acting Person*, "Wojtyła believes that he has uncovered one sturdy piece of evidence confirming the fact that man is *ad imaginem Dei*. Namely, that he is unrepeatable, inalienable, and incommunicable."[84] Yet Hittinger emphasizes the unity of the human person and construes this unity so as to account for the participation of human reason in divine reason (and thus of the natural law in the eternal law). This participation requires that the human person, through rationality, be an "image of God."[85]

Is there a case, then, for a more positive assessment of the traditional view that the human person, through rationality, is the image of God? It seems to me that the answer is yes, and I will seek to make this case by examining Thomas Aquinas's approach to the image of God. Given the profundity of Novak's concerns, I will pursue my examination of Aquinas's doctrine in light of questions raised by Novak. Among these questions are the following:

If the image of God is an inherent and substantial property of human nature, does the image of God name a power exercised in isolation from God's activity, and thereby foster human presumption and pride? Does the affirmation that humans are in the image of God through rationality include or even allow for the active mutuality of God and human beings? Does it constitute a true locus of intimacy between God and humans? Does it fit either with the God who commands Israel in the Torah, or with the biblical emphasis upon divine love? Does it emphasizes reason above freedom, and thereby reduce God's transcendence and God's freedom? Would humans who cannot exercise rationality thereby not be made in the image of God, and not be the objects of God's concern? Is historical revelation necessary if reason is already the image of God? How would such revelation not merely be a refurbishing of reason?

Thomas Aquinas on the Image of God

Aquinas holds that, in Novak's words, "reason is what distinguishes humans from the rest of creation,"[86] and that humans are in the image of God because of the possession of rationality.[87] Does Aquinas thereby fall into the problems that Novak, citing Philo, identifies with this traditional account of the image—namely, fostering an illusion of human autonomy, excluding humans who cannot exercise rationality, and undermining divine transcendence by claiming for humans an area of substantial identity with God?

The Image of God and Autonomy

Aquinas accepts the dictum that "an image leads to the knowledge of that of which it is the image."[88] In its fullest expression, therefore, the image of God is found in humans when human rationality is in act. Following Book XIV of Augustine's *De Trinitate*, Aquinas points out that "in our soul word 'cannot exist without actual thought.'"[89] He concludes that the image of God, insofar as it is an image of the Trinity, exists primarily "in the acts of the soul, that is, inasmuch as from the knowledge which we possess, by actual thought we form an internal word; and thence break forth into love."[90] In Book XIV, Augustine goes on to say that the image of the Trinity does not reveal itself merely in any acts of the soul but more properly in those acts that have God as their object. In Augustine's words, quoted by Aquinas, "The image of God exists in the mind, not because it has a remembrance of itself, loves itself, and understands itself; but because it can also remember, understand, and love God by Whom it was made."[91] As an image of the Trinity, then, the human image of God is not self-enclosed but rather is our knowing and loving *God.*

In other words, the image of the Trinity in human beings is an image formed in relationship with God, in the "active mutuality" and mutual intimacy that Novak commends. The human person cannot be the image of God in this fullest sense unless the person fulfills God's law. As Aquinas points out, the Torah commands that "you shall love the Lord your God with all your heart, and with all your soul, and with all your might" (Deut. 6.5).[92] Lacking such charitable intimacy with God, one cannot love in the way requisite for the image of the Trinity and so one does not fully manifest the image.[93]

Aquinas thus would agree with Novak that the fullness of the human image of God comes about within the covenantal relationship that God bestows upon his people, although Aquinas understands this in light of the New Covenant in Christ and the Spirit. Does this emphasis on human relationship with God hold also when the human image of God is understood as an image of divine unity? Aquinas notes that because God's unity is not opposed to God's Trinity, "to be to the image of God by imitation of the divine nature does not exclude being to the same image by the representation of the divine Persons: but rather one follows from the other."[94] In this regard, Aquinas turns from Augustine to the Greek Fathers, notably Gregory of Nyssa and John of Damascus. For Gregory of Nyssa this image is ontological, involving human participation in divine goodness, whereas for John of Damascus "the image of God in man belongs to him as 'an intelligent being endowed with free-will and self-movement.'"[95] Aquinas agrees that these attributes give the human being an "image" rather than merely a "trace" of God.[96]

When understood in this way, however, is the image of God reduced to being "constituted phenomenologically without reference to God?" Much depends upon how one understands ontological goodness and free will. For the ancient philosophers and their patristic and medieval inheritors, goodness had a richer signification than it does in modern thought. Aquinas remarks that "according to the Platonists . . . goodness is more extensively participated than being," and he cites Pseudo-Dionysius in favor of the view that "goodness, since it has the aspect of desirable, implies the idea of a final cause, the causality of which is first among causes, since an agent does not act except for some end."[97] For Aquinas, to say that human ontological goodness is a likeness of God's goodness thus includes reference not only to God's creative activity (as final cause), but also to our activity as ordered to God as our end or goal. In this way, ontological goodness means that human beings never exist in a state of neutrality toward good; we are always in motion toward God in some way, and it is this inclination that undergirds our intentional activity toward God through knowledge and love.

It follows that the "active mutuality" in the relationship of human beings and God extends all the way down, as it were, rather than being solely based upon human intentionality. While the fullness of such active mutuality takes place on the intentional level, it cannot be restricted to that level without ignoring the basis for the human drive toward relationship with the Creator. As Aquinas points out, goodness requires "a form, together with all that precedes and follows upon that form"—that is, its proper inclination and action—"for everything, in so far as it is in act, acts and tends towards that which is in accordance with its form."[98]

In short, regarding Gregory of Nyssa's understanding of the image of God as the human participation in the divine goodness, one should recognize that created goodness, for Gregory and Aquinas, involves teleological ordering to God. This dynamism toward God belongs intrinsically to all creatures: "All things desire God as their end, when they desire some good thing . . . because nothing is good and desirable except forasmuch as it participates in the likeness to God."[99] In human beings, as intentional agents, this desire grounds the intimate active mutuality that attains its pinnacle in the consummation of the covenantal relationship. As Aquinas states, "The intellectual soul approaches to the divine likeness, more than inferior creatures, in being able to acquire perfect goodness."[100]

What about John of Damascus's view that the image of God consists in human free will and self-movement? Does this view require reference to God, or does it open the door for the modern portrait of the human being as autonomous? Nothing other than the divine will, Aquinas observes, causes the divine willing.[101] God's knowledge does not determine God's will, because while God knows all things that are possible, he does not will all things that are possible. Yet the divine will is not autonomous from the divine wisdom. Regarding the role of divine wisdom, Aquinas notes that "effects proceed from His own infinite perfection according to the determination of His will and intellect."[102] With respect to freedom of choice, he points out that the divine goodness is the "proper object" of the divine will, which wills the divine goodness by absolute necessity.[103] This is so because the act of will does not begin from a position of neutrality toward all objects; rather, the will is a rational appetite for the good. The good attracts and draws the will. The divine goodness, as infinite perfection, supremely fulfills this appetitive movement.

Yet this necessary movement of the divine will, willing the divine goodness that the divine intellect knows, does not mean that God wills creatures by a necessary movement. God freely loves creatures into existence: "since the goodness of God is perfect, and can exist without other things inasmuch as no perfection can accrue to Him from them, it follows that His willing things apart from Himself is not absolutely necessary."[104] Were this not the case, God would not truly transcend the creaturely realm. But since it is the case, God's will, by which he necessarily wills his goodness and freely wills creatures, is uncaused. Even so, if goodness necessarily draws the divine will, is God truly "free?" Yes, because the embracing of perfect goodness is true freedom. True freedom requires the ordering of appetite to being as good: will is not a neutral appetite, but a rational appetite for being as good. God's freedom consists in his willing his own infinite goodness, rather than being "free" to hate his infinite goodness.[105]

What does this mean for human free will and self-movement? Aquinas points out that "by the will we are masters of our own actions. But we are not masters of that which is of necessity."[106] It would seem, therefore, that human free will is incompatible with any kind of necessitation. Yet all people desire happiness, even though people identify diverse goods with happiness.[107] Does "happiness" then necessitate the will? Aquinas points out that coercion, which implies violence, is quite different from inclination. If we incline toward knowing and loving others, this does not mean that others are coercing us or even that our own nature is coercing us. When the will inclines toward a good, it acts in a voluntary fashion. Thus, even a "natural necessity" is not coercive: "as the intellect of necessity adheres to the first principles, the will must of necessity adhere to the last end, which is happiness: since the end is in practical matters what the principle is in speculative matters."[108] But what constitutes happiness? Aquinas examines various candidates, including wealth, honors, fame, power, health, pleasure, and care of the soul. He concludes: "It is impossible for any created good to constitute man's happiness. For happiness is the perfect good, which lulls the appetite altogether; else it would not be the last end, if something yet remained to be desired."[109] From this perspective, humans are in the image of God because human free will leads toward intimate relationship with God as the constitutive element of happiness. When understood in this way, the image of God in human beings does not render us autonomous, but instead leads us upward to the fulfillment of volition in the happiness that consists in communion with God.[110]

This account of divine and human freedom has important consequences with respect to John of Damascus's (and Aquinas's) view that human free will and self-movement constitute humans in the image of God. To act consciously for an end is intrinsic to rational freedom.[111] The "end" toward which the rational appetite tends does not constrain the will, even though the will's movement is not free in the sense of determining its own ends. These ends are inscribed in human nature—and indeed the very postulate of a human nature with determinate ends leads ultimately to the presence of a Creator. Aquinas also observes that the ultimate source of the movement from potency to act, in every movement, is God (not simply the ultimate source in the sense of a chain that stretches back in time, but the ultimate source, presently active, of the requisite actuality).[112] The human free will, in other words, does not constitute itself in autonomy from God. Even phenomenologically speaking, one cannot correctly conceive of the free action of the human will apart from inscribed ends or apart from a source of the will's being.

Holding that humans are in the image of God through human rationality, therefore, does not put the doctrine of the image of God in the service of human autonomy. This is especially true with regard to the image of the Trinity, which is fulfilled in the covenantal relationship of knowing and loving God. Aquinas emphasizes that Augustine's famous triad—the mind remembering itself, understanding itself, and loving itself—is in the image of God "due to the fact, not that the mind reflects on itself absolutely, but that thereby it can furthermore turn to God."[113] In this respect Aquinas is agreeing with the teaching of Augustine: "Augustine says (*De Trin.* xiv. 12): 'The image of God exists in the mind, not because it has a remembrance of itself, loves itself, and understands itself; but because it can also remember, understand, and love God by Whom it was made.'"[114] As we have seen, neither does emphasizing the divine unity connect the image of God with human autonomy, once goodness and freedom are rightly understood.

The Image of God and Rational Activity

Novak's second concern has to do with the possibility that locating the human image of God in rationality excludes human beings who cannot exercise rationality, including the unborn, the permanently and seriously mentally disabled, and the comatose. In modern societies, where abortion and euthanasia are common, the affirmation that God has bestowed the image of God upon all human beings, including those who cannot exercise rationality, is as Novak puts it "anything but academic."[115] Does the traditional view of the human image of God as constituted by rationality provide, however unwittingly, a foundation for horrific contemporary violations of the commandment "You shall not kill" (Exod. 20.13)?[116]

For his part, Aquinas states that "since [the mind] is not always actually understanding, as in the case of sleep, we must say that these acts, although not always actually existing, yet ever exist in their principles, the habits and powers."[117] The habits qualify the powers, and so virtues and vices denote habits of the powers of the soul.[118] The powers themselves are not the soul's essence, since only in God is operation the same as essence.[119] Aquinas notes that "if the very essence of the soul were the immediate principle of operation, whatever has a soul would always have actual vital actions, as that which has a soul is always an actually living thing."[120] It will be clear that this distinction between the essence and powers of the soul already provides a basis for denying that human beings who lack the exercise of rationality thereby lack the image of God.

Can one possess the rational powers of the soul without being able to exercise them? It would seem not: if the spiritual soul is the "primary principle" of human intellection,[121] how could the body prevent such intellection from occurring? Aquinas's answer is that since human intellection requires sense knowledge, human intellection cannot occur without a fitting "corporeal instrument," and so bodily disorders (as is well known from observation) may impede intellection.[122] No bodily disorder, however, can erase the powers of intellect and will from the soul, despite their seeming absence. In the case of unborn children, permanently and seriously mentally disabled persons, and the comatose, the rational powers are present in the soul. Such persons simply "lack the use of reason accidentally," due to bodily immaturity or impairment.[123]

Aquinas therefore holds that human beings who cannot exercise rationality may be baptized and enjoy the life of grace, including friendship with God through the elevation of the rational powers.[124] With regard specifically to unborn children, Aquinas observes that while they cannot be baptized while living inside the womb, they can already "be subject to the action of God, in Whose sight they live, so as, by a kind of privilege, to receive the grace of sanctification."[125] The grace of sanctification heals and elevates the essence of the soul, and through the essence flows into the powers of the soul so as to infuse the virtues.[126] The same holds for newborn infants and young children. Although as yet unable to exercise rational acts, they can possess the infused habits that qualify the soul's rational powers in grace.

How can one have habits in the rational powers, however, without being able to act rationally? In this regard Aquinas observes that while "it belongs to every habit to have relation to an act," nonetheless a habit is "in a state of potentiality in respect to operation."[127] In general, of course, it requires at least one act, and often many acts, to cause a habit to form in one of the soul's powers.[128] Yet since a habit is not an act, but rather is ordered to action, actions on the part of the person are not absolutely necessary for the presence of a habit. It can happen that even before being able to act, a human being may possess habits—infused by a special divine sanctifying action or by baptism—that qualify the powers of intellect and will. Among such habits are faith and charity.[129]

The view that humans are in the image of God through rationality does not, then, exclude human beings who are unable to exercise rationality. Does the above argument, however, hinge on the claim that human beings possess a spiritual soul? Certainly, were one to hypothesize that the human soul is solely material, then one would have trouble defending the full humanity of human beings who cannot exercise rationality.[130] Novak's position, however, does not solve this difficulty: were one to suppose that human beings were simply well-developed animals, one would also have trouble defending the view that all human beings, and not just some, possess a unique "shadow"-image.

With regard to human beings who cannot exercise rationality, recall Novak's remark about the image of God: "The only way one can constitute the intimacy of the relationship *with* God, which Scripture suggests is a possibility *for* humans from the very beginning and continually thereafter, is to see the 'image of God' as that which God *and* humans share in what they do *together*."[131] It seems to me that the position that humans are in the image of God through rationality accomplishes what Novak has in view. This can be seen particularly clearly in the case of human beings who cannot exercise rationality. It might appear that such human beings do nothing together with God; they cannot obey God's commandments or even be rational subjects of God's commandments, although they can be passive objects. But as we have seen, the image of God enables God to work even with those who cannot exercise reason and will. God enables them already to possess the habits of faith and charity. They become full members of the mystical Body that seeks, by the grace of the Holy Spirit, to instantiate Christ's charity in the world until the fullness of the new creation arrives. The fullness of the image of God is this working together to bring about the restoration and fulfillment of creation in wisdom and holiness, by means of human beings' sharing in the divine life.[132]

The Image of God and Divine Transcendence

What about Novak's third concern, namely that the traditional approach exaggerates the image of God by understanding it not as a shadow but as "a transfer of some divine power"[133] that enables "humans to have something substantial in common with God?"[134] If humans possess "some divine power" that is possessed "in common with God," what happens to the God who commands Israel, the God who relinquishes "some of his own space, as it were, to allow his human creatures a place on which to stand before him—but never successfully against him?"[135] If humans already have divine power, will humans fear God (let alone have "terror" of him[136])? Will humans desire to be "the objects of God's concern?"[137] In other words, having received divine power, why could not human beings stand on our own and be self-sufficient? As Novak cautions in light of the view that the rational soul (as an incorruptible image of God) is immortal, "Were even humans, whom Scripture teaches are the highest of all creatures, to believe themselves to be immortal, that would blur the difference between God and creation. . . . Were humans immortal, being born without having to die, could they not even assume that they have succeeded God in the order of things?"[138]

Aquinas addresses such concerns by emphasizing that the image of God is "some likeness to God, copied from God as from an exemplar; yet this likeness is not one of equality, for such an exemplar infinitely excels its copy."[139] Because of this infinite difference, no attribute can be predicated univocally of God and of human beings. God cannot "transfer" anything divine to human beings, nor can human beings possess anything "in common" with God. The infinite difference between God and humans is such that even though creatures can analogously have a likeness to the Creator, "it must nowise be admitted that God is like creatures."[140] Even so, in claiming that human beings are the image of the infinite God in some positive way, rather than limiting the image to the *via negativa* of the shadow, how can we avoid fostering the illusion that humans "have succeeded God in the order of things?"

Aquinas suggests that the fact that "God understands and loves Himself" is the root of the image of God in human beings.[141] Among bodily creatures, only human beings can know God. The fact that other animals do not share the perfection of rationality (intellect and will) has significance, Aquinas suggests, for the interpretation of human beings' special creation in the image of God in Gen. 1.[142] As he points out, how do humans image God more distinctively than in knowing and loving? He has in view not the mere knowing and loving of anything, but rather the supreme relationship made possible by intellect and will, namely knowing and loving God. But does this mean that humans do what God does, so that, in our own domain at least, humans "have succeeded God in the order of things?" What kind of power is the power to know and love God? To what degree is it something that humans have "in common" with God?

Aquinas here distinguishes between our natural knowing and loving, and the knowing and loving that grace and glory make possible for us. To avoid misunderstanding, I should make two points at the outset. First, Aquinas does not conceive of our natural knowing and loving as a neutral realm, impervious to God or to the grace of the Holy Spirit. Rather, he conceives even of our created powers of knowing and loving as always being drawn by God toward himself as Truth and Goodness. The distinction between nature and grace does not indicate an opposition between the two, but rather expresses the scope of the gift of creation, in and through which the grace of the Holy Spirit transforms and deifies human beings. Second, Aquinas does not conceive of even our glorified powers of knowing and loving as divine. Even heavenly glory is simply a "likeness" of God, a participation in God rather than a full crossing of the gap between finite creatures and infinite Creator.[143]

Aquinas sets forth three ways in which human knowing and loving imitates or images God's knowing and loving. The first way is our "natural aptitude for understanding and loving God," an aptitude that "consists in the very nature of the mind."[144] As I noted above, the intellect and will are never neutral vis-à-vis God, even when we do not consciously know and love God. The second way comes through the grace of the Holy Spirit elevating our natural powers, "inasmuch as man actually or habitually knows and loves God, though imperfectly."[145] Aquinas presents this as an imperfect "conformity" to God, and it leads into the third way, which consists in a perfect human knowledge and love of God.[146] Far from displacing God, the three levels of the image depict God's activity in human beings in creation, re-creation, and heavenly conformity. As Aquinas states, "The first is found in all men, the second only in the just, the third only in the blessed."[147]

Understood in this way, the image of God is not something that raises us to God's level or makes us his competitors. On the contrary, the image of God describes God's activity in us, with us; it is a theocentric reality. In and through the image of God, God acts in and with us to accomplish historically and covenantally his purpose of salvation. When we imagine that the image of God describes primarily our own activity rather than God's activity in us, we fall into pride. But the fact that the image of God can be distorted does not mean that we would do better to think of it as a shadow. This is so because our knowing and loving are more than a mere shadow; they are what constitute the possibility, through their teleological ordering, of the gratuitous gift of the covenantal relationship. Only those who know and love can enter joyfully into a relationship with the God who teaches and commands.

Image and Incarnation

In affirming that humans are the image of God through rationality, therefore, one does not isolate the human being from God's activity or undermine God's transcendence; nor does one exclude human beings who cannot exercise rationality. Rather, the image of God, when construed as rationality, highlights the intimacy between God and human beings, fulfilled in the "active mutuality"[148] that takes place when human beings know and love the God who creates and redeems them in covenantal love. Yet, given this account of the image of God, one might still ask what exactly revelation accomplishes. Does God's covenantal election of Israel, as fulfilled in Christ Jesus, merely refurbish (without elevating) human rationality? Likewise, does the image of God as human rationality have a place for Novak's insight that the image of God is ultimately "that which God *and* humans share in what they do *together*?"[149]

For Aquinas, these questions require contemplation of the union of the Image and the image, that is to say the incarnate Word.[150] It would take us too far afield to enumerate all the ways in which this is so. For our purposes, it will suffice to explore Aquinas's analysis of why it was particularly fitting that the Word (and not the Father or the Holy Spirit) became incarnate. The first reason for this fittingness is that the Word expresses all the ways that God can be participated. Therefore, the Word is the "exemplar likeness" of all creatures, because God knows all creatures in knowing his Word.[151] Just as a craftsman turns to his original idea of his artwork in order to restore his tarnished work, God the Father sends his Word or Image in order to refurbish his fallen creation, so that creatures might participate in God as they were intended to do. Commenting on 2 Cor. 5.19, "God was in Christ reconciling the world to himself," Aquinas emphasizes the aspect of new creation: "The first creation of things was made by the power of God the Father through the Word; hence the second creation ought to have been brought about through the Word, by the power of God the Father, in order that restoration should correspond to creation."[152]

It will be already clear that the Word/Image's taking up of the human image of God (in the hypostatic union) enriches the notion of the image of

God. The divine Image renews the rational understanding and volition of the human image. As Aquinas says, the renewal and elevation of our rationality comes "by participating the Word of God, as the disciple is instructed by receiving the word of his master."[153] This master is Christ, in whom the image of God has been taken up and perfected by the divine Image. In his human image, Christ displays the divine Image; he is "the image of the invisible God" (Col. 1.15). As Christ says in response to the question of his disciple Philip, "He who has seen me has seen the Father" (Jn 14.9). Reflecting upon the renewal of the image in the Image, Aquinas remarks that "for the consummate perfection of man it was fitting that the very Word of God should be personally united to human nature."[154] The Word incarnate leads us to the Word, from whom our wisdom comes.

In this first reason of fittingness, we see that the Word incarnate, the Messiah of Israel, does more than simply renew the image of God; he also accomplishes "the consummate perfection of man" by transforming human participation in the Word. Human nature now does not merely participate distantly in the Word. Through the hypostatic union, human nature belongs to the Word, so that Christ is the Word. This profound elevation of the human image means that in Christ, who as human is the image of God, we see the very Image of the Father. It is through the mutual activity of the humanity and divinity of Christ that the image of God in us is restored. In this sense, the image of God, as consummated in Christ, becomes a "theandric" reality. When the Holy Spirit configures us to Christ's image/Image, we too share in the perfected and elevated image of God. This mutual activity of God and humans resonates with Novak's view of the image of God as "that which God *and* humans share in what they do *together*." In Christ, we experience the image of God as the "active mutuality" emphasized by Novak.

This point is strengthened by Aquinas's second reason for why the Word, in particular, fittingly became incarnate. The first reason proceeds on the basis of the claim that "such as are similar are fittingly united."[155] The second reason proceeds from the goal of the union, namely salvation through adoptive sonship. In this vein Aquinas quotes Rom. 8.17, which teaches that we are to be "fellow heirs with Christ".[156] As Aquinas goes on to observe, we are "conformed to the image of his Son" (Rom. 8.29) and become adopted sons. This happens when Christ, by his external and interior teaching, configures us through the Holy Spirit to the divine Image. It is fitting that the Word/Image be the one who conforms the human image to the divine Image. Once again we find a strong emphasis on the mutual activity of God and human beings in the perfection and elevation of the human image of God.

Aquinas's third reason for the fittingness of the Word's incarnation comes from his reading of Gen. 3, the fall of Adam and Eve. He points out that Adam and Eve sought knowledge, but sought it in an inordinate way. The serpent promises Eve, "For God knows that when you eat of it your eyes will be opened, and you will be like God, knowing good and evil" (Gen. 3.5). Eve determines to eat the fruit partly on the ground "that the tree was to be desired to make one wise" (Gen. 3.6). Disobedience to God's commandment, however, results not in a deeper participation in God's Word, but in alienation from God's Word/Image and correspondingly in loss of wisdom.[157] In this context, Aquinas observes that "it was fitting that by the Word of true knowledge man might be led back to God, having wandered from God through an inordinate thirst for knowledge."[158] By obeying the incarnate Word's teaching and commandments human beings receive, in love, the true knowledge that Adam and Eve mistakenly sought to claim for themselves by disobedience. This true knowledge exceeds the limits of natural human knowledge: "For now we see in a mirror dimly, but then face to face. Now I know in part; then I shall understand fully, even as I have been fully understood" (1 Cor. 13.12).

Concluding Reflections

In his recent book on the image of God according to Gen. 1.26–27, the biblical scholar Richard Middleton points out that in contemporary Old Testament scholarship, "the royal-functional interpretation of the image" has "come virtually to monopolize the field."[159] Although this interpretation of the image of God in terms of power has medieval parallels (Middleton mentions the tenth-century Jewish thinker Saadiah), Middleton takes special note of the importance of this interpretation for fifteenth-century Italian humanists. Their view of the *imago dei*, indeed, sounds rather close to the view that Novak fears, namely that humans "have succeeded God in the order of things."[160] With such thinkers as Pico della Mirandola in mind, Middleton comments that "these Renaissance thinkers imagined a creative, transformative energy by which humans (in imitation of God's own creative activity) shaped earthly life through cultural-historical action, whether in city-building, alchemy, politics, scholarship, or the arts."[161] Middleton draws a connection, rooted in his own evangelical background, to the Reformed theologian Abraham Kuyper's "world-transformative vision,"[162] which he views with caution due to the danger of theocratic politics.

Like Novak, therefore, Middleton is particularly concerned that the interpretation of the image of God not lead to a misunderstanding of human power. Undertaking a detailed comparison of Gen. 1.26–27 with Near Eastern parallels, he arrives at a position similar to Jürgen Moltmann's, who also accepts the "royal" interpretation of the image. For both thinkers, the primary meaning of Gen. 1.26–27 is an egalitarian view of human power: "the use of *imago Dei* language in Gen. 1 (derived from the ancient Near East) functions to delegitimate any intrinsically hierarchical social structure and to affirm the dignity and agency of all humanity."[163] On this basis, Middleton argues that Gen. 1.26–27 stands as a corrective to the central place of priestly and royal mediation in Israelite religion: "the democratization of the image suggests that human beings do not need institutional mediation of God's presence by either kings or priests. Rather, just as the *imago Dei* in Gen. 1 democratizes royal ideology, the text suggests that human beings as the image of God are *themselves* priests of the creator of heaven and earth."[164]

Leaving aside the audacious claim that Gen. 1.26–27 critiques the fundamental institutions of the people of Israel (as well as the biblical theology of mediation), how does Middleton's approach, which interacts with the majority position of contemporary biblical scholarship, relate to Novak's and Aquinas's readings? Like Middleton, Novak reads Gen. 1.26–27 in terms of power, but he does so by emphasizing that we begin in a condition of "terror" before God. Since we cannot stand before God on the basis of our own resources, God graciously allows us room to stand before him. In this relationship of intimate "active mutuality," which is one of commandment and obedience (whether constituted covenantally by Noahide law or by Torah), we find the basis for envisioning ourselves as God's "image." Novak also argues that one can fruitfully conceive of the image of God as a shadow, by means of a *via negativa* that exposes a profound neediness in human beings that requires a transcendent referent. In this way, one avoids reifying the "image" as something humans autonomously possess rather than as something that God freely bestows upon us. By denying that the image of God puts an end to the hierarchical pattern of human existence, Novak enters more deeply into the meaning of Gen. 1.26–27 than, in my view, Middleton's egalitarian reading can do.

For his part, Aquinas's reading of Gen. 1.26–27 emphasizes not mere power, but the spiritual power of knowing and loving. By so doing, Aquinas transcends the limits of the "royal" interpretation's this-worldly understanding of power. But does Aquinas's approach adequately address Novak's concerns regarding human autonomy, the exclusion of those who cannot exercise rationality, and the ascription of a divine power to human beings? In each of these areas, Novak's concerns enhance the interpretation of Aquinas's reading of the *imago dei*. In accordance with the dictum that an image leads to that which it images, the theology of the image of God should emphasize relationality vis-à-vis God. Second, the theology of the image of God should underscore that God and the human soul can be in relationship even if the human person lacks an adequate bodily instrument for the normal processes of cognition and volition. Third, the theology of the image of God should stress that the image of God does not name a "divine" power. Along the way, Aquinas's reading of the *imago dei* also avoids the difficulties raised by Novak's views of divine power, divine transcendence, and the constitution of human nature in the free response of humans to God.

With respect to Christian theology, Aquinas's interpretation attains its highest point in the personal unity of the divine Image and the human image in the incarnate Son, whose humanity is formed by the Holy Spirit. From this perspective, the human image of God has its fullest meaning in the covenantal fulfillment that accomplishes the unity of divine and human knowing and loving. In the *imago dei* as the meeting point of nature and grace, we find the revelation of "the holy city, new Jerusalem, coming down out of heaven from God, prepared as a bride adorned for her husband" (Rev. 21.2). To quote John Paul II's favorite passage from the Second Vatican Council: "Christ the new Adam, in the very revelation of the mystery of the Father and of his love, fully reveals man to himself and brings to light his most high calling" (*Gaudium et Spes* §22).[165]

Chapter 4

Natural Law and Noahide Law

Discussing natural law, Joseph Ratzinger recounts the story of Nineveh in the book of Jonah: "Nineveh was a heathen city, a city with many gods. But at the call of the prophet, they believe God. They know in their inmost hearts that he exists, the one God, and they recognize the voice of that God in the preaching of the foreign prophet. Even sin has not quite extinguished in the heart of man the capacity to recognize the voice of God."[1] Since human beings are in the "image of God," even those not included in the covenants nonetheless can worship God and know right and wrong. How should this ability be understood theologically? In response to this question, David Novak consistently has recourse to the rabbinic doctrine of Noahide law, as appropriated by Maimonides. Novak thus finds theological support for natural law doctrine in the rabbinic understanding of the gentiles. By contrast, the natural law doctrine of Thomas Aquinas finds its theological support in the Mosaic law and especially in the Decalogue.[2] The Christian theologian focuses on Israel, whereas the Jewish theologian focuses on the gentiles. Are these two approaches to natural law compatible?

By comparing Novak's Maimonidean view of "Noahide law" and Aquinas's view of the Decalogue/moral precepts of Mosaic law, can we enrich our understanding of natural law?[3] I focus on Novak's *Natural Law in Judaism* and Aquinas's *Summa theologiae*. In their natural law doctrine, Novak and Aquinas are particularly concerned to understand the relationship between creation and covenant, which are united by the fact that (in Ratzinger's words) both are "a gift, a creative act of God's love."[4] This interplay between creation and covenant is the leitmotif of Jewish-Christian dialogue on providence/theonomy, the image of God, and natural law.

Novak on Noahide Law

What Is Noahide Law?

All human beings descend, according to Scripture, from Noah (Gen. 9.19). On the basis of the Tosefa and the Talmud, Novak lists seven "Noahide laws" that, according to the rabbinic tradition, bind all of Noah's descendents, whether Jew or gentile:

(1) the requirement to establish a judicial system in society (*dinim*); (2) the prohibition of blasphemy (*birkat ha-shem*); (3) the prohibition of idolatry (*avodah zarah*); (4) the prohibition of wanton destruction of human life (*shefikhut damim*); (5) the prohibition of adultery, incest, homosexuality, and bestiality (*gillui arayot*); (6) the prohibition of robbery (*gezel*); (7) the prohibition of eating a limb torn from a living animal (*ever min ha-hai*).[5]

The Rabbis derived these laws from scriptural texts, but they are not part of the rabbinic exposition of Jewish law (*halakhah*). First, the Rabbis did not claim that the Torah taught Noahide law directly; rather, Novak says, the biblical texts cited in support of the seven Noahide laws "are used as allusions (*asmakhta*) at best."[6] Second, the Noahide laws' purpose differed from the purpose that normal *halakhah* served. The Rabbis did not promulgate them so as to be observed by Jews. Neither did the Rabbis intend to promulgate laws for gentiles, because Jews did not possess lawmaking power over gentiles when these laws were formulated. Novak suggests that "the Rabbis were engaged more in speculating about the overall teaching of Scripture and its analogues in the outside world than they were engaged in strictly legal exegesis when they were developing the doctrine of Noahide law."[7]

The Noahide laws begin with the particularity of Scripture, but they have in view the universal community of all humankind, inclusive of but by no means limited to the particular community of Israel that is the subject of *halakhah*. The Noahide laws do not follow from an understanding of the "good" for human beings: Novak holds that knowing this good requires Revelation.[8] Instead, in a manner comparable to the image of God as understood by Novak, the Noahide laws are negative laws that sketch certain limits inscribed in human finitude and contingency, limits that if infringed would evidence "the arrogant pretensions of humans acting as if they themselves were infinite."[9] Novak emphasizes that of the seven Noahide laws, six involve negative commandments, and the seventh—the requirement that each society establish a judicial system—serves to enforce the six negative commandments.

For Noahide law to be "law," and for human nature to be demonstrably shared, requires the existence of a lawgiving Creator. Against Hugo Grotius, Novak states that "the cosmic relation of nature and law, where neither term is a metaphor, ultimately requires the affirmation of a cosmic lawgiver, who is simultaneously the creator of nature."[10] Lacking this "ontological dimension,"[11] one could not persuasively articulate the "commonality" of Noahide humanity, because one could not claim for human beings a stable and normative "nature." For Novak therefore the theology of creation, revealed in the Torah, stands as a constitutive part of any natural law doctrine. Without their particularity, the Rabbis could not have persuasively defended a universal (Noahide) human nature subject to certain laws.

Israel, the Gentiles, and Noahide Law

What is the relationship of Jews to Noahide law? On the one hand, Novak observes that the *ben Noah*, or children of Noah, stand for non-Jews. They are the descendents of Noah who are not children of Abraham. In this respect, the Rabbis sketched Noahide law so as to account for what non-Jews were obligated to do. On the other hand, Novak points out that the concept of "Noahide" depends upon a notion of "pre-Judaic man" that is broader than would be otherwise suggested by the differentiation of gentile/Noahide and Jew/Torah. Prior to the giving of the Torah, Noahide law obligated all human beings on the grounds of their sharing a created human nature. The Torah does not negate this sharing of created human nature; rather, the Jews who received the Torah at Sinai did so as persons bound to observance of the Noahide laws. The universality of the created order thus preceded the particularity by which the Rabbis were able to know the universality of the Creator's Noahide law.

Novak suggests that the Jews' observance of the Noahide law enabled them to receive the Torah at Sinai. In this regard he cites a rabbinic text on Deut. 33.2: "'When the Holy-One-blessed-be-He appeared (*nigleh*) to give the Torah to Israel, he did not appear to Israel alone but to all the nations.'"[12] While some interpreters of this text suppose it to mean that Israel alone freely chose to observe the Torah, Novak argues that the text is instead about Noahide law. He notes that "the text continues with the Edomites refusing the Torah when they hear that it prohibits murder. The Ammonites and Moabites refuse it because it prohibits incest. And the Ishmaelites refuse it because it prohibits theft."[13] Having rejected Noahide law, the other nations were too disordered to be able to enter into a covenant with the Lord. For Novak, in short, "the acceptance of the Noahide laws is the very precondition for Israel's entrance into the covenant."[14] Failure to follow the Noahide laws makes relationship with God impossible. As Novak says, "Noahide standards are what first had to be fulfilled in order for Israel to be able to accept revelation and its law with cogency."[15]

Does this mean that God's election of the Jews, their acceptance of covenantal relationship with him, depended upon a moral righteousness that Israel, uniquely among nations, possessed prior to the reception of the Torah? Novak makes three points that are helpful in answering this question. First, God did not give Israel the choice of accepting or rejecting the Torah. Rather, according to "the great preponderance of scriptural and rabbinic teaching," Israel "could accept the covenant and develop its life together with God, or she could reject the covenant and have it imposed upon her by God anyway."[16] Second, God did not reveal the Torah to the other nations directly, but did so only through Israel; and the other nations remain free to reject "the covenant with impunity," without facing moral condemnation on this basis.[17] Third, "acceptance" of Noahide law, like Israel's "acceptance" of the Torah, does not form the basis for that law being binding. On the contrary, "such acceptance only confirms a prior normative order already in place."[18] Thus, Israel's "acceptance" of the Torah at Sinai rests upon God's election, not upon her own Noahide righteousness. And the fact that other nations were not thus elected does not mean that they necessarily lacked commitment to Noahide law. As Novak remarks, "Not all the nations of the world are viewed by the Jews as being on the same submoral level as are the nations mentioned in the rabbinic text, who were culturally unable to accept even the natural Torah let alone the specifically revealed one."[19]

As regards Noahide law, the key point for Novak is not what differentiates Israel from the other nations, but what unites all nations as children of Noah. Noahide law is not a universalism that allows one to bypass Israel's particularity.[20] Noahide law *is* a "universalism," however, in the sense of grounding moral obligation not solely on laws that pertain to covenantal particularity, but also on laws that pertain to the sharing of created human nature. Jews share a created human nature with all other children of Noah, even though for Jews this common nature is lived out within the particularity of covenantal intimacy. Novak affirms that "human nature and its normative requirement are something she [Israel] has in common with all the other nations of the world,"[21] a universality expressed historically in the shared possession of Noahide laws by "other real historical communities which have accepted these norms for themselves."[22]

Novak combines his insistence upon "certain basic moral norms held in common" due to shared human nature, with an equal insistence that "[b]ecause Israel has so completely accepted the natural law and included it as a standard for guiding her own unique convential law, she is in a special position to teach the world about natural law."[23] Novak is referring to the people of Israel rather than to the modern State of Israel, which he observes "is structured by a totally secular system of law, one whose ties to classical Jewish law are at most highly selective."[24] His view that the people of Israel are "in a special position to teach the world about natural law" stems from the particularity of Israel's covenantal relationship, via the Torah, with God: Israel has been given covenantal intimacy with the Creator, and the Noahide law has received confirmation in the Torah.

Aquinas on Israel and the Nations

A Gratuitous Election

Like Novak, Aquinas strongly affirms the dignity of the people of Israel: "The more a man is united to God, the better his state becomes: wherefore the more the Jewish people were bound to the worship of God, the greater their excellence over other peoples."[25] At Sinai, and in preparation for the Messiah, the people of Israel received "a prerogative of holiness."[26] This prerogative consisted in the whole Torah, and not merely the Decalogue that "showed forth the precepts of the natural law."[27] For this reason gentiles were welcomed into the observance of the Torah, as shown by Exod. 12.48, "And when a stranger shall sojourn with you and would keep the Passover to the Lord, let all his males be circumcised, then he may come near and keep it; he shall be as a native of the land."[28] On this basis, Aquinas affirms that "Gentiles obtained salvation more perfectly and more securely under the observances of the Law than under the natural law alone."[29] He has particularly in view the ceremonial precepts, which, while never binding upon the gentiles,[30] fostered the worship of the one God in accord with the mandate of the Decalogue.

Aquinas recalls the warning in Deut. 9.6 about Israel's election: "Know therefore, that the Lord your God is not giving you this good land to possess because of your righteousness; for you are a stubborn people."[31] Israel's election, he emphasizes, is completely a "gratuitous election," even in Abraham.[32] Against the view that Israel observed the natural law at the time of receiving Torah at Sinai, Deut. 9 continues, "Remember and do not forget how you provoked the Lord your God to wrath in the wilderness; from the day you came out of the land of Egypt, until you came to this place, you have been rebellious against the Lord. Even at Horeb [Sinai] you provoked the Lord to wrath, and the Lord was so angry with you that he was ready to destroy you" (Deut. 9.7–8). In this light, the natural law cannot easily be seen as (in Novak's words) "what first had to be fulfilled in order for Israel to be able to accept revelation and its law with cogency."[33] From Aquinas's perspective, it seems more promising to look for natural law precepts *within* the Torah, since Israel as much as the gentiles needed instruction even as regards the natural law.

The Divine Pedagogy

Aquinas holds that the Torah both marks Israel's covenantal intimacy with God and serves as a pedagogue after the failure of natural law among all nations, including Israel. Lest the latter aspect seem to overwhelm the former, Aquinas insists that the Torah gives Israel a covenantal intimacy with God, even if by itself (i.e., outside its ordination to the Messiah) it cannot bring human beings to the perfection of this covenantal intimacy. Aquinas observes that "just as the principal intention of human law is to create friendship between man and man; so the chief intention of the divine law is to establish man in friendship with God."[34] Covenantal intimacy itself therefore requires the law's pedagogical aspect. This is so because the fulfillment of covenantal intimacy, on the human side, requires that humans be holy. As Aquinas puts it, "Now since likeness is the reason of love, according to Ecclus. xiii.19: *Every beast loveth its like*, there cannot possibly be any friendship of man to God, Who is supremely good, unless man become good: wherefore it is written (Levit. xix.2; cf. xi.45): *You shall be holy, for I am holy.*"[35] In order to be holy, human beings need the pedagogy of the Torah.

In what does this pedagogy consist? Aquinas offers a theology of history according to which the period after Noah constitutes a slide "into idolatry and the most shameful vices."[36] This history of the nations' idolatry exposes the impotence of human reason to "suffice him [man] for salvation."[37] Once human beings have recognized their insufficiency, God elects Abraham, who relies upon faith rather than trusting in himself. The election of Abraham prepares for the giving of the Torah to Abraham's descendents, because only a people can receive a law: "at the time of Abraham God gave men certain familiar, and, as it were, household precepts: but when Abraham's descendants had multiplied, so as to form a people, and when they had been freed from slavery, it was fitting that they should be given a law."[38] Israel's inability to follow the Torah's commandments shows the impotence of fallen humans to instantiate holiness. The Torah thus pedagogically disbars human beings from presuming to rely upon natural law alone. In this regard Aquinas, following St. Paul, comments that "after man had been instructed by the Law, his pride was convinced of his weakness, through his being unable to fulfil what he knew."[39]

Negatively, then, the Torah teaches Israel (and through Israel all humankind) that human beings require resources beyond our own to be able to turn from sin: "all men, both Jews and Greeks, are under the power of sin, as it is written: 'None is righteous, no, not one; no one understands, no one seeks for God. All have turned aside, together they have gone wrong; no one does good, not even one'" (Rom. 3.10–12; cf. Ps. 14.1–3, Is. 59). Does the Torah also teach positively? As we have already suggested, Aquinas makes clear that the answer is yes. This is the case even for the Torah's ceremonial precepts, those regarding sacrifices, festivals, clothing, food, and so forth. Following Maimonides, Aquinas finds a literal reason, an intelligible purpose, in each ceremonial law. The ceremonial laws "refer to the shunning of idolatry; or recall certain divine benefits; or remind men of the divine excellence; or point out the disposition of mind which was then required in those who worshipped God."[40] At the same time the ceremonial laws prefigure Christ and his Body the Church. Likewise the laws of the Torah that have to do with human-to-human relationships—"not only litigious matters, but also voluntary contracts which are concluded between man and man, and whatever matters concern the community at large and the government thereof"[41]—teach both literally and figuratively.[42] Praising the wisdom of the Torah's judicial laws, Aquinas observes, "The people of Israel is commended for the beauty of its order (Num. xxiv.5): *How beautiful are thy tabernacles, O Jacob, and thy tents, O Israel.*"[43] Aquinas values the judicial laws regarding property, for example, because "the Law provided a threefold remedy against the irregularity of possessions."[44] Even in their literal sense, the judicial laws, like the ceremonial ones, have a spiritual purpose: "the purpose of the Law was to accustom men to give of their own to others readily."[45] Lastly, the moral precepts of the Torah possess a permanent positive pedagogy, because "all the moral precepts belong to the law of nature."[46]

Thus the Torah both teaches the impotence of the natural law for salvation and teaches the natural law, whose norms Christ Jesus does not abrogate. This simultaneously positive and negative pedagogy relies upon the presence of shared created human nature. Sin does not erase natural law principles, the first principles of practical reason, from human minds.[47] Despite the slide "into idolatry and the most shameful vices,"[48] human beings continue to apprehend "a prior normative order already in place,"[49] in Novak's phrase. Aquinas notes that "human reason could not go astray in the abstract, as to the universal principles of the natural law; but through being habituated to sin, it became obscured in the point of things to be done in detail."[50] Human beings can therefore know natural law without the Torah, despite the weakened character of this knowledge after sin.

God reveals the natural law in the Torah because the obscuring of the natural law by sin blocks the fulfillment of the Torah in covenantal friendship with God: "As the Apostle says (1 Tim. i.5), *the end of the commandment is charity.*"[51] This inclusion in Revelation does not change natural law's character as "natural." Rather, as Aquinas puts it, "The Old Law is distinct from the natural law, not as being altogether different from it, but as something added thereto. For just as grace presupposes nature, so must the divine law presuppose the natural law."[52] The created "normative order," the norms of justice in relationships between human beings and between human beings and God, is taken up, not overturned, in the covenantal friendship promised by the Torah and fulfilled in Christ.

Novak on the Covenantal *Gestalt*

Creation and Revelation

How close is Aquinas's position to Novak's? Novak is concerned that by integrating natural law and Mosaic law too closely, one runs the risk of a rationalistic interpretation of Torah. In *The Guide of the Perplexed*, Maimonides observes that "the Law, although it is not natural, enters into what is natural."[53] Novak explains that for Maimonides,

> one moves up from the life of the body to the life of the soul, and then one brings the enlightenment of the soul back down to properly rule the life of the body. The excellence of the soul entails the excellence of the body. And the excellence of the soul presupposes an ordered bodily life. ... Maimonides saw all the commandments of the Torah in the context of this reciprocal relation of body and soul, a relation that participates in the cosmic relation of matter and form. In this sense, all of the commandments of the Torah are natural law. They all contribute either to spiritual betterment or to political betterment.[54]

According to Novak, this teleological view of natural law lacks "a truly responsive role for God"[55]; teleology tends to separate the commandments of the Torah from the covenantal God's responsive activity. Novak argues that "[t]his is the theological problem with Maimonides' natural law theory. Minimally, it is noncovenantal; maximally, it is counter-covenantal."[56]

The separation of the commandments from the covenantal God characterizes modern Jewish thought even more radically. Novak explains that "by identifying revelation essentially with natural law instead of seeing natural law functioning at the juncture of revelation and creation, liberal Jewish theology has confused the necessary distinctions and interrelations between all three prime events [creation, revelation, eschatological redemption] Judaism affirms."[57] If the Torah is at its heart simply the revelation of the givens of creation, accessible to natural reason, then the Torah is hardly revelation at all.

No more than Aquinas, however, does Novak wish to deny that many commandments of the Mosaic law belong to natural law. Indeed, Novak remarks that "we can appreciate the wisdom of the commandment 'you shall not murder' (Exod. 20.13) before we eventually understand that its prescription is part of God's wisdom as creator of the universe and its nature in which moral law is an inherent ingredient."[58] In this respect Novak differentiates between the commandment prohibiting murder and the commandment prohibiting the eating of pork. Both derive from God's wisdom, but the prohibition of murder is accessible also to created human reason, whereas the prohibition of eating pork requires Revelation since it "is not immediately universal."[59] Does this thereby relegate the prohibition of murder to the realm of universal reason, for which the particularity of communal laws and the lawgiving God are unnecessary?

Novak argues that particularity cannot be gotten rid of so easily: just as the universal concept of (secular) "society" emerges from, rather than grounds, particular (religious) "communities," so also "technical languages are . . . abstractions *from* these prior historical languages, not the transcendental ground *of* them. They are abstractions designed to function in particular areas where condensed precision is called for."[60] If this is so, then the prohibition of murder cannot be subsumed by Enlightenment universalism by discarding its connection with the particularity of God's wisdom, as known covenantally in the community for which God has also prohibited eating pork. For the Jew, both prohibitions make sense in light of "the wisdom by which God creates, structures, and sustains the world,"[61] the wisdom by which God also elects the Jews. As Novak goes on to say, "unlike the idea of human rights, it [natural law] does not claim to be self-constituting. By its real assertion of *nature*, it indicates that it is rooted in an order that transcends any immanent society. Here is where it parts company with liberalism and reconnects itself to the religions of revelation from whence it emerged, in our case, to Judaism."[62]

For Novak, therefore, the key is that "creation and its order, that is, nature, is the necessary precondition for revelation to occur."[63] Revelation refers to the particular covenantal relationship of God to the community of Israel, while the created order refers to all human beings and communities.

But since Revelation is given to a human community, covenantal Revelation between God and a people must be prepared for in the created order. Thus "natural law or its equivalent . . . had to be in place for Israel to be enough of a human community, with insight into the nature of human sociality, to be able to accept the Torah from God. Only then can their existing polity be elevated and become a holy people, God's portion in the world."[64] Natural law describes the "limits" that preserve the social bonds of every successful human community, whereas human communities that repudiate these limits chart a path of violence and chaos.

Novak takes his examples of natural law in Scripture from the pre-Sinai period, when the community is being formed: Adam and Eve's "sin of idolatry"; Cain's criminal guilt prior to the existence of any written law or divine commandment against murder;[65] the criminal connection between sexuality and violence, absent the institution of marriage, both before and after the Flood; the dialogue between God and Abraham over justice as regards Sodom and Gomorrah; Abraham's unjust deception of Abimelech; the rape of Dinah; Joseph's refusal to commit adultery with Potiphar's wife;[66] Jethro's attraction to the pre-Sinai community of Israel under Moses' leadership. By means of these examples, Novak develops his insight that "Noahide standards are what first had to be fulfilled in order for Israel to be able to accept revelation and its law with cogency,"[67] or in other words that natural law is best understood as the standards of justice that precede the Mosaic law and that form Israel as the kind of community that can receive the Mosaic law, by contrast with Sodom, Egypt, and other such communities that "were in violation of the natural law of God."[68]

The Covenantal *Gestalt*

After giving the above examples of natural law from the pre-Sinai narratives of Scripture, Novak does not give examples from the Mosaic law of Sinai. But he does grant that commonality between the Mosaic law's norms and those found in other communities should be expected, precisely because of the natural law that emerges from the created order. He observes that

> the normative content of the Sinai covenant need not be regarded as originally instituted at the event of the Sinai revelation. Even much of that content which is cultic, historical research has been showing to have analogues and precedents in other cultures. And that commonality is even more evident in the ethical teaching of Scripture, which, being more universal in essence, will have more easily discovered cognates elsewhere.[69]

Where then is the uniqueness and particularity of Israel and the Mosaic law? Novak finds it "in its overall *Gestalt*, which constitutes a full and abiding relationship between God and a people on earth,"[70] and which, precisely in its particularity, opens up to the universal because it "has future significance for humankind as a whole."[71] Elsewhere he makes the same point: "Sinai establishes the divine-human relationship *de novo* whereas it only confirms the basic interhuman relationships."[72] The particularity of Israel consists in the covenantal relationship established by Sinai. The Sinai commandments express this particularity when viewed covenantally, but insofar as they incorporate pre-Sinai (Noahide) norms grounded in creation, the Sinai commandments also have a universal dimension. The Sinai covenant gives the created order, in Israel, an intimate friendship with God.[73] As Novak puts it, "even if we are able to discern the specific reasons for each and every one of the individual commandments, that would in no way detract from the overall revealed *Gestalt* of the commandments as *Torah*. That *Gestalt* is that each of the commandments bespeaks God's own personal involvement in the life of the elected community in the world."[74]

Aquinas on Sinai and Natural Law

Does Aquinas retain a similar emphasis on the covenant in his account of the Decalogue/moral precepts of the Torah? Or in his handling of the Decalogue/moral precepts as natural law, does he cut them off from the covenant and thereby fall into a rationalistic account of the Torah? Can we discern any consequences of Aquinas's choice of the Mosaic law, rather than the pre-Sinai narratives, for exemplifying natural law?

Sinai and the Pre-Sinai Narratives

As we have seen, the theology of history in which context Aquinas understands the Sinai covenant emphasizes human sin, with the Mosaic law as a positive and negative pedagogue against human pride. The pre-Sinai narratives, however, seem to make God himself complicit in violations of the Decalogue. Among the examples cited by Aquinas, consider the Lord's command to the people of Israel through Moses after the ninth plague: "Speak now in the hearing of the people, that they ask, every man of his neighbor and every woman of her neighbor, jewelry of silver and gold" (Exod. 11.2). Since the Lord intends for the people to leave Egypt with this jewelry, never to return, does not the Lord here command theft—contrary to "You shall not steal" (Exod. 20.15)? Similarly, God commands Abraham to offer Isaac as a human sacrifice: "Take your son, your only son Isaac, whom you love, and go to the land of Moriah, and offer him there as a burnt offering upon one of the mountains of which I shall tell you" (Gen. 22.2). This appears to violate the commandment "You shall not kill" (Exod. 22.13).[75] If each commandment, as Novak says, "bespeaks God's own personal involvement in the life of the elected community in the world,"[76] is God's involvement so arbitrary that he can change his mind about what to command Israel? Is God a reliable covenant partner, or does he violate the moral norms that he has inscribed in his own creation?

Aquinas answers by appealing to the covenantal context of the Decalogue. He quotes Isa. 24.5, "The earth lies polluted under its inhabitants; for they have transgressed the laws, violated the statutes, broken the everlasting covenant."[77] If God has transgressed his laws, then he has broken his covenant. But just as his covenant is "everlasting," so are his laws. Sinai confirms that the God who is personally involved in Israel is also the God who created the world and established the universal norms for human nature. Quoting 2 Tim. 2.13's commendation of this God, "if we are faithless, he remains faithful—for he cannot deny himself," Aquinas affirms that God "would deny himself if he were to do away with the very order of his own justice, since he is justice itself."[78] He argues that the apparent dispensations of the Decalogue in the pre-Sinai narratives, such as God's command to Abraham to slay Isaac, do not in fact violate the natural law but rather involve the divine lawgiver acting directly to achieve the just end, known by God, that the law entails. Thus, with regard to the near-slaying of Isaac, Aquinas comments that God "is the Lord of life and death: for He it is who inflicts the punishment of death on all men, both godly and ungodly, on account of the sin of our first parent."[79] Elsewhere I have explored Aquinas's position on this issue in some detail.[80] Rather than pursuing the issue here, let me simply underscore that for Aquinas, God's commands never contradict Sinai, because God can directly will the end toward which the law aims.

In short, the laws of Sinai cannot be dispensed, nor does God do so. Aquinas notes that "the intention of every lawgiver is directed first and chiefly to the common good; secondly, to the order of justice and virtue, whereby the common good is preserved and attained. If therefore there be any precepts which contain the very preservation of the common good ... such precepts contain the intention of the lawgiver, and therefore are indispensable."[81] The Decalogue consists of just such precepts. The first three laws, concerning human-to-God relations, "contain the very order to the common and final good, which is God."[82] The last seven laws, concerning human-to-human relations, contain the "very order of justice and virtue." Insofar as all the moral laws included in the Mosaic law are good moral laws, and thus are in accord with reason (divine and human), "all the moral precepts belong to the law of nature,"[83] and cannot be dispensed.

Creation and Revelation

Aquinas adds, however, that the moral precepts of the Decalogue do not all belong to the law of nature "in the same way": the Decalogue includes both precepts of natural law and precepts inaccessible to human reason alone.[84] With respect to the former, Aquinas notes that "there are certain things which the natural reason of every man, of its own accord and at once, judges to be done or not to be done: e.g., *Honor thy father and thy mother*, and, *Thou shalt not kill*, *Thou shalt not steal*: and these belong to the law of nature absolutely."[85] While these precepts of the Decalogue are not absent from the covenantal particularity of Israel—on the contrary, the history of Israel amply illustrates them[86]—nonetheless they flow from the created order. Other precepts of the Decalogue, however, are not accessible to natural human reason. As an example Aquinas gives, "Thou shalt not take the name of the Lord thy God in vain."[87] Only by Revelation can we know "the name of the Lord."

In Aquinas's view, the covenantal particularity of the Decalogue explains the Decalogue's combination of natural law with law inaccessible to reason alone. Uniquely among the laws given to Israel, the Decalogue is God's direct instruction: "God himself is said to have given the precepts of the decalogue; whereas He gave the other precepts to the people through Moses."[88] The Decalogue does not include either the first principles of practical reason (which need not be promulgated anew) or those precepts that must be more laboriously deduced from natural law principles, which God teaches through the mediation of "wise men" such as Moses.[89] Instead, the purpose of the Decalogue is to renew creation by recalling the basic precepts of the natural law, and to elevate creation by placing it within the context of covenantal Revelation, of knowing the very "name" of the Lord. Recall Jacob's plea: "Tell me, I pray, your name" (Gen. 32.29)—and his exultation that same night, "For I have seen God face to face, and yet my life is preserved" (Gen. 32.30).

The Sabbath Commandment

For Aquinas as for Novak, then, the Decalogue calls into question efforts to isolate natural law doctrine, rooted in our natural knowledge of the created order, from the covenantal particularity in which it comes fully to light. Consider Aquinas's treatment of the commandment of Sabbath observance. Against Hesychius's exclusion of the commandment regarding the Sabbath from the Decalogue, Aquinas notes that "it seems unbecoming for the precept of the Sabbath-day observance to be put among the precepts of the decalogue, if it nowise belonged to the decalogue."[90] Following Origen's and Augustine's commentaries on Exodus, Aquinas argues for the inclusion of the Sabbath in the Decalogue.[91] One might ask, however, why observing the Sabbath should have a special place among the "ten words" (Deut. 4.13) that Moses singles out as the heart of the Law. Would it not fit better among the ceremonial precepts, which are "determinations of the precepts of the decalogue,"[92] laws that apply the principles articulated by the Decalogue to Israel's particular time and place? If, as Aquinas states, "the precepts of the decalogue need to be such as the people can understand at once,"[93] is Sabbath observance such a precept?

In reply, Aquinas suggests that the Sabbath commandment can at the same time be universal (grounded in the order of creation) and covenantal. The Sabbath commandment is a universal moral precept, knowable by natural law, "in so far as it commands man to give some time to the things of God, according to Ps. xlv.11: *Be still and see that I am God.*"[94] As Aquinas points out, the Sabbath commandment, understood as a moral precept, is the foundation of all the ceremonial precepts.[95] Worship is not an irrational impulse: "It belongs to a dictate of natural reason that man should do something through reverence for God."[96] In principle, therefore, human beings can understand the Sabbath commandment "at once," although in practice those who do not believe in God reject the commandment. In addition to being a moral precept, however, the Sabbath commandment is also a ceremonial precept as regards God's choice of the seventh day for the people of Israel to worship him.[97] The seventh day need not be set apart for human beings to "give some time to the things of God"; God could have chosen another day, and in the New Covenant God does so.

The determination of the seventh day as a day of rest and worship for the Israelites is not the only way in which the Sabbath commandment is covenantal as well as universal. Aquinas argues that the Sabbath commandment points back to creation and points forward to the elevation of creation in eschatological new creation. Understanding the Decalogue as law for the human community under God, Aquinas notes that "man owes three things to the head of the community: first, fidelity; secondly, reverence; thirdly, service."[98] The Sabbath pertains to the service of the "head," God. Such service arises in response to the divine gifting that constitutes the community: "Service is due to his master in return for the benefits which his subjects receive from him: and to this belongs the third commandment of the sanctification of the Sabbath in memory of the creation of all things."[99] The Sabbath hearkens back to the seven days of creation, as the commandment makes clear: "for in six days the Lord made heaven and earth, the sea, and all that is in them, and rested the seventh day; therefore the Lord blessed the sabbath day and hallowed it" (Exod. 20.11, repeating Gen. 2.3).

Human community under God, rooted in creation, is ordered by God's grace to the perfect Sabbath, union with God. Aquinas notes that "it is right that the seventh day should have been sanctified, since the special sanctification of every creature consists in resting in God."[100] This special sanctification is already envisioned by God in creating from all eternity. Aquinas differentiates between the "first perfection" of a creature, in which it fully receives its substantial form, and the creature's "second perfection," which is the attainment of the creature's end or goal. This "end" can be "either an operation, as the end of the harpist is to play the harp; or something that is attained by the operation, as the end of the builder is the house that he makes by building."[101] In this sense the "end" is caused by the form as the principle of operation. What then are the "first perfection" and "second perfection" of the universe? Aquinas answers, "Now the final perfection, which is the end of the whole universe, is the perfect beatitude of the Saints at the consummation of the world; and the first perfection is the completeness of the universe at its first founding, and this is what is ascribed to the seventh day."[102]

By calling to mind both the beginning and the end, creation and new creation, the Sabbath commandment illustrates how the Decalogue weaves together creation and covenantal particularity. As Aquinas explains, this union of creation and (covenantal) new creation is why the Decalogue includes the Sabbath but not the other festivals or sacrifices:

> Now of all the divine favors to be commemorated the chief was that of the creation, which was called to mind by the sanctification of the Sabbath; wherefore the reason for this precept is given in Exod. xx.11: *In six days the Lord made heaven and earth*, etc. And of all future blessings, the chief and final was the repose of the mind in God, either, in the present life, by grace, or, in the future life, by glory; which repose was also foreshadowed in the Sabbath-day observance: wherefore it is written (Isa. lviii.13): *If thou turn away thy foot from the Sabbath, from doing thy own will in My holy day, and call the Sabbath delightful, and the holy of the Lord glorious.*[103]

Aquinas notes that the first three commandments can also be viewed as teaching the right ordering of deeds, words, and thoughts, the last of which applies to the Sabbath commandment, since "the sanctification of the Sabbath, as the subject of a moral precept, requires repose of the heart in God."[104]

The Decalogue and Natural Law

Posing the question of whether the "ten precepts of the decalogue are set in proper order," Aquinas answers in the affirmative on the basis of his contention that "the precepts of the Decalogue are such as the mind of man is ready to grasp at once."[105] It would seem, however, that the three commandments about God are not "such as the mind of man is ready to grasp at once." Idolatry, irreverence, and lack of worship have been prevalent in human history, which seems to show a lack of readiness on the part of human apprehension.

In reply, Aquinas holds that sin obscures, but without effacing, human apprehension of the natural obligation to worship God. Describing the consequences of sin, he says that "when man turned his back on God, he fell under the influence of his sensual impulses: in fact this happens to each one individually, the more he deviates from the path of reason, so that, after a fashion, he is likened to the beasts that are led by the impulse of sensuality" rather than by rational reflection.[106] Sin cannot efface the natural law in its first principles, including love of God and love of neighbor, from the human mind. But the natural law "is blotted out in the case of a particular action, in so far as reason is hindered from applying the general principle to a particular point of practice, on account of concupiscence or some other passion."[107] In idolatry, irreverence, irreligion, and so forth, we lose touch with what is reasonable.[108]

Despite the fact that the natural law precepts are in accord with reason, therefore, the Mosaic law contains such precepts because human beings, weighed down by sin, have difficulty making right judgments in moral reasoning. As Aquinas puts it,

> It was fitting that the divine law should come to man's assistance not only in those things for which reason is insufficient, but also in those things in which human reason may happen to be impeded. Now human reason could not go astray in the abstract, as to the universal principles of the natural law; but through being habituated to sin, it became obscured in the point of things to be done in detail. But with regard to the other

moral precepts, which are like conclusions drawn from the universal principles of the natural law, the reason of many men went astray, to the extent of judging to be lawful, things that are evil in themselves.[109]

It follows that the Decalogue can be expected to be the central source of natural law, not despite of the Decalogue's covenantal character, but because of it. God makes covenant with Israel so that Israel might become holy: "You shall be holy, for I the Lord your God am holy. Every one of you shall revere his mother and his father, and you shall keep my sabbaths: I am the Lord your God. Do not turn to idols or make for yourselves molten gods: I am the Lord your God" (Lev. 19.2–4). The Decalogue holds a central covenantal place because it communicates to Israel the natural law as elevated into the covenantal context of God's call to supernatural friendship with him.

This covenantal context becomes even more evident in light of Aquinas's threefold ordering of the moral precepts of the Mosaic law. He begins with the moral principles that are "so evident as to need no promulgation; such as the commandments of the love of God and our neighbor."[110] Rather than solely being mere commandments, these principles provide "the ends of the commandments."[111] Thus the Mosaic law commands the act of charity toward God and neighbor: "you shall love the Lord your God with all your heart, and with all your soul, and with all your might" (Deut. 6.5) and "[y]ou shall not take vengeance or bear any grudge against the sons of your own people, but you shall love your neighbor as yourself" (Lev. 19.18).[112] Following upon these commandments, about which "no man can have an erroneous judgment," are commandments that are first conclusions from basic natural law principles. As we have seen, the Decalogue reveals these first conclusions, whose truth most people recognize.[113] Lastly, following upon the commandments of the Decalogue stand the moral precepts that require further reasoning to deduce. God reveals these precepts, which follow from the law of charity and the Decalogue, through wise intermediaries—Moses and Aaron.

The Goal of Charity

The foremost place of the commandments regarding charity indicates the relationship of covenant and creation in Aquinas's theology of the Decalogue. As he does with respect to all the precepts of the Mosaic law, he argues that the moral precepts point intrinsically to the New Law: "Man cannot fulfil all the precepts of the law, unless he fulfils the precept of charity [Deut. 6.5, Lev. 19.18], which is impossible without charity."[114] Aquinas specifically means the supernatural virtue of charity, as becomes clear from his conclusion: "Consequently it is not possible, as Pelagius maintained, for man to fulfil the law without grace."[115] In this covenantal context the commandments of the Decalogue, including those commandments that are knowable solely from within the created order, have charity as their goal. Thus, inquiring whether "peace is the proper effect of charity," Aquinas quotes Ps. 119.165, "Great peace have those who love thy law."[116] To love the Mosaic law, Aquinas explains, requires both loving God with one's "whole heart, by referring all things to Him," and loving "our neighbor as ourselves."[117] Such love comes about not through our natural powers, which are insufficient to make us friends with God, but through "the infusion of the Holy Spirit, Who is the love of the Father and the Son, and the participation of Whom in us is created charity."[118]

It follows that the precepts of the Torah are far from a mere list of rules. Rather, Aquinas treats them under the rubric of Ps. 19.8, "the precepts of the Lord are right, rejoicing the heart; the commandment of the Lord is pure, enlightening the eyes."[119] As Ps. 19 goes on to say of the precepts of the Mosaic law, "More to be desired are they than gold, even much fine gold; sweeter also than honey and drippings of the honeycomb. Moreover by them is thy servant warned; in keeping them there is great reward" (19.11–12). They belong to the covenantal narrative of the law and the prophets. Aquinas remarks in this respect, "As anyone can see, who reads carefully the story of the Old Testament, the common weal of the people prospered under the Law as long as they obeyed it; and as soon as they departed from the precepts of the Law they were overtaken by many calamities."[120]

This covenantal narrative, as Novak likewise sees, provides a commentary on the natural law (the created order) as it is taken up into friendship with God. Recall Novak's insistence that "the overall revealed *Gestalt* of the commandments as *Torah* . . . is that each of the commandments bespeaks God's own personal involvement in the life of the elected community in the world."[121] Aquinas strongly affirms this point, although he emphasizes that the "elected community in the world" is the people of God constituted around the divine Messiah. For Aquinas the commandments "disposed men to the justifying grace of grace of Christ, which they also signified."[122] In this emphasis on the need for grace, he does not part ways with Novak. Novak remarks in this regard that "both Judaism and Christianity are convinced that humans are doomed if basically left to their own devices; that grace is a necessity for the human condition. The difference between them . . . is whether one is connected to the grace of God by the Torah or by Christ."[123]

The End of the Law

Nonetheless, by holding that the moral precepts continue to bind Christians while the ceremonial and judicial ones do not, has Aquinas rationalistically removed the Decalogue from what Novak calls the "the overall revealed *Gestalt* of the commandments as *Torah?*" Here one recalls the strictures of Martin Luther, who holds that the Mosaic law and the Decalogue pertain, as such, solely to the Jews. He grants that "the Gentiles have certain laws in common with the Jews, such as these: there is one God, no one is to do wrong to another, no one is to commit adultery or murder or steal, and others like them."[124] For Luther, however, Christians do not receive these shared laws from Moses as lawgiver: "If I were to accept Moses in one commandment, I would have to accept the entire Moses. Thus the consequence would be that if I accept Moses as master, then I must have myself circumcised, wash my clothes in the Jewish way, eat and drink and dress thus and so, and observe all that stuff."[125] On this view, because the Mosaic law can only be accepted whole or rejected whole, the seemingly shared laws are actually not shared. Luther embraces the radical implications of his position: "That Moses does not bind the Gentiles can be proved from Exod. 20[:1], where God himself speaks, 'I am the Lord your God, who brought you out of the land of Egypt, out of the house of bondage.' This text makes it clear that even the Ten Commandments do not pertain to us. For God never led us out of Egypt, but only the Jews."[126] For Luther, "the New Testament and the natural law" suffice to provide the moral precepts that Christians require,[127] and so the Mosaic law's sole ongoing role is to remind Christians of the impossibility of fulfilling God's commandments and of the mercy of Christ.

Does Aquinas preserve "the overall revealed *Gestalt* of the commandments as *Torah*," or does his position open itself to Luther's critique that following the Mosaic law in any particular requires one to follow the whole Mosaic law? Commenting on Bar. 4.1, "She is the book of the commandments of God, and the law that endures for ever," Aquinas states, "The Old Law is said to be *for ever* simply and absolutely, as regards its moral precepts; but as regards the ceremonial precepts it lasts for ever in respect of the reality which those ceremonies foreshadowed."[128] The Sabbath, insofar as it is a ceremonial precept, offers an example. Aquinas remarks that "its place is taken by the *Lord's Day*, which recalls the beginning of the new creature in the Resurrection of Christ."[129] This is not a negation but a fulfillment: Aquinas holds that Christ Jesus, as Israel's Messiah, fulfills the whole Mosaic law for us in his Paschal mystery.[130] Since Moses' law belongs to Christ's ordering of human beings to friendship with God, the moral precepts retain their covenantal *Gestalt.* Aquinas, like Novak, gives a covenantal account of natural law as a reality in human history.

Obedience to the Natural Law

Aquinas raises the question of human obedience to natural law precepts in light of Jesus' teaching to a young man of Israel, "If you would enter life, keep the commandments" (Mt. 19.17).[131] Full obedience, Aquinas observes, can only be achieved in the context of covenantal union with God. Deepening God's promise that Israel would be his own people, Jesus makes us his friends by giving us a share in his Spirit. But if obedience to the commandments requires charity, what about the striving of human beings who lack charity? Can such persons follow the natural law?

Recall that Novak argues that the Decalogue (and the whole Mosaic law) adds a covenantal dimension or *Gestalt* to natural law for Israel, and that other peoples experience natural law ("Noahide law") outside this covenantal context. Broadly speaking, Aquinas's position is similar. He proposes that outside covenantal charity, human beings can certainly understand, and often follow, the basic precepts of the natural law. The commandment "Honor your father and your mother" (Exod. 20.12), for example, "does not mean that a man must honor his father from charity, but merely that he must honor him. Wherefore he that honors his father, yet has not charity, does not break this precept."[132] In this sense, Aquinas, like Novak, leaves an important place for natural law even outside the covenantal relationship with God. No human beings, even those who have no share in covenantal relationship with God, stand outside natural law.

Yet Aquinas could not agree fully with the distinction that Novak seeks to make through the rabbinic positing of a "Noahide law." At least as I understand Aquinas's position, the view that the nations receive Noahide/natural law, while Israel receives Noahide and covenantal Mosaic law, does not sufficiently account for the participation of the nations in the Abrahamic covenantal promise: "by you all the families of the earth shall bless themselves" (Gen. 12.3). Without some (proleptic) participation in the covenantal relationship, how could the "Noahides" have any hope of fulfilling even the seven Noahide commandments? Interpreting Rom. 2.14–15, Aquinas holds that the "Noahides" who are able to fulfill the natural law do so by a certain graced participation in "the Israel of God" (Gal. 6.16).[133] He explains that implicit faith allows for participation in the covenant: "If, however, some [gentiles] were saved without receiving any revelation, they were not saved without faith in a Mediator, for, though they did not believe in Him explicitly, they did, nevertheless, have implicit faith through believing in Divine providence, since they believed that God would deliver mankind in whatever way was pleasing to him" (cf. Heb. 11.6).[134] For Aquinas, therefore, at least some of the Noahides already have a salvific, though implicit, relationship with the God of the covenant.

Aquinas's position here involves his understanding of what law is. He holds that God draws human beings toward himself by means of law: "the extrinsic principle moving to good is God, Who both instructs us by means of His Law, and assists us by His Grace."[135] Through the very constitution of human reason, God in natural law moves us interiorly to good. Thus, even Noahide/natural law is already relational and "already bespeaks God's own personal involvement."[136] Since natural law belongs to the teleological constitution of the rational creature, the goal of natural law in the concrete historical order cannot be fulfilled without covenantal charity. This is so because only charity unites us to the ultimate end for which we were created, namely God himself. Lacking charity, human actions miss the good toward which God has ordained human beings.[137] It is better to honor one's father and mother than not to do so; and yet if one does so for self-seeking reasons, one has failed to fulfill the commandments "you shall love the Lord your God" (Deut. 6.5) and "you shall love your neighbor as yourself" (Lev. 19.18). These commandments are certainly in accord with natural reason, but they require charity to be fulfilled. Lacking charity, one can neither "keep the commandments" nor "enter life" (Mt. 19.17).

Natural Law and Justification

Can the moral precepts of the Mosaic law make human beings just? Numerous Pauline texts, Aquinas observes, answer in the negative. He quotes 2 Cor. 3.6, for example, where Paul writes that God "has qualified us to be ministers of a new covenant, not in a written code but in the Spirit; for the written code kills, but the Spirit gives life."[138] Here Paul is emphasizing the insufficiency of fallen human resources to attain covenantal life with God: "Such is the confidence that we have through Christ toward God. Not that we are sufficient of ourselves to claim anything as coming from us; our sufficiency is from God" (2 Cor. 3.4–5). In the same vein, Aquinas recalls Gen. 15.16, "And he [Abraham] believed the Lord; and he reckoned it to him as righteousness," which Paul interprets in Rom. 4.2, "For if Abraham was justified by works, he has something to boast about, but not before God."[139] Although the moral precepts command certain human actions, therefore, the moral precepts themselves, on their own, cannot bring about the divine action needed for the restoration of "that justice which is before God."[140]

Aquinas takes equal notice of Rom. 2.13, "For it is not the hearers of the law who are righteous before God, but the doers of the law who will be justified," as well as of such Old Testament texts as Lev. 18.5, "You shall therefore keep my statutes and my ordinances, by doing which a man shall live."[141] In this regard Aquinas distinguishes between possessing justice as a virtuous "habit"—in which case the infused virtue of justice justifies the human person—and doing "works of justice."[142] Doing "works of justice," as commanded by the moral precepts of the Mosaic law (and by the natural law), does indeed pertain to the justified person.[143] Indeed, in this sense obeying all the precepts of the Mosaic law pertains to justification, although the mode of obedience differs before and after Christ. As Aquinas puts it, "The fulfilment of the commandments of the Law, even those which are about the acts of the other virtues, has the character of justification, inasmuch as it is just that man should obey God: or again, inasmuch as it is just that all that belongs to man should be subject to reason."[144] The Mosaic law commands good actions, and doing good actions pertains to justification, even though human beings cannot justify themselves by their actions alone without the grace of the Holy Spirit.

We thus arrive back at the difference between Christianity and Judaism identified by Novak: "whether one is connected to the grace of God by the Torah or by Christ."[145] Perhaps this difference should be specified further: Aquinas grants that the Torah connects one to the grace of God, although it does so only in a dispositive fashion, because the grace of the Holy Spirit flows through the Messiah who fulfills the Torah. Aquinas affirms that "the Old Law ordained men to Christ in two ways. First, by bearing witness to Christ. . . . Secondly, as a kind of disposition, since by withdrawing men from idolatrous worship, it enclosed (*concludebat*) them in the worship of one God, by whom the human race was to be saved through Christ."[146] The Torah and the "law of Christ" (Gal. 6.2) "have the same end, namely, man's subjection to God."[147] In this sense, divine law is one. Aquinas, in other words, can affirm that both the Torah and Christ connect one to the grace of God, so long as one allows for the key distinction as regards causality: the Messiah of Israel accomplishes the Torah's covenantal promises of full intimacy between Israel and God. As Aquinas observes, "the proper effect of law is to lead its subjects to their proper virtue."[148] Christ leads us to this end by uniting us to himself. "Do we then overthrow the law by this faith? By no means! On the contrary, we uphold the law" (Rom. 3.31).

Conclusion

Must disagreement about Christ and Torah be the last word in our comparison of Novak and Aquinas on Noahide/natural law? Without minimizing this disagreement, I would draw attention to three positive conclusions that are shared by the two thinkers and that lead in fruitful directions for natural law reflection.

First, Novak and Aquinas agree that Jews and Christians need not view natural law in rationalistic terms: natural law is appropriately viewed in covenantal context, in which the rich interweaving of creation and covenant becomes apparent. With Aquinas, I take the further step of locating natural law primarily in the context of Sinai rather than primarily in the normative human limitations manifested in the pre-Sinai narratives, but this does not mean that natural law is not what Novak calls "Noahide" law.

Second, Novak and Aquinas agree that the people of Israel, due to their knowledge of the "name" and law of the Creator God, have much to teach other peoples about natural law. For Aquinas, this can be particularly clearly seen in the Sabbath commandment, whose linking of creation's beginning with its eschatological goal exhibits natural law's theocentric and teleological character.

Third, Novak and Aquinas agree that while obeying natural law precepts is good, more than Noahide/natural law is needed in order to achieve the justification of human beings. Humans accomplish Noahide/natural law (which as we have seen Aquinas identifies with the moral precepts of the Mosaic law) through the grace of God. Yet neither can the justification of fallen human beings be separated from their observance of the precepts of natural law, since to be justified is to act justly.

Natural law doctrine thrives best when not isolated, in Novak's words, from "God's own personal involvement in the life of the elected community in the world."[149] Without this hope for intimacy with God, the justice entailed by Noahide/natural law could not satisfy the human person. It is indeed this hope that enables Jews and Christians to bear unique witness to the world about the natural law.

Chapter 5

Election and the Life of Wisdom

When Jews and Christians converse together qua Jews and Christians, their identity arises from the doctrine of election, that is, from being chosen freely by God to be his people. Most of the controversies between Jews and Christians, however, have arisen precisely with regard to the doctrine of election. Why then should we pursue the quest for wisdom from the standpoint of covenantal election? The danger, as Regina Schwartz points out with respect to the discourses of monotheistic religions, is that we might thereby inscribe our shared quest for wisdom within the fratricidal story of Cain and Abel.[1] In seeking greater wisdom through Jewish-Christian dialogue, can we ultimately avoid what Schwartz terms "the curse of Cain?"

With this question in mind, this final chapter examines three approaches to the life of wisdom: Harold Bloom's *Where Shall Wisdom Be Found?*, Leon Kass's *The Beginning of Wisdom: Reading Genesis*, and David Novak's *The Election of Israel: The Idea of the Chosen People*. All three authors are Jewish, but as far as I know, only Novak is Torah-observant and fully committed to the doctrine of election. I hope to show that Novak's approach, with its embrace of Jewish covenantal particularity, sustains Jewish-Christian dialogue about what it means to live wisely as creatures of God.

Harold Bloom on Wisdom

In his preface to *Where Shall Wisdom Be Found?*, Harold Bloom reflects upon his reasons for writing a book on the topic of "wisdom." His reasons are not merely academic, although the book consists of essays on seminal authors—poets, philosophers, and theologians from the past three millennia—to whom Bloom has repeatedly returned over his long career. Instead, his reasons are existential. As he says, *"Where Shall Wisdom Be Found?* rises out of personal need, reflecting a quest for sagacity that might solace and clarify the traumas of aging, of recovery from grave illness, and of grief for the loss of beloved friends."[2] In this quest, he seeks to be nourished by the "aesthetic splendor, intellectual power, [and] wisdom" of the greatest works of the human intellect.[3] How does such wisdom, expressed with intellectual power and aesthetic beauty by great human authors, "solace and clarify" Bloom's experience of the human condition, especially as regards the passage of time, which ultimately will "triumph" over his evasion of death?[4] What is the use of seeking to acquire the "sagacity" of the great authors?

Bloom first points out that, whether useful or not, human beings all "learn to crave wisdom, wherever it can be found."[5] Not only believers in God, but also secularists who doubt or deny God's existence, "thirst for human wisdom."[6] He finds, however, that this wisdom "immediately goes out the door when we are in a crisis."[7] Even the wise person cannot avoid fear of dying, anguish at the suffering and death of loved ones, and the misery of suffering. Indeed, for Bloom the greatest wisdom does not seek to comfort; instead it places before us our condition, illumined by commitment to truth and the power of aesthetic beauty. Rather than comforting, wisdom "teaches us to accept natural limits."[8] It is a mistake, Bloom thinks, to equate wisdom with human transcendence. In this regard he cites the wisdom of *Don Quixote* and *Hamlet*, both of whose heroes end simply in the grave. But if wisdom is neither an antidote to existential fear nor a taste of human transcendence, how does wisdom enable us "to accept natural limits?"

Bloom suggests that true wisdom enables us to do the right thing in the time that we have. This true wisdom, he holds, characterizes the best of the Rabbinic tradition. Citing a saying of Rabbi Hillel as "a perfect, balanced wisdom," Bloom summarizes its import: "I affirm myself, but if I am for myself only, it is inadequate, and unless standing up both for myself and for others happens right now, whenever can it happen?"[9] In the same vein, he quotes Rabbi Tarphon, who taught the necessity of perseverance even when it becomes clear that one's labor can never be completed. As Bloom says of his own experience of living in accord with this wisdom, "However many classes had to be taught and however much writing had to be done, when I was ill, depressed, or weary, I rallied, with Tarphon's cognitive music in my inner ear."[10] Nonetheless, he closes his preface with a note of transcendent hope, taken from Rabbi Akiba. Akiba teaches that "everything is given against a pledge and a net is cast over all the living," so that we will soon have to pay everything back. To this supreme awareness of death, however, Akiba adds, "And everything is prepared for the feast."[11] Bloom comments: "This sharpens the Covenant, as little else can. If wisdom is trust in the Covenant, then I cannot see how wisdom can go further."[12] Rabbi Akiba has in view the eschatological feast, the World-to-Come.

How does Bloom both deny transcendence and affirm trust in the Covenant? What Bloom calls the "secular wisdom tradition" tries, he thinks, "to teach us that there is a god in us who can, for a time anyway, hold out against Nemesis."[13] By trusting in our human resources (our "personal daemon, or genius"[14]), we find a wisdom that enables us to overlook our failures, neuroses, and the impending dissolution of our being. We thereby live in the moment fully and without fear—or, as Bloom makes clear, at least we can imagine that we do so. Such "prudential wisdom" or willingness to "overlook what cannot be surmounted"[15] serves at times as a helpful crutch: if wisdom can accomplish nothing else, at least it can hold off for a time those realities that threaten to cripple us.

But such wisdom, Bloom suggests, needs to be combined with a variant of the "monotheistic hope" that he appropriates by reading the Rabbis and other authors influenced by theistic commitments. By "hope" he means not a belief in God or in the rabbinic expectation of the World-to-Come, but rather a sense that there is something more to strive toward and hope for, even while in wisdom we also know that it is unattainable. This hope stimulates our striving and provides a place, within wisdom, for a kind of trust. Bloom thus concludes: "We cannot embody it, yet we can be taught how to know wisdom, whether or not it can be identified with the Truth that might make us free."[16] Such wisdom is "trust in the Covenant," not as covenant, but as the refusal to reject all hope for some kind of transcendence. As Bloom puts it in a book that he published a year after *Where Shall Wisdom Be Found?*, "The need (or craving) for transcendence may well be a great unwisdom, but without it we tend to become mere engines of entropy."[17]

Leon Kass on Wisdom

The quest for wisdom proposed by Leon Kass in his *The Beginning of Wisdom: Reading Genesis* takes shape within a close reading of the book of Genesis. Kass observes that although contemporary science and technology provide humans with a longer lifespan and make communication and travel much easier, science and technology cannot provide an understanding of human purpose and meaning.[18] Indeed, in the modern period wisdom became disjoined from natural science, which rejected purposefulness in nature. Given the success of science and technology in providing human beings with new "powers for genetic, somatic, and psychic human engineering," the need for wisdom about human life is ever more pressing.[19]

Kass places this general need for wisdom in the context of his own existential search for wisdom. During the years he spent earning his M.D.

at the University of Chicago and his Ph.D. in biochemistry at Harvard, the Judaism of his forebears did not engage his interest. As an undergraduate, he was "inclined to think all religions were fossils, superstitious leftovers from before the Age of Enlightenment."[20] He observes with respect to his undergraduate understanding of Judaism, "Little did I then imagine that I would later come to see the insufficiency of the scientific understanding of human life and the Enlightenment's view of the world. It would have been inconceivable to me that I would later find a most compelling kind of wisdom in the oldest of the still living religions."[21] Kass is careful to note, however, that his reading of Genesis, while offering him "a compelling kind of wisdom," has not yet led him to the practice of Judaism, that is, to observance of Torah.[22]

As an alternative to either faith or doubt as regards the Bible's veracity, Kass proposes "the attitude of thoughtful engagement, of suspended disbelief, eager to learn."[23] To arrive at the wisdom that Genesis teaches, we need to trust that the words we hear merit our full attention. Ultimately, Kass suggests, the reader will discover in Genesis a path of wisdom that should structure how we live both as individuals and as communities. Genesis has in view a "new human way—the way of the Children of Israel, launched as a light unto the nations."[24] This "way," characterized by righteousness vis-à-vis others and holiness vis-à-vis God, makes clear the choice that all persons and societies face. Wisdom is instantiated when "all human beings, mindful of their limitations and standing in awe-and-fear of the Lord, can be treated as equal creatures, equally servants of the one God toward whose perfection we may strive to align our lives."[25] The other alternative, equally depicted by Genesis, is the opposite of wisdom: "a world in which the rational mastery of nature and the pursuit of immortality leads ultimately to the enslavement of mankind under the despotic rule of one man worshiped as a god."[26]

In interpreting Genesis in this manner, Kass knows that his account of covenantal Israel is more universal than particular and that he therefore develops a position that somewhat separates him from Torah-observant Jews and, in a different way, from many Christians as well.[27] He comments that most readers, even those whose background is secular, come to the biblical text through a "tradition" shaped by the biblical text. He emphasizes, however, that standing within a tradition does not substitute for the work that each reader must undertake in order to appropriate biblical wisdom.[28] For Kass, it is in this work of appropriation that philosophic openness—the effort to approach the text as much as possible "without presuppositions or intermediaries"[29]—has its value.

Kass grants in his introduction that some prior knowledge is helpful before beginning to read any book: "What kind of book are we reading? In what spirit and manner should we read?"[30] But he does not think that these questions need answering at the outset. He argues instead that "[f]or the beginning reader, answers to these questions cannot be had in advance. They can be acquired, if at all, only as a result of reading."[31] He is confident that wisdom should be pursued "through the direct and unmediated encountering of the text" and "in a spirit and manner that is simultaneously naïve, philosophic, and reverent."[32] By contrast, as he points out, religious communities insist upon the role of interpretative traditions. In choosing to do without any interpretive tradition, Kass states that he is "acutely mindful of what I am sacrificing."[33] Nevertheless, he lays more emphasis on what he is avoiding, namely, the danger that the meanings of the text might be obscured by the lens of the interpretive tradition.

Wisdom, as Kass conceives of it, consists primarily in the ethical discovery that "all human beings, mindful of their limitations and standing in awe-and-fear of the Lord, can be treated as equal creatures, equally servants of the one God toward whose perfection we may strive to align our lives."[34] Certainly, the intellectual and aesthetic power of the narrative leads one toward affirmation of the truth of the narrative's witness. Yet, can the living God's relationship with his covenantal people in history be bracketed without distorting this witness? In this regard one might question the dichotomy that Kass posits between philosophy, which "begins in wonder and seeks understanding for its own sake," and the Bible, which roots wisdom in "awe and reverence" leading to righteousness through obedience to God's commandments.[35] Jacob/Israel wrestles with God in order to learn God's (or the angel of God's) name; Jacob sees a vision of a ladder uniting earth and heaven. In both cases, a vision linked with the knowledge of God is followed by a covenantal blessing that shapes Jacob/Israel's action. Here, contemplative openness to truth is a *covenantal* openness, in which the living God constitutes the ground for what would otherwise seem an unattainable yearning.

For this reason, God's election of Israel has much more to do with the possibility of the life of wisdom than one would first suppose. Bloom's and Kass's accounts of the life of wisdom lead us to David Novak's work on the doctrine of election. If Bloom's view of the life of wisdom turns on the aesthetic and the esoteric, while Kass's view of the life of wisdom hinges on the philosophic and the ethical, does Novak's emphasis on the doctrine of the election of Israel offer deeper insight?[36]

Election and the Life of Wisdom: David Novak

While affirming that God elects Israel freely rather than on the basis of Israel's merits, Novak argues that election can be forfeited, at least by particular Jews.[37] Were the Torah entirely subordinate to election, how could the Torah's norms stand above and judge the elect community's actions? Likewise, were the Torah entirely subordinate to election, how could Israel be truly related to other nations of the world? Just as other nations do not stand above or outside of law, so also Israel could not advert to her election so as to justify a lawless action undertaken to preserve Israel among the other nations of the world. Like Kass, then, for Novak the election of Israel cannot be understood outside of the Torah's ethical teaching, much of which applies to each and every human being.

More forcefully than Kass (let alone Bloom), Novak holds that God has acted powerfully in Israel. As Novak says, "we must positively realize that if God's presence had not been with us we would have died as a people."[38] Election consists in this active presence of God. With regard to the other nations of the world, Israel's vocation is "to remind them by our very vulnerable and incomplete life that God is not present in the world, that redemption is not to be expected by human criteria, that redemption will only come when God decides by his own mysterious criteria that the time is right for us and for them along with us."[39] Here Novak's view has affinities not only with Kass's interest in the ethical dimensions of creatureliness, but also with Bloom's gesture toward wisdom as trust. As Novak remarks, "the final redemption can only be hoped for; it cannot be predicted, let alone achieved by humans. We can only have faith *that* it will come; we cannot have any knowledge of *what* it will be."[40] Yet Novak's trust is not entirely contentless, since he affirms that "the estrangement between God and Israel and God and the world will ultimately be overcome. And God's redemption of Israel will be central to this cosmic redemption."[41] Whereas Bloom does not possess this eschatological hope—and therefore perches on the very edge of despair—Kass's reading of Genesis leads him in Novak's direction.

By contrast to Kass's bracketing of the question of the living God, Novak places it at the very center: "But *with whom* does this historical relationship occur? Certainly, it is one with ourselves inasmuch as we are a people. But if it is only an interhuman relationship, then what gives it the total existential claim that serious Jews sense it makes on every Jew?"[42] Novak has especially in view the challenge posed philosophically to the doctrine of election by Baruch Spinoza. Seeking a post-Spinozan philosophical retrieval of the doctrine, he warns against two mistakes. The first mistake is to assume that all wisdom belongs to the Torah alone, a position he attributes to the medieval kabbalists.[43] If the Torah contains all wisdom, then both the elect people and the Torah itself can be understood in utter isolation from the world and from human wisdom, since the created order provides nothing of value to the elect. The Torah thereby subsumes the world and renders it at best redundant. Novak states, "When the world is reduced to the level of the Torah alone, there is no room for philosophy at all. All wisdom comes from specific revelation, and philosophy is considered to be an intrusion from a realm that is ultimately an illusion."[44]

The second mistake consists in allowing the world to subsume the Torah, so that the Torah becomes at best a reprising of this-worldly wisdom. On this view, the created order makes revelation unnecessary. It is this second mistake that particularly inspires Novak's understanding of the life of wisdom. Recognizing that most people have been persuaded by Spinoza's philosophical arguments, in which the world subsumes the Torah, Novak seeks to offer philosophical reasons for the classical of divine election. He remarks that "if traditionalists want to counter external charges of myopia, and the internal charge that we are ignoring the relationship that we have with God as creator of the world, then we must expose the roots of the modern denial of the election of Israel."[45]

In seeking these roots, Novak proposes to show how "the deepest wisdom the world has to offer"—that is, philosophical wisdom—supports the life of wisdom made possible by divine election. He is well aware, however, of the danger that the philosophical wisdom might thereby seem to be the ground of divine election (the Torah) rather than the other way around. As he observes, "we must be outspoken in insisting that the Torah can never and, therefore, must never be justified by the world or anything in it. The Torah comes from God, and it is for God's sake that it is given to us."[46] Philosophical wisdom cannot provide the justification for the Torah, because the relationship must always be the other way around: even though it might appear that philosophy is a broader wisdom, in fact the Torah is broader. Divine election (covenantally instantiated in the gift of the Torah) grounds philosophical wisdom.

How so? Novak argues that "how one views God's singular relationship with the world is going to determine how one views God's general relationship with the world—and vice versa."[47] Put simply, the world's wisdom contains a part of what the Torah contains: "God gave the complete Torah to Israel and a partial Torah to the world."[48] In this view, the life of wisdom consists fundamentally in learning how to live in accord with "divine law."

Philosophical reflection, itself God's gift through the gift of created rationality, attains the divine law partly, whereas the Torah fully expresses the divine law.

Spinoza's mistake, according to Novak, was to disjoin the quest for truth from historical revelation. In making this disjunction, Spinoza goes beyond Maimonides, who also somewhat ahistorically conceived of revelation as (in Novak's words) "the highest degree of intellection of eternal truth that is possible for finite intelligence," but who still maintains the privileged place of the Torah and the elect people of Israel "in the universal apprehension of that truth."[49] By contrast, Spinoza deliberately severs himself from the rabbinic tradition and religious observance of the people of Israel.[50] As Novak says, "For Spinoza, a relationship with an intelligible and scientifically legitimate God and a relationship with the Jewish people as traditionally constituted were mutually exclusive. He opted, then, for God over Israel."[51] Novak points out that in the following centuries, many Jews have followed in Spinoza's path by choosing secularity over Torah observance on the grounds that only thereby could they lead rational lives. Such secular Jews, however, have generally rejected Spinoza's depiction of "God" and remained committed to their Jewish identity, only now without God or Torah. Their bond with Spinoza consists in their agreement with his claim that a life of wisdom requires breaking with the scriptural and rabbinic witness to a transcendent God who elected Israel.

After reviewing the responses to Spinoza set forth by Hermann Cohen and Franz Rosenzweig, Novak undertakes a constructive philosophical retrieval of the biblical doctrine of the election of Israel. He identifies three central steps in this retrieval. First, God's transcendence, attested throughout the Bible, must be philosophically reclaimed. Only a transcendent God, Creator of the whole world, can be more than a local deity. In response to philosophical worldliness, theological use of philosophy requires insisting upon a deeper "worldliness" framed by God's creative presence.

Second, theological/philosophical work must overcome "historicism's separation of the reader from the biblical text itself."[52] Here Novak points to Spinoza's rejection of rabbinic readings of Scripture that constitute biblical interpretation within the living community of Israel.[53] Spinoza finds valid only the meanings available within the (isolated) text itself. The difference, Novak notes, is similar to that between the Pharisees and the Sadducees, the latter of whom opted for "the more literally confined reading of the Bible."[54] Novak argues that the Pharisaic approach remains the correct one, because only such an approach can account for the community's living participation in the realities revealed in Scripture.[55] As Novak says, "By rejecting the continuing and uninterrupted historical connection of the people of Israel with the Bible *by* and *through* tradition, a tradition both theirs and that of the Bible itself, the Sadducees and their modern admirer Baruch Spinoza precluded philosophical reflection on the Bible."[56] They did so because the Bible, and thus also the realities revealed in the Bible, became simply part of the historical past.

Novak observes that biblical interpretation that limits itself strictly to attempting to understand biblical texts in their original historical contexts undercuts the participation of the elect people of God in the realities revealed in the Bible, which now come to be seen strictly as past. By contrast, for the Rabbis, "the Torah speaks far beyond the time in which it was originally uttered."[57] The Torah can speak in this way because of the realities revealed in the Torah remain present and active in the interpretive community that engages the Torah. Understood in this light, "the Bible is the book that Jews have never stopped reading. It is a book addressed to them in all their generations."[58] The point is that the elect community is always taken up into the Torah so that God's words and deeds instruct the people in the present. Thus the tradition of interpretation, even in failing to measure up to the standards of historical research into the Bible, does not thereby fail. Interpretation of the Bible that focuses solely on the past cannot account for the kind of reality that the Bible is: as Novak puts it, "Modern historical research on the Bible . . . has been conducted on the assumption that contemporary readers of the Bible are reading about someone other than themselves."[59]

If the Bible is not past in this way, how does this fact encourage *philosophical* reflection vis-à-vis the Bible? It would seem that it might have the opposite effect, since it obviously goes against the philosophy of history that has been widely accepted since the Renaissance. This brings us to Novak's third step. He holds that the ongoing participation of the elect community in the realities of Scripture presumes that a fully historical reading of Scripture needs to attend to the historical engagement of the ongoing elect community with its Scriptures. This means affirming the "primary traditional context of and for the Scriptural text,"[60] including "the role of tradition in the redaction and canonization of the text of Scripture."[61]

What would otherwise seem to be the fragmented and strictly past character of biblical texts thus appears in an entirely different light. The texts of the Bible can be seen as a unified revelation incarnated by the living and ongoing interpretive community whose Scriptures the texts are. Moreover, the present normativity of biblical revelation and its unity as revelation allow for the work of philosophy. Novak explains that "philosophical reflection requires that its prime datum be present, indeed that datum which is most consistently present to us."[62] If the datum be of solely historical interest, then philosophers will pay it no attention. Additionally, the datum must elicit existential/ethical concern, because philosophy seeks to know how to live. As Novak observes, "The consistent presence of Scripture and the full range of its normative potential was one of the prime bequests of Pharisaism to its rabbinic (and Christian) heirs. Because of that, some of them have been able to reflect on the Bible philosophically."[63]

To sum up the three steps requisite for philosophical retrieval of the doctrine of election: (1) philosophical reclamation of truth of the biblical testimony to the transcendence of the electing God; (2) a philosophy of history that, as regards Scripture, overcomes historicism; (3) philosophical affirmation of the interpretive value of the elect community's ongoing exegetical tradition. What kind of life of wisdom do these three steps promote?

Edot, Huqqim, Mishpatim

Novak's answer consists in correlating election with the Torah, in order to understand the "phenomenological constitution of the commandments and their intentionality."[64] In order to work out this correlation, he turns to the three kinds of commandments specified in Deut. 6.20, which he translates as, "What (*mah*) do these testimonies (*edot*), statutes (*huqqim*), and norms (*mishpatim*) mean which the Lord our God has commanded you?" In Judaism's liturgical life, Deut. 6.20 has particular importance because "[i]n the Passover Haggadah this question becomes the all-inclusive question of the 'wise son.'"[65] These three kinds of commandments—*edot, huqqim,* and *mishpatim*—comprise the life of wisdom that marks the elect people of God. To understand how wisdom relates to election, one needs to understand what the practice of these three kinds of commandments requires.

Novak first takes up the *mishpatim*, which relate to his philosophical effort to overcome the assumption that biblical interpretation has to do primarily with the past. The *mishpatim* are the "laws that justly govern interhuman relationships" and which, belonging to the natural law, are not unique to Israel. Novak observes, "According to the Rabbis, reason would have dictated them even if they had not been written in the Torah."[66] Through the Torah's *mishpatim*, we see the elect community's shared bond with all other nations of the world. Does this link with the order of creation mean that the *mishpatim* do not belong to divine revelation? No, answers Novak, because "they participate in a larger covenantal context, one that reason could not dictate since it is rooted in unique historical events, not uniform universal processes (nature)."[67] These norms demonstrate that seeking to understand the Bible solely in its original historical context is mistaken. Unique as the events of covenantal events of revelation are, the *mishpatim* show that the covenant's normative force continues beyond the original historical context. The Torah lays claim to the obedience of every generation of Jews, in part because it is grounded through the *mishpatim* in "the universal order of nature (specifically, human nature)."[68]

By contrast to the *mishpatim*, which human rationality could derive for itself, the *edot* underscore the historical singularity of the elect people and relate to Novak's philosophical insistence upon the role of tradition. He comments that these laws "testify to covenantal events by symbolic celebration. They comprise that part of revelation that gives tradition its historical intentionality and continuity."[69] The *edot* make manifest especially what distinguishes Israel as God's elect people.[70] With Passover as the preeminent instance, the *edot* "are most directly concerned with the election of Israel because they celebrate it."[71] In the liturgical celebrations commanded by the Torah, the meaning of the whole Torah appears in its most concise form: God's action to redeem his elect people and to accomplish his covenantal promises. As Novak says, therefore, "the election of Israel . . . is most directly experienced and celebrated in the study and practice of the *edot*."[72]

When compared with the *mishpatim*, the *edot* bear witness to the covenantal particularity of Israel. Whereas all nations, including Israel, must observe the *mishpatim*, Israel alone has the special privilege of partnership with God through the *edot*: "The *edot* are the modes of Israel's active, responsive experience of God's electing and nurturing love for her in the covenant. Hence the *edot* are intercovenantal, involving the collective relationship of Israel with the Lord and simultaneously with each other."[73]

Third, the *huqqim* correspond to Novak's philosophical retrieval of God's transcendence. The *huqqim* are the laws in the Torah that have no evident reason; human rationality cannot make sense of them, other than by saying that God gave them in order to set Israel apart. Novak explains that "the *huqqim* are those laws having neither natural nor historical reasons, laws accepted because of God's authority alone. They are laws that have no analogues in the positive law of any other people."[74] While the *mishpatim* unite Israel to the other nations, the *edot* and the *huqqim* separate Israel from the nations. The covenantal separation to which the *edot* testify is reinforced by the *huqqim*, which establish the parameters of the covenant: Israel does not stand on a level of equality vis-à-vis God. Indeed, Novak emphasizes that without the *huqqim*, the *edot* (as well as the *mishpatim*) would be misinterpreted. Although Israel experiences herself in the *edot* to be a full covenantal partner, Israel is not an *equal* partner. The *huqqim* undercut any pretensions of equality, because the *huqqim* flow from God alone rather than being mediated by human reason.

Novak describes the *huqqim* as "the limits of Israel's election,"[75] by which he means that these laws undercut any sense of symmetry between God and Israel. Contrasting the *huqqim* with both the *mishpatim* and the *edot*, he observes, "Precisely because they [the *huqqim*] have neither universal nor historical reasons, because their sole authority is God's mysterious will, they are able to function as active reminders that Israel is totally defined by the covenant, whereas God participates in the covenant but is not defined by it."[76] In this sense, the *huqqim* stand against any theological rationalism, including any rationalism built upon pride in the privilege of covenantal election.

Among the examples of *huqqim*, Novak gives a special place to God's command to Abraham to slay his son Isaac (Gen. 22). God's responses to Job similarly depend for their force upon an appreciation of the *huqqim*. Novak remarks in this vein, "The *huqqim* intend the unassimilable surd of revelation. . . . The *huqqim* intend God's primal authority, which transcends both humanity in general and even the specific history of the covenant with Israel."[77] For Novak, this absolute transcendence does not call into question God's goodness, as if God were an arbitrary despot. Rather, Novak envisions the *huqqim* in light of the mysteries of creation and covenantal redemption. Far from positing a despotic God behind these mysteries of God's generosity, the *huqqim* simply ensure that human beings cannot grasp God: "everything is contingent upon that which no finite creature can ever comprehend."[78]

Election and the Life of Wisdom

It follows that the election of Israel reveals three interrelated aspects of the true life of wisdom, which is grounded in the gifting of the living God. The first aspect consists in following the ethical norms of justice, which are rationally derivable but which God has covenantally revealed so as to facilitate obedience. These norms, the *mishpatim*, have to do with "wise dealing, righteousness, justice, and equity" (Prov. 1.2–3), and through these norms God "stores up sound wisdom for the upright; he is a shield to those who walk in integrity, guarding the paths of justice and preserving the way of his saints" (Prov. 2.7–8). As a later proverb puts it with more specificity, "He who oppresses a poor man insults his Maker, but he who is kind to the needy honors him. The wicked is overthrown through his evil-doing, but the righteous finds refuge through his integrity" (Prov. 14.31–32).

The second aspect of the life of wisdom consists in the worship of the living God. The greatest possible joy is to worship God as he wishes to be worshipped, and this fullest joy is reserved for God's covenantal partner through the *edot*: "Praise God in his sanctuary, praise him in his mighty firmament! Praise him for his mighty deeds; praise him according to his exceeding greatness!" (Ps. 150.1–2). Nonetheless, sincere worship, even when unaided by the covenant, will not be despised: as the psalm continues, "Let everything that breathes praise the Lord!" (Ps. 150.6).

Lastly, the third aspect of the life of wisdom is to recognize God as transcendent mystery. The psalmist understands creatureliness in light of this divine mystery: "What is man that thou art mindful of him, and the son of man that thou dost care for him? Yet, thou hast made him little less than God, and dost crown him with glory and honor" (Ps. 7.4–5). Or as a later Psalm puts it, "Man is like a breath, his days are like a passing shadow" (Ps. 144.4)—and therefore only God can give lasting gifts to human beings: "Stretch forth thy hand from on high, rescue me and deliver me from the many waters" (Ps. 144.7), waters that threaten to capsize and bring to ruin our fragile existence. As we read in the prophet Isaiah, "To whom then will you compare me, that I should be like him? says the Holy One. Lift up your eyes on high and see: who created these? He who brings out their host by number, calling them all by name; by the greatness of his might, and because he is strong in power not one is missing" (Is. 40.25–26). No creature can compare to God. To remind Israel of this truth is the purpose of the *huqqim*. "For my thoughts are not your thoughts, neither are your ways are my ways, says the Lord. For as the heavens are higher than the earth, so are my ways higher than your ways and my thoughts than your thoughts" (Is. 55.8–9).

In short, the wise person will act justly, worship God, and acknowledge that God and God's purposes cannot be measured or controlled by humans. Election thereby perfects the life of wisdom, since the Torah's threefold commandments set forth such wisdom most perfectly. The life of wisdom thus understood is not ahistorical, since the Torah, as covenantal, is historical and concrete: it is the "study and practice of the *edot*," the covenantal commandments that detail how Israelites must worship, that stand at the center of daily life and which provide the framework in which the universal commandments of justice (*mishpatim*) and the truth of divine transcendence (*huqqim*) do not become overwhelming.

Election not only perfects, but also grounds the life of wisdom. Election does so first of all by its rootedness in the created order. Novak states that "the Torah in toto is concerned with more than Israel, but also with elementary norms that the creator has enabled all humans to discover with intelligence and good will in their own social nature."[79] The Torah does not cease to recall human beings to their createdness, and the life of wisdom flows from appreciation of one's createdness. But this recollection of createdness does not alone suffice to ground the life of wisdom. Given human brokenness and the destruction caused by sin, the life of wisdom also requires eschatological hope as a ground. In this regard, Novak affirms, "The ultimate consequent of the election of Israel is the final redemption itself (*ge'ulah*)."[80] Election grounds redemption, but does not do so in a way that imposes a necessary framework upon God. In some way, redemption, in which the life of wisdom will take on an unimaginable fullness, will bring together election's particularity and universality, without minimizing either. It will supremely fulfill the universal *mishpatim*, but it will also supremely fulfill "the irreducible singularity of Israel's historical existence,"[81] displayed in the *edot*. It will do so in a way that reveals God's transcendence, by revealing a God who stands outside the confines of what human rationality can measure and evaluate (*huqqim*). In this final redemption, God, Israel, and the world will be united in a universal reconciliation that takes place in and through the particularity, whose form can neither be predicted nor achieved by human beings, of "God's redemption of Israel."[82]

Concluding Reflections

What then is the life of wisdom? It certainly is, as Bloom remarks, "trust in the Covenant"—a trust that depends upon Rabbi Akiba's assurance that "'everything is prepared for the feast.'"[83] It also certainly is, as Kass puts it, a "new human way—the way of the Children of Israel, launched as a light unto the nations" and "built on two related principles: the practice of *righteousness* in relations toward others, informed by the pursuit of *holiness* in relation to the divine."[84] If it is the "way of the Children of Israel," then it must be the way of divine election, "concerned with the irreducible singularity of Israel's historical existence"[85] as the people of the living God.

As Novak grants, much wisdom is already to be found in the *mishpatim*, in which the peoples of the world share through natural law and philosophical ethics. Since the worship of God belongs to the *mishpatim*—the *edot* specify how Israel is to worship God—the peoples of the world are not cut off from the life of wisdom. Yet, the *mishpatim* and the *edot*, precisely as revealed to God's elect people Israel, sustain the life of wisdom by displaying God's active and redemptive presence in history. Without this revelation of God's care, the life of wisdom falters in the face of death, as Bloom recognizes despite his rejection of Israel's God.

Because humans cannot overlook suffering and death, our own resources, whether aesthetic or ethical, cannot sustain us. Thus, it is most importantly the revelation of the *huqqim*, the binding of Isaac (and for Christians the Cross of Christ), that, in the context of a life of *mishpatim* and *edot*, provides for the fullness of the life of wisdom, in which we lift up our minds and hearts to the God who escapes our grasp and who therefore can save us. It is only in the context of election and covenant that the living God is found. Although Jews and Christians understand our place in this election differently because of Christ Jesus, together we can affirm and await the fullness of the life of wisdom, a fullness that humans cannot achieve on our own and whose time and nature are known only to the God who will accomplish it. In this fullness, as Novak says, "the estrangement between God and Israel and God and the world will ultimately be overcome. And God's redemption of Israel will be central to this cosmic redemption."[86]

Conclusion

Jacob Neusner remarks: "No two communities irritate one another more than do Judaism and Christianity: the continuation of Judaism despite Christianity, the formation of Christianity in the face of Judaism."[1] Can this irritation be assuaged? According to Neusner—who is of course a preeminent contributor to Jewish-Christian dialogue—the answer is to understand Judaism and Christianity as "a family sharing a complex inheritance," so that "the task of Judaisms and Christianities in dialogue [is] to compare and contrast their many-splendored readings of the Scriptures of ancient Israel."[2] As Neusner puts it, "The two religions, classical, catholic and orthodox Christianity and its competition, classical, normative, and Rabbinic Judaism, do intersect: they turn out to be debating about issues in common, drawing on a shared body of holy books, and appealing to universal reason and a single logic."[3]

Neusner's insight is Novak's as well. Indeed, it is precisely this engagement with "issues in common, drawing on a shared body of holy books, and appealing to universal reason and a single logic"—or what Novak calls "open philosophical exegesis of Scripture"[4]—that has guided the chapters of this book. Novak shows that not only Jews and Christians, but also the world as a whole, needs the covenantally grounded insights that inform Jewish-Christian dialogue about the meaning of life, the big issues about what constitutes human reality. Having carefully carved out theological space for Jewish-Christian dialogue (Chapter 1), Novak assists Jews and Christians in moving beyond "autonomy" so as to think together about God's guidance of human beings in providential theonomy (Chapter 2). As Novak helps us see, providential theonomy makes sense because the living God is required to understand the human person: human beings bear the imprint of transcendence, the "image of God" (Chapter 3). Given the kind of creatures humans are, the door is opened to understanding the moral order through reason and revelation, and Novak finds in natural law or Noahide law the precepts without which a human community cannot survive (Chapter 4). Having taught us about life in the presence of the living God, Novak also teaches us about living with hope in the face of death, that is to say living the life of wisdom that God's redemptive election sustains (Chapter 5).[5]

These fruitful conversations between Jews and Christians about what it means to be human take place "at the border between theology and philosophy."[6] Yet Novak also rightly argues that Jewish-Christian dialogue has significance for engaging adherents of a purely secular worldview. In this regard, Novak proposes a shared witness to transcendent hope:

> Jews and Christians begin at the same starting point, and both are convinced that we will meet at the all-mysterious end. Yet we cannot deny that our appointed tasks in this world are very different and must remain so because the covenant is not the same for both of us. It is God alone who will bring us to our unknown destination in a time pleasing to him. That time has not yet come. In the meantime, the constitution of the Jewish-Christian dialogue might have a message for the larger body of humankind for whose peace we must all be concerned. Our dialogue might be able to show the world that the hope it needs for its very survival can only be hope for its final redemption.[7]

In the chapters of this book, we have sketched via Jewish-Christian dialogue a portrait of human reality that is profoundly hopeful. As Novak suggests, hope becomes possible when humans recognize themselves as created in the image of a God who governs and guides them, and who thereby fosters the survival of themselves and their communities. The life of wisdom takes place within such communities of hope.

As such, the present book seeks to offer a hopeful "message for the larger body of humankind for whose peace we must all be concerned." In this regard, of course, Novak's appeal to eschatology remains crucial, since the peace that Jews and Christians proclaim is not yet the fullness of peace. Here we can appreciate Novak's exhortation to Jews and Christians "to engage in *cooperative* work, which will enable us together to formulate universal norms that are not, in effect, one cultural particularity becoming universal by absorbing all others into itself, or one cultural particularity eliminating all others altogether."[8] When Jews and Christians, obedient to revelation, understand themselves as people called uniquely by God, this "particularity" does not destroy the ability of humans to work together cooperatively. On the contrary, such particularity fosters the development of communities of justice, founded upon the recognition of creatureliness and transcendence.

Here an insight of the Jewish biblical theologian Jon Levenson proves helpful. Levenson observes that on the one hand, "The old expression 'the fatherhood of God and the brotherhood of man' captures one important dimension of the legacy of the Old Testament/Tanakh."[9] On the other hand, as Levenson says, this dimension attains its truth only through God's electing (covenantal) love: "another, more prominent dimension speaks of God's mysteriously singling out one son from his brothers for a special destiny, to be reenacted in the experience of the ongoing community . . . . There is, in short, a kind of *supersessionism internal to the Hebrew Bible*, and no appeal to the common scripture of Judaism and Christianity can overcome it."[10] This "internal" supersessionism is God's election of Israel. In Novak's words, "God chooses the Jewish people"—the descendents of Abraham, Isaac, and Jacob, not the descendents of Ishmael or Esau—"for a continuing covenantal relationship with himself for which he gave them the Torah."[11] Christians hold that this covenantal relationship attains its fulfillment in Christ Jesus, and Novak does not disallow this "mild" supersessionism. Recall Novak's challenge: "If Christianity does not regard itself as going beyond Judaism, why should Christians not become Jews? It is always a ready possibility."[12]

In a truly theological Jewish-Christian dialogue, this possibility—and its converse—are required. It therefore follows, as we have seen, that Jewish-Christian dialogue can never merely be a "message for the larger body of humankind for whose peace we must all be concerned."[13] In other words, Jews and Christians always discuss the life of wisdom—inclusive of election, providence, theonomy, the image of God, and natural law/Noahide law—not only for the sake of the world, but for the sake of salvation. The life of wisdom remains dependent for both Jews and Christians on specific covenantal commitments.

It should not surprise, however, that from within these commitments Jews and Christians attest to a life of faith and hope that speaks to "the larger body of humankind for whose peace we must all be concerned." Indeed, exploring and proclaiming this peace is the task of a Jewish-Christian dialogue inspired, as Jews and Christians should be, by the theology of David Novak.

Notes

Introduction

[1] Franz Rosenzweig, "Towards a Renaissance of Jewish Learning," in *On Jewish Learning*, ed. N.N. Glatzer (Madison, WI: University of Wisconsin Press, 1955), 59–60.

[2] Martin Buber, Letter to Franz Rosenzweig, July 13, 1924, in Franz Rosenzweig, *On Jewish Learning*, 115.

[3] Hans Urs von Balthasar, *Martin Buber and Christianity: A Dialogue between Israel and the Church*, trans. Alexander Dru (London: Harvill, 1961). For a detailed discussion of Buber's impact on von Balthasar's thought, see Anthony C. Kieke-Sciglitano, "Hans Urs von Balthasar and 'The Jewish Critique': Intramural Appropriation and Response," *Toronto Journal of Theology* 14 (1998): 177–96.

[4] See Martin Buber, *Two Types of Faith*, trans. Norman P. Goldhawk (Syracuse, NY: Syracuse University Press, 2003). See also Buber, *I and Thou*, trans. Walter Kaufman (New York: Simon & Schuster, 1996) and *On Judaism*, ed. Nahum N. Glatzer (New York: Schocken Books, 1996). In *Two Types of Faith* Buber comments on Christianity and Rabbinic Judaism: "If we consider the Synoptic and Johannine dialogues with the disciples as two stages along one road, we immediately see what was gained and lost in the course of it. The gain was the most sublime of all theologies; it was procured at the expense of the plain, concrete and situation-bound dialogicism of the original man of the Bible, who found eternity, not in the super-temporal spirit, but in the depth of the actual moment. The Jesus of the genuine tradition still belongs to that, but the Jesus of theology does so no longer. We have taken our stand at that point in the midst of the events reported in the New Testament where the 'Christian' branches off from the 'Jewish'. . . . The difference between this 'It is true' and the other 'We believe and know' is not that of two expressions of faith, but of two kinds of faith" (34–35). One sees here how Buber has appropriated and redirected the concerns of Moses Mendelssohn. For Novak's view of dogma, which follows Rosenzweig rather than Buber, see Novak's "The Role of Dogma in Judaism," in *Tradition in the Public Square: A David Novak Reader*, ed. Randi Rashkover and Martin Kavka (Grand Rapids, MI: Eerdmans, 2008), 73–87.

[5] David Novak, "Buber and Tillich," in *Talking with Christians: Musings of a Jewish Theologian* (Grand Rapids, MI: Eerdmans, 2005), 89–107, at 106.

[6] Ibid., 107.

[7] R. Kendall Soulen, *The God of Israel and Christian Theology* (Minneapolis, MN: Fortress Press, 1996), 29.

[8] Ibid., 30.

[9] Ibid., 32.

10. Ibid., 170. For his part, Novak reads Acts 15 as "a radical reconception of what the election of the people of God is to be" that constitutes a break with "the field of Jewish normativity" (Novak, "The Role of Dogma in Judaism," in *Tradition in the Public Square: A David Novak Reader*, 86). As Novak says, "The schism did not occur because Judaism affirmed the Law and Christianity denied it, but rather because Christianity put forth its own new law as part of its new covenant," and therefore entered into a new halakhah ("The Role of Dogma in Judaism, 86–87).
11. See Mark S. Kinzer, *Postmissionary Messianic Judaism: Redefining Christian Engagement with the Jewish People* (Grand Rapids, MI: Brazos, 2005).
12. This position builds upon my earlier work, which is generally assumed (rather than reprised) in Chapter 1. See *Christ's Fulfillment of Torah and Temple: Salvation according to Thomas Aquinas* (Notre Dame, IN: University of Notre Dame Press, 2002) and *Participatory Biblical Exegesis: A Theology of Biblical Interpretation* (Notre Dame, IN: University of Notre Dame Press, 2008). See also my *Sacrifice and Community: Jewish Offering and Christian Eucharist* (Oxford: Blackwell, 2005), chapters 1 and 2.
13. Randi Rashkover and Martin Kavka, "Introduction," in *Tradition in the Public Square: A David Novak Reader*, xv. See also my *Biblical Natural Law: A Theocentric and Teleological Approach* (Oxford: Oxford University Press, 2008).
14. David B. Burrell, C.S.C., "Can We Be Free without a Creator?," in *God, Truth, and Witness: Engaging Stanley Hauerwas*, ed. L. Gregory Jones, Reinhard Hütter, and C. Rosalee Velloso Ewell (Grand Rapids, MI: Brazos, 2005), 35–52, at 37. See also George Steiner's connection of aesthetic truth and communication with the doctrine of creation: Steiner, *Real Presences* (Chicago, IL: Chicago University Press, 1989), 229.
15. For an introduction (from a Jewish perspective) to such vigorous and largely deleterious debates in the medieval period, marked by Christian oppression of Jews, see David Berger, *The Jewish-Christian Debate in the High Middle Ages: A Critical Edition of the Nizzahon Vetus* (Northvale, NJ: Jacob Aronson, 1996).
16. Miroslav Volf, *Exclusion and Embrace: A Theological Exploration of Identity, Otherness, and Reconciliation* (Nashville, TN: Abingdon Press, 1996), 206. See especially Alasdair MacIntyre's *Whose Justice? Which Rationality?* (Notre Dame, IN: University of Notre Dame Press, 1988) and *Three Rival Versions of Moral Enquiry: Encyclopaedia, Genealogy, and Tradition* (Notre Dame, IN: University of Notre Dame Press, 1990). See also Novak's "A Jewish View of War," in *Tradition in the Public Square: A David Novak Reader*, 253–65 (originally published in 1974 and explaining, from within Jewish theology, Novak's opposition to the Vietnam War).
17. Volf, *Exclusion and Embrace*, 207.
18. Ibid., 208.
19. Ibid., 211.
20. Michael Fagenblat and Nathan Wolski, "Revelation Here and Beyond: Buber and Levinas on the Bible," in *Levinas and Buber: Dialogue and Difference*, ed. Peter Atterton, Matthew Calarco, and Maurice Friedman (Pittsburgh, PA: Duquesne University Press, 2004), 157–78, at 169.
21. J.A. Di Noia, O.P., *The Diversity of Religions: A Christian Perspective* (Washington, D.C.: Catholic University of America Press, 1992), 9; cf. George Lindbeck, *The Nature of Doctrine* (Philadelphia, PA: Westminster, 1984), 32–41. Novak points out

that Lindbeck's *The Nature of Doctrine* offers an account of doctrine similar to the account that Novak, as a Jew, affirms: "Is not Lindbeck asserting that Christian doctrine is necessarily correlated with Christian halakhah?" (Novak, "The Role of Dogma in Judaism," in *Tradition in the Public Square: A David Novak Reader*, 87).

[22] Novak, *Jewish-Christian Dialogue: A Jewish Justification* (Oxford: Oxford University Press, 1989), 105. For discussion of Rosenzweig see, in addition to Novak, Leora Batnitzky, *Idolatry and Representation: The Philosophy of Franz Rosenzweig Reconsidered* (Princeton, NJ: Princeton University Press, 2000); Michael Wyschogrod, "Franz Rosenzweig's *The Star of Redemption*," in *Abraham's Promise: Judaism and Jewish-Christian Relations*, ed. R. Kendall Soulen (Grand Rapids, MI: Eerdmans, 2004), 121–30.

[23] Cf. Rodney Clapp, "Tacit Holiness: The Importance of Bodies and Habits in Doing Church," in *Border Crossings: Christian Trespasses on Popular Culture and Public Affairs* (Grand Rapids, MI: Brazos, 2000), 63–74.

[24] Peter J. Leithart, "Marcionism, Postliberalism, and Social Christianity," *Pro Ecclesia* 8 (1999): 85–97, at 85. Cf. Scott Bader-Saye's effort to move beyond the "inwardness tradition": Bader-Saye, *Church and Israel after Christendom: The Politics of Election* (Boulder, CO: Westview Press, 1999). See also Walter Lowe, "The Intensification of Time: Michael Wyschogrod and the Task of Christian Theology," *Modern Theology* 22 (2006): 693–99, as well as Charles Taylor's reflections on Descartes's "epoch-making" "radical twist" of "Augustinian inwardness": Taylor, *Sources of the Self: The Making of the Modern Identity* (Cambridge, MA: Harvard University Press, 1989), 143.

[25] See David Novak's lament regarding the condition of much of Judaism in the United States, in his "Response to Michael Wyschogrod," *Modern Theology* 11 (1995): 211–18, at 213–14. Novak appropriately adds that "my Christian friends tell me that Christian religious communities have, *mutatis mutandis*, all the above spiritual problems" (214). See also, for Rosenzweig on revelation, Randi Rashkover, *Revelation and Theopolitics: Barth, Rosenzweig and the Politics of Praise* (New York: T & T Clark, 2005), 177.

[26] See, for example, David Novak, "What Does Edith Stein Mean for Jews?," in *Talking with Christians*, 164.

[27] Joseph Cardinal Ratzinger, "The Dialogue of Religions and the Relationship between Judaism and Christianity," in *Many Religions—One Covenant: Israel, the Church and the World*, trans. Graham Harrison (San Francisco, CA: Ignatius Press, 1999), 89–113, at 112. Ratzinger explains that "the encounter of the religions is not possible by renouncing truth but only by a deeper entering into it" (109), a task that requires "respect for the beliefs of others and the readiness to look for the truth in what strikes us as strange or foreign; for such truth concerns us and can correct us and lead us farther along the path. What we need is the willingness to look behind the alien appearances and look for the deeper truth hidden there. Furthermore, I need to be willing to allow my narrow understanding of truth to be broken down. I shall learn my own truth better if I understand the other person and allow myself to be moved along the road to the God who is ever greater, certain that I never hold the whole truth about God in my own hands but am always a learner, on pilgrimage toward it, on a path that has no end" (110).

28 Pierre Hadot, *Philosophy as a Way of Life*, ed. Arnold I. Davidson, trans. Michael Chase (Oxford: Blackwell, 1995), 132. For Christian appropriation of Hadot's understanding of "spiritual exercises," see David B. Burrell, C.S.C., "Friends in Conversation: The Language and Practice of Faith," in *Friendship and Ways to Truth* (Notre Dame, IN: University of Notre Dame Press, 2000), 19–35.

29 Walter Kasper, "Paths Taken and Enduring Questions in Jewish-Christian Relations Today: Thirty Years of the Commission for Religious Relations with the Jews," in *The Catholic Church and the Jewish People: Recent Reflections from Rome*, ed. Philip A. Cunningham, Norbert J. Hofmann, S.D.B., and Joseph Sievers (New York: Fordham University Press, 2007), 3–11, at 10.

30 Reinhard Hütter, "'In.' Some Incipient Reflections on *The Jewish People and Their Sacred Scriptures in the Christian Bible*," *Pro Ecclesia* 13 (2004): 13–24, at 22. See also David B. Burrell, C.S.C., "Some Requisites for Interfaith Dialogue," *New Blackfriars* 89 (2008): 300–10, along with his *Knowing the Unknowable God: Ibn-Sina, Maimonides, Aquinas* (Notre Dame, IN: University of Notre Dame Press, 1986); *Freedom and Creation in Three Traditions* (Notre Dame, IN: University of Notre Dame Press, 1993); and "Friendship with God in al-Ghazali and Aquinas," in *Friendship and Ways to Truth*, 67–86. In an earlier book review, Burrell criticizes David Novak's *Talking with Christians: Musings of a Jewish Theologian* (Grand Rapids, MI: Eerdmans, 2006) and Michael Wyschogrod's *Abraham's Promise: Judaism and Jewish-Christian Relations* (Grand Rapids, MI: Eerdmans, 2004) for "two lacunae": "the state of Israel and Islam—two subjects on which both books are virtually silent!" (Burrell, review of *Talking with Christians* and *Abraham's Promise*, in *Modern Theology* 22 [2006]: 705–9, at 707). In Novak's Preface to his *The Jewish Social Contract: An Essay in Political Theology* (Princeton, NJ: Princeton University Press, 2005), xvi, Novak identifies himself as "a religious Zionist (in the theological if not the current partisan sense)," but he makes clear that his work situates itself, quite rightly in my view, not vis-à-vis the state of Israel but vis-à-vis the situation of Judaism in North America, which explains his primary engagement with Christianity rather than with Islam (or with the state of Israel). See, for example, his "What Is Jewish about Jews and Judaism in America?" in *Tradition in the Public Square: A David Novak Reader*, 187–201. For Novak on Islam, see "The Treatment of Islam and Muslims in the Legal Writings of Maimonides," in *Tradition in the Public Square*, 231–50, as well as *Talking with Christians*, 15.

31 Rabbi Giuseppe Laras, "Jewish Perspectives on Christianity," in *The Catholic Church and the Jewish People*, 23–28, at 28. See also in the same volume Massimo Giuliani, "The Shoah as a Shadow upon and a Stimulus to Jewish-Christian Dialogue," 54–70. Regarding the Shoah and the goal of remembering, see Miroslav Volf's superb *The End of Memory: Remembering Rightly in a Violent World* (Grand Rapids, MI: Eerdmans, 2006). On Christian religious persecution of non-Christians, see more broadly Mark A. Noll, "Have Christians Done More Harm than Good?," in *Must Christianity Be Violent? Reflections on History, Practice, and Theology*, ed. Kenneth R. Chase and Alan Jacobs (Grand Rapids, MI: Brazos, 2003), 79–93.

32 Pope John Paul II, *Spiritual Pilgrimage: Texts on Jews and Judaism 1979–1995*, ed. Eugene J. Fisher and Leon Klenicki (New York: Crossroad, 1995), 63; quoted in §86 of the Pontifical Biblical Commission's *The Jewish People and Their Sacred Scriptures in the Christian Bible* (2001), as well as by Reinhard Hütter in his

"'In.' Some Incipient Reflections on *The Jewish People and Their Sacred Scriptures in the Christian Bible.*"

33 John Paul II, *Spiritual Pilgrimage*, 63. *Nostra Aetate* §4 urges the overcoming of prejudices: "Since, therefore, the spiritual heritage common to Christians and Jews is so great, this synod wishes to promote and recommend that mutual knowledge and esteem which is acquired especially from biblical and theological studies and from friendly dialogues" (translation in *Decrees of the Ecumenical Councils*, vol. 2, ed. Norman P. Tanner [Washington, D.C.: Georgetown University Press, 1990], 970).

34 Bruce Marshall, "Elder Brothers: John Paul II's Teaching on the Jewish People as a Question to the Church," in *John Paul II and the Jewish People: A Jewish-Christian Dialogue*, ed. David G. Dalin and Matthew Levering (Lanham, MD: Rowman and Littlefield, 2008), 113–29, at 120. Cf. my *Christ's Fulfillment of Torah and Temple*, chapter 5: "Israel, the Church, and the Mystical Body of Christ."

35 Cf. Jacob Taubes, *The Political Theology of Paul*, trans. Dana Hollander (1993; Stanford, CA: Stanford University Press, 2004). Against Carl Schmitt, Taubes argues that "the separation of powers between worldly and spiritual is *absolutely necessary*. This boundary, if it is not drawn, we will lose our Occidental breath" (103).

36 On this point see Novak's "The Dialectic between Theory and Practice in Rabbinic Thought," in *Tradition in the Public Square: A David Novak Reader*, 21–33. For Novak's work on particular moral problems see, for example, his published doctoral dissertation, *Suicide and Morality: The Theories of Plato, Aquinas and Kant and Their Relevance for Suicidology* (New York: Scholars Press, 1975); *Halakhah in a Theological Dimension* (Chico, CA: Scholars, Press, 1985), with essays on such topics as nuclear war, divorce, drug abuse, and bioethics; *Law and Theology in Judaism*, 2 vols. (New York: KTAV, 1976), with essays on such topics as slavery, euthanasia, and the relationship of parents and children; *Jewish Social Ethics* (Oxford: Oxford University Press, 1992), with essays on such topics as human sexuality, AIDS, nuclear war, technology, criminal violence, and economics. Randi Rashkover and Martin Kavka give an important place to Novak's work on particular moral issues in *Tradition in the Public Square: A David Novak Reader*, but because they disagree with some of his ethical conclusions, they "hope to persuade readers that Novak's logic can be detached from the positions on social-ethical issues that he holds" ("Introduction," in *Tradition in the Public Square: A David Novak Reader*, xvi). Actually detaching Novak's "logic" from his "positions on social-ethical issues," however, would likely require significantly reformulating his theology of revelation, election, theonomy, the image of God, and natural law.

37 Novak, *The Sanctity of Human Life*, (Washington, D.C.: Georgetown University Press, 2007), 32. In his summary of Noahide law in *The Sanctity of Human Life*, Novak states, "Jewish tradition recognizes that the Torah did not come into a normative vacuum: The people Israel were already living under an earlier law before the revelation at Mount Sinai. That law is what the rabbis called the seven Noahide commandments (*sheva mitsvot bnei Noah*). For the purposes of ethical enquiry, pertaining to the realm of interhuman relationships, the pertinent norms to consider are the prohibitions of shedding the blood of innocents (*shefikhut damim*); robbery (*gezel*); and sexual immorality (*gilui arayot*), which includes prohibitions of incest, adultery, homosexuality, and bestiality" (31–32).

Comparing Mosaic law with Noahide/natural law, Novak observes, "The difference between the two forms of divine law is that natural law is discovered by human reason within its experience of human life as naturally communal—specifically, through the rightful claims humans make on each other, collectively and individually. Assuming that natural law comes from divine creative wisdom is to give an irreducible metaphysical reason for the justifiable human claims that deserve to be codified into positive law. Revealed law, on the other hand, is God's way of directly claiming human beings for a positive relationship with Himself, even if that relationship at present can be with only one people in the world" (33).

[38] Ibid., 33.
[39] Ibid., 35.
[40] Ibid., 72.
[41] Ibid., 52.
[42] Novak explains with regard to the approval of abortion by some traditionalist Jewish ethicists: "Erroneous inferences have been made from the 'mere water' texts because certain distinctions in Talmudic jurisprudential logic have been overlooked" (ibid., 55). The cases that Rashi has in mind deal with "conflicts of economic interests," not cases in which human life is at issue (57).
[43] Ibid., 58.
[44] Novak cites Aristotle's *History of Animals*, 7.3/583b1-20 (see ibid., 85, fn. 153).
[45] Does this scientific development thereby overturn the four instances in which the embryo's status as "mere water" shapes authoritative Jewish legal tradition? Novak answers "no" on the grounds that these four instances have to do with "highly specialized matters of Jewish ritual law," and thus with theology proper rather than "reasoning about universal moral questions" (ibid., 62).
[46] Ibid., 68.
[47] Ibid., 70. As Novak asks with embryo research in mind (the primary topic of his discussion, although his discussion also includes abortion), "Do we want to contribute to a moral culture for which human life at every stage of its development, is essentially a commodity to be bought and sold, used or discarded, and ultimately the property of whoever has the most power?" (70–71).
[48] Commenting on Bachrach's view that allowing elective abortion would increase sexual promiscuity, Novak states, "The situation is not very different today. Abortion is still largely the recourse of persons who either did not practice birth control or whose birth control device failed them" (ibid., 70). See also Novak's similar appeal to Bachrach's decision in his "A Jewish View of Abortion," in *Tradition in the Public Square: A David Novak Reader*, 266–78, at 272 (originally published in 1974).
[49] Novak, *The Sanctity of Human Life*, 38–39.
[50] Ibid., 39. Novak explains, "That does not mean that the prohibition of murder was not binding and known to be binding before the Mosaic revelation; it simply means that before that direct revelation of God's fuller law, the prohibition of killing innocent life was the commandment of the 'hidden God' (Isa. 45.15) rather than the commandment of the God 'who arrived at Sinai . . . who appeared at Mount Paran' (Deut. 33.2)—the God from whom 'Moses commanded us the Torah' (Deut. 33.4). In fact, Gen. 9.6 is a re-presentation of a norm that has no

single historical origin but is coterminous with human being in the world, at all times and everywhere" (39).
51 Ibid., 39. Novak remarks that some Jewish theologians, while accepting this rabbinic teaching on Gen. 9.6, have nonetheless concluded "that only an embryo literally in utero could be the object of an illicit abortion" (42), but Novak argues against this interpretation.
52 Ibid., 45.
53 Ibid., 44.
54 Ibid., 43.
55 Ibid., 42.
56 Ibid., 47.
57 Ibid.
58 See Gilbert Meilaender, *Bioethics: A Primer for Christians*, 2nd edn. (Grand Rapids, MI: Eerdmans, 2005), 34–35. See also R. Kendall Soulen's critique of abortion as a form of eugenics, of "selection" rather than the recognition of divine election, in his "Election, not Selection," *Pro Ecclesia* 15 (2006): 379–86. While advocating exceptions, Soulen says, "In God's household, it is not only the weak who are dependent on the strong. Time and again, the well-being of the strong turns out to be dependent on those who by human reckoning are least" (385). Soulen calls for extending "at least the most basic constitutional protections to every member of the human family, regardless of stage of biological development, from conception onward" (385). Cf. Vincent Bourguet, "Bioéthique et dualisme ontologique," *Revue Thomiste* 97 (1997): 619–39.
59 Obviously this issue is a profoundly difficult one, not least because of the existential agony that such situations involve—an agony that is not taken away by the decision to abort the baby, as Novak recognizes (see Novak, *The Sanctity of Human Life*, 82, fn. 116). See also *Evangelium Vitae* §58.
60 *Evangelium Vitae* §61.
61 Novak, "A Jewish View of Abortion," 274.
62 Richard Dawkins, *The God Delusion* (Boston, MA: Houghton Mifflin, 2006), 57. See also Edward O. Wilson's *Consilience* (New York: Vintage, 1999) and the response by Wendell Berry, *Life Is a Miracle: An Essay against Modern Superstition* (Washington, D.C.: Counterpoint, 2001); as well as Daniel Dennett, *Darwin's Dangerous Idea* (New York, NY: Touchstone, 1995), and the brief but telling response by David Burrell, *Friendship and Ways to Truth*, 88–90.
63 Burrell, *Friendship and Ways to Truth*, 5.

Chapter 1

1 George Lindbeck, "The Church as Israel: Ecumenism and Ecclesiology," in *Jews and Christians: People of God*, ed. Carl E. Braaten and Robert W. Jenson (Grand Rapids, MI: Eerdmans, 2003), 78–94, at 80.
2 Ibid., 83.
3 Ibid., 83–84. He rejects as a "supersessionist absurdity" the condemnation of "Christian Jews for Torah-observance, that is, for worshiping God as did Jesus and the apostles" (84). In an essay published 8 years earlier, Lindbeck affirms that

"[e]xclusively gentile churches vaccilate between legalism and antinomianism. They need Torah-observant Christian Jews to teach them a better way, a law-abidingness rooted in doxology, not self-righteousness" (Lindbeck, "Response to Michael Wyschogrod's 'Letter to a Friend,'" *Modern Theology* 11 [1995]: 205–10, at 208). Lindbeck underscores, however, that such Torah observance should be optional for Christian Jews. For postliberal Christian affirmation of the claims of Messianic Judaism see also John Howard Yoder, *The Jewish-Christian Schism Revisited*, ed. Michael G. Cartwright and Peter Ochs (Grand Rapids, MI: Eerdmans, 2003), 32 and elsewhere; R. Kendall Soulen, *The God of Israel and Christian Theology* (Minneapolis, MN: Fortress, 1996). Cf. Novak's review of Soulen's book in *First Things* 81 (March 1998): 58–60. David J. Rudolph discusses Yoder's and Soulen's contributions in "Messianic Jews and Christian Theology: Restoring an Historical Voice to the Contemporary Discussion," *Pro Ecclesia* 14 (2005): 58–84, at 72–76 and 77–78, respectively.

4. Lindbeck, "The Church as Israel: Ecumenism and Ecclesiology," 87.
5. Markus Bockmuehl, *Seeing the Word: Refocusing New Testament Study* (Grand Rapids, MI: Baker Academic, 2006), 224.
6. Ibid., 225. Quoting Gabriele Boccaccini's *Middle Judaism: Jewish Thought 300 B.C.E.–200 C.E.* (Minneapolis, MN: Fortress Press, 1991), Francis Watson suggests that the distinction between "Judaism" and "Christianity," at least as regards the first century, "must be 'recognized as a consequence of confessional bias' (p. 18). While Christianity and Rabbinism chose to disinherit one another, 'a reciprocal excommunication cannot cancel the truth of their common origin' (p. 16)—an origin within a 'plurality of groups, movements, and traditions of thought coexist[ing] in a dialectical relationship, which was sometimes polemical but never disengaged' (p. 14)" (Watson, *Paul and the Hermeneutics of Faith* [London: T & T Clark International, 2004], 5 fn. 3).
7. Bockmuehl, *Seeing the Word*, 226.
8. David Novak, "What Does Edith Stein Mean for Jews?" in Novak, *Talking with Christians: Musings of a Jewish Theologian* (Grand Rapids, MI: Eerdmans, 2005), 146–66, at 164. Novak observes with regard to Edith Stein that "Jewish tradition regards such persons as apostates (*meshumadim*), who have removed themselves from the assembly of Israel (*keneset yisrael*) in a radical way, even if they still consider themselves personally part of the body of the Jewish people. That general judgment stands even if the apostate is a person of extraordinary intellectual and moral virtues like Edith Stein" (148). Elsewhere he emphasizes that even if such conversion is a sincere effort to follow one's conscience, it is still a sin because of the character of God's relationship with Israel.
9. Ibid., 164.
10. Ibid.
11. Ibid., 149. See also Novak's "Jews and Catholics: Beyond Apologies," *First Things* (January 1999): 20–25, where he evaluates the Vatican document "We Remember: A Reflection on the Shoah" (March 1998).
12. Ibid., 163.
13. Ibid.
14. Alasdair MacIntyre, *Whose Justice? Which Rationality?* (Notre Dame, IN: University of Notre Dame Press, 1988), 370; quoted by Novak in "What Does Edith Stein Mean for Jews?," 164.

[15] Novak, "What Does Edith Stein Mean for Jews?," 164.
[16] Ibid.
[17] Novak notes that the Vatican document "We Remember: A Reflection on the Shoah" contains the following remark: "The Nazi regime was determined to exterminate the very existence of the Jewish people, a people called to witness to the one God and the law of the covenant." Commenting on that sentence, Novak observes, "This statement of the Catholic Church recognizes the chosenness of the Jewish people, a fact nothing short of *qiddush ha-shem*, 'the sanctification of the name of God.' If the Church, from the top down, recognizes this as the reason for the survival and continuing strength of the Jewish people, then, despite any reservations, Jews have to see this document as making a positive contribution to the always complex relationship between the Jewish people and the Catholic Church" (Novak, "Jews and Catholics: Beyond Apologies," 25). Novak also recognizes the role of atheism in Nazi ideology: "Perhaps the true source of the Nazi venom against the Jewish people is that for which or for Whom the Jews are to survive" (ibid.).
[18] Novak, "What Does Edith Stein Mean for Jews?," 164. Christians who do seek more often posit two separate paths of salvation rather than remaining within the fulfillment/participation model that retains the Christian affirmation that Jesus is Israel's Messiah and is the one Mediator. Cf. the issues that arise in Albert Vanhoye, S.J., "Salut universel par le Christ et validité de l'Ancienne Alliance," *Nouvelle revue théologique* 116 (1994): 815–35 and the response by Emmanuelle Main, "Ancienne et Nouvelle Alliances dans le dessein de Dieu. À propos d'un article recent," *Nouvelle revue théologique* 118 (1996): 34–58. For elaboration of the two-path account of salvation (one for Jews and one for gentiles), see, for example, Friedrich-Wilhelm Marquardt, *Das christliche Bekenntnis zu Jesus, dem Juden. Eine Christologie*, 2 vols. (Munich: 1990–91). For a similar approach on a more popular level, see Rosemary Radford Ruether, *Faith and Fratricide: The Theological Roots of Anti-Semitism* (1974; Eugene, OR: Wipf and Stock, 1996); Philip A. Cunningham, *A Story of Shalom: The Calling of Christians and Jews by a Covenanting God* (New York: Paulist Press, 2001). Against the two-path model of salvation, see also John M. McDermott, S.J., "The Jews, Jesus, and the Church," *Josephinum Journal of Theology* 11 (2004): 26–48.
[19] Novak, "What Does Edith Stein Mean for Jews?," 164.
[20] Ibid.
[21] Novak comments in this regard, "Faith (*emunah*) is the human existential response to God's revealed grace (*gillui Shekinah*). One's experience of that grace realizes whatever possibilities that person brings up with him or her to that revelation. *Where* that revelation fundamentally occurs is *the* existential question. Our [Jewish and Christian] fruitful conversations of late have had to largely bracket *the* existential question confronting us for good worldly reasons. It is, nevertheless, the crucial question that leaves us both at an impasse. . . . At this theological level, which is the most profound aspect of our understanding of ourselves and each other, Edith Stein is a great manifestation of our impasse. She cannot be invoked as a bridge in dialogue between Jews and Catholics because in this world one cannot be both a faithful Jew and a faithful Catholic in tandem. These necessarily communal identities are mutually exclusive here and now" (ibid., 165).

[22] David Novak, "Avoiding Charges of Legalism and Antinomianism in Jewish-Christian Dialogue," in *Talking with Christians*, 26–45, at 40. Cf. Leon Menzies Racioner, "Hebrew Catholicism: Theology and Politics in Modern Israel," *Heythrop Journal* 45 (2004): 405–15.

[23] Novak, "Avoiding Charges of Legalism and Antinomianism in Jewish-Christian Dialogue," 41.

[24] Ibid. For further discussion see Bruce W. Longenecker, "On Israel's God and God's Israel: Assessing Supersessionism in Paul," *Journal of Theological Studies* 58 (2007): 26–44; Longenecker, "Different Answers to Different Questions: Israel, the Gentiles and Salvation History in Romans 9–11," *Journal for the Study of the New Testament* 36 (1989): 95–123. In "On Israel's God and God's Israel," Longenecker finds that "Paul evidences a supersessionism that stands opposed as much to the 'two ways' approach that has gained some recent popularity as it stands in opposition to the replacement interpretations that have marked out Christian theology at various points throughout Christian history. The 'two ways' and replacement interpretations stand together in the shared belief that, for Paul, salvation in Christ is of little relevance to the Jewish people. We have seen reason to believe that, if fact, Paul maintained a form of supersessionism whereby the Christian gospel was thought to be of key relevance to the Jewish people, offering the way of salvation not only for Gentiles but also for Jews. But in this conviction Paul also studiously avoided (at least in Rom. 9–11) any suggestion that God's covenant with Israel had been abrogated" (38–39).

[25] Novak, "Avoiding Charges of Legalism and Antinomianism in Jewish-Christian Dialogue," 41.

[26] Ibid.

[27] Ibid., 41, fn. 36. In this footnote Novak takes note of some Christian theologians who are seeking to move beyond supersessionism of any kind—he names Paul van Buren, Kendall Soulen, and Scott Bader-Saye—and he judges that their work "makes a new form of dialogue possible from the Christian side." Novak holds, however, that if Christian theology is to remain Christian, it has to hold the milder form of supersessionism.

[28] Novak, "From Supersessionism to Parallelism in Jewish-Christian Dialogue," in *Talking with Christians*, 8–25, at 9. Novak adds, "Thus the longest and perhaps deepest Jewish debate over Christianity, one that began when the church became a decidedly non-Jewish community and that has by no means ended, has been the question of whether the Christians do or do not worship *our* God. If they do not, then they are idolaters ipso facto" (9). It seems likely that Novak has in view, within the longstanding Jewish debate, the controversy prompted among Jewish theologians by *Dabru Emet*. For criticism of *Dabru Emet*, see especially Jon D. Levenson, "The Agenda of *Dabru Emet*," *Review of Rabbinic Judaism* 7 (2004): 1–26, especially 7–9, 26; Levenson, "How Not to Conduct Jewish-Christian Dialogue," *Commentary* 112, no. 5 (December 2001): 31–37; Levenson, "Did God Forgive Adam? An Exercise in Comparative Midrash," in *Jews and Christians: People of God*, ed. Carl. E. Braaten and Robert W. Jenson, 148–70, especially 169. Novak agrees with Levenson that the doctrines of the Trinity and the Incarnation have no place in Jewish-Christian dialogue and deeply divide Jews from Christians (cf. Novak, "When Jews Are Christians," in *Talking with Christians*, 218–28, at 224). Nonetheless,

Novak holds that Christians should be taken at their word when they profess to worship the one Creator God of Israel, even if Christians worship this God in the wrong way. Michael Wyschogrod and David Berger likewise withdrew from *Dabru Emet* when, in Berger's words, "it became clear that it would not contain a forthright assertion that Christian belief and worship, at least if practiced by a Jew, are *avodah zarah*, or foreign worship, the term usually translated, imprecisely to be sure, as idolatry" (Berger, "Introducing Michael Wyschogrod," *Modern Theology* 22 [2006]: 673–75, at 674). For a Christian response to Levenson's concerns, see John McDade, S.J., "Christians and Jews: Competitive Siblings or the Israel of God?" *New Blackfriars* 89 (2008): 267–79. For explanation of how Christians hold that God is "one" and "simple," see Gilles Emery, O.P., *Trinity in Aquinas* (Naples, FL: Sapientia Press, 2006). See also the discussion of God in *Christianity in Jewish Terms*, ed. Tikva Frymer-Kensky et al. (Boulder, CO: Westview Press, 2000): Peter Ochs, "The God of Jews and Christians," 49–69; David Ellenson, "A Jewish View of the Christian God: Some Cautionary and Hopeful Remarks," 69–76.

[29] In the conclusion to his *Paul and the Hermeneutics of Faith* (New York: T & T Clark International, 2004), which compares Paul's reading of passages from the Torah with contemporaneous Jewish readings of the same passages, Francis Watson asks of the first century: "May we perhaps understand the Christian community itself as just another Jewish sect? To raise these questions is not at all to suggest that we can or should erase the difference between Pauline Christian Judaism (for want of a better expression) and non-Christian Judaisms. . . . As our readings of early readings of scripture have shown, the difference is ineradicable—the difference summed up in the Christian invocation of Jesus as Lord" (532–33). For Watson, "Pauline Christian Judaism" holds that Torah observance is a dead end which has been covenantally replaced by faith in Christ. For his part, Novak considers that "Judaism" requires accepting Torah observance as the obligatory covenantal path for all Jews, and he also holds that Christian faith in Jesus as the Son of God incarnate separates Christians from "Judaism."

[30] Novak, "From Supersessionism to Parallelism in Jewish-Christian Dialogue," 10.

[31] Novak adds, "The election of Israel as the Jewish people would only be terminable if one held with supersessionists as diverse as Baruch Spinoza and Friedrich Schleiermacher that the Jews elected God rather than that God elects the Jews. . . . Whenever the Jews reject God's covenant with them, God keeps offering it to us again and again" (11–12).

[32] Ibid., 13.

[33] Ibid., 19.

[34] Ibid., 14. Novak is responding to the view of Rabbi Joseph B. Soloveitchik, whom he otherwise admires. In an influential essay titled "Confrontation," *Tradition: A Journal of Orthodox Thought* 6 (1964): 5–9, Soloveitchik indicated serious reservations about Jews engaging in dialogue with Christians. For a valuable response to Soloveitchik by Michael Wyschogrod, see "A Jewish View of Christianity," in Wyschogrod, *Abraham's Promise: Judaism and Jewish-Christian Relations*, ed. R. Kendall Soulen (Grand Rapids, MI: Eerdmans, 2004), 149–64, at 155–57. See also in the same volume Wyschogrod's "The Impact of Dialogue with Christianity on My Self-Understanding as a Jew," 225–36.

[35] It will be clear that Hegel's philosophy of religion, as Novak says, makes Hegel "the greatest logician of supersessionism" (Novak, "From Supersessionism to Parallelism in Jewish-Christian Dialogue," 12). Novak also points to Friedrich Schleiermacher, who views the Old Testament as entirely valueless for Christians (11, fn. 4). See also Martin Luther, "How Christians Should Regard Moses" (1525), in *Martin Luther's Basic Theological Writings*, ed. Timothy F. Lull (Minneapolis, MN: Augsburg Fortress, 1989), 135–48.

[36] Novak, "From Supersessionism to Parallelism in Jewish-Christian Dialogue," 22.

[37] Ibid.

[38] Ibid. Novak adds, "In talmudic logic this is called *bereirah*, that is, when the present defines the past in a way in which the past could never define the present. Later Talmudic logic called this process *asmakhta*, namely, the 'association' of norm and text, which is neither the derivation of the norm *from* the text nor the overcoming of the text *by* the norm" (ibid.).

[39] Ibid., 24. In *Natural Law in Judaism* (Cambridge: Cambridge University Press, 1998), Novak criticizes the medieval Jewish thinker Saadiah's teleology on the grounds that it reduces "revelation to creation" (129), and thus cannot account for covenant. He commends instead Franz Rosenzweig's insistence that covenant "enables our relation *to* the world to be ontologically (even if not usually chronologically) subsequent to our direct relationship *with* God" (130). Novak aims to uphold the primacy and freedom of God's active (covenantal) relationship with humans.

[40] Novak, "From Supersessionism to Parallelism in Jewish-Christian Dialogue," 24. Cf. the statement by the delegates involved in the consultation organized by the National Council of Synagogues and the United States Conference of Catholic Bishops' Committee for Ecumenical and Interreligious Relations, "Reflections on Covenant and Mission," *Origins* 32, no. 13 (September 5, 2002): 218–24, and the critical response by Avery Cardinal Dulles, S.J., "Covenant and Mission," *America* 187, no. 12 (October 21, 2002): 8–11.

[41] Novak, "From Supersessionism to Parallelism in Jewish-Christian Dialogue," 25.

[42] Novak, "Theology and Philosophy: An Exchange with Robert Jenson," in *Talking with Christians*, 229–46, at 230.

[43] Ibid. Novak explains why he does not include Islam here: "Jews, Christians, and Muslims commonly worship the God of Abraham, but that commonality is not nearly as specific and concrete as the common Jewish-Christian worship of the Lord God of Israel since it is not made over the proper interpretation of the same Scripture and does not involve a dispute over the nature of the community covenanted with this God" (ibid.). Other Jewish theologians argue that Islam is more truly monotheistic and therefore more cognate with Judaism than is Christianity: Novak cites in this regard L.E. Goodman, *God of Abraham* (Oxford: Oxford University Press, 1996), 34–35 (Novak, "Theology and Philosophy," 230, fn. 1).

[44] Novak, "When Jews Are Christians," in *Talking with Christians*, 218–28.

[45] Ibid., 218.

[46] Ibid.

[47] Ibid.

[48] Ibid., 220.

[49] Ibid., 222.

50 Ibid.
51 Ibid. See, for example, N.T. Wright, *Jesus and the Victory of God* (Minneapolis, MN: Fortress Press, 1996), 463–72; Pope Benedict XVI/Joseph Ratzinger, *Jesus of Nazareth: From the Baptism in the Jordan to the Transfiguration*, trans. Adrian J. Walker (New York: Doubleday, 2007), chapter 3.
52 Novak, "When Jews Are Christians," 222. Debates over biblical interpretation are difficult to resolve, as Novak points out, because at least at times "scriptural exegesis is much more a process whereby the teachings of the tradition of a religious community (what Jews call *Oral Torah* and Catholics call the *magisterium*) are *connected to* Scripture than it is one in which these teachings are simply *derived from* Scripture in some unproblematic fashion. Thus, it is that Jews and Christians can read a common text so differently and therefore cannot resolve their differences by appealing to the authority of Scripture" (224).
53 Ibid., 222. Novak explains his view of what the Messiah will do and be, and why Jesus could not have been the Messiah: "Messiahhood is a political designation for a divinely restored (or, at least, divinely sanctioned) Jewish king in Jerusalem, who will gather in the exiles, establish a state governed by the Torah, and rebuild the Temple. . . . Jesus was not the Messiah precisely because he did not bring about the full restoration of the Jewish people to the Land of Israel and God's universal reign of peace" (ibid.). See also Novak, *Covenantal Rights: A Study in Jewish Political Theory* (Cambridge: Cambridge University Press, 2000), x.
54 Novak, "When Jews Are Christians," 221. Cf. John McDade, S.J., "Christians and Jews: Competitive Siblings or the Israel of God?" *New Blackfriars* 89 (2008): 267–79, at 279.
55 Novak, "When Jews Are Christians," 223.
56 Ibid., 223. Novak remarks, "The commonality between Judaism and Christianity can be affirmed and developed only in those areas where our respective traditions do indeed overlap. But on the whole question of who Jesus is, they do not overlap" (224).
57 Ibid., 226.
58 McDade, "Christians and Jews," 274. McDade goes on to note, "Christianity will say, classically for example in the writings of Thomas Aquinas, that Christ fulfils the whole Torah—the spiritual, juridical and ritual commandments—and that the church by sacramental union and participation in him observes Torah" (278). This is the argument of my *Christ's Fulfillment of Torah and Temple: Salvation according to Thomas Aquinas* (Notre Dame, IN: University of Notre Dame Press, 2002). However, McDade adds that "this enters Christian consciousness only minimally and implicitly" (278).
59 Novak, "When Jews Are Christians," 220.
60 Ibid., 220–21.
61 Novak differentiates between "proselytizing, specifically directed at Jews" and "a general Christian proclamation of the Gospel to the entire world" (ibid., 220).
62 Ibid., 225.
63 Ibid., 220.
64 See Mark S. Kinzer, *Postmissionary Messianic Judaism: Redefining Christian Engagement with the Jewish People* (Grand Rapids, MI: Brazos, 2005). His book develops for a (gentile) Christian audience the arguments that he made in an earlier study

directed to an audience of Messianic Jews, *The Nature of Messianic Judaism: Judaism as Genus, Messianic as Species* (West Hartford, CT: Hashivenu Archives, 2000). Some of the questions that I pose to Kinzer have already been raised by R. Kendall Soulen (although Soulen is more positive than I am about Kinzer's proposal for Torah observance) in his review of *Postmissionary Messianic Judaism*, published in *Pro Ecclesia* 16 (2007): 105–7, which I read after drafting this chapter. John P. Yocum, too, raises similar questions in his review essay "On Mark S. Kinzer's *Postmissionary Messianic Judaism: Redefining Christian Engagement with the Jewish People*," *Nova et Vetera* 5 (2007): 895–906. In addition to querying Kinzer regarding the role of the Holy Spirit, Yocum observes that "to say that the 'schism between the Jewish people and the *ekklesia* can be healed without coming to full agreement over Yeshua's messianic identity' (307) is also rather troubling" (Yocum, "On Mark S. Kinzer's *Postmissionary Messianic Judaism*," 905).

[65] Kinzer, *Postmissionary Messianic Judaism*, 12.

[66] In his response to Michael Wyschogrod's "Letter to a Friend," *Modern Theology* 11 (1995): 165–71, David B. Burrell, C.S.C., rightly remarks, "The liturgical celebration of fulfillment is quite different, however, from the theological (or pseudo-theological) conceptualization of 'displacement'" (Burrell, "Response to Michael Wyschogrod's Letter," *Modern Theology* 11 [1995]: 181–86, at 182). For a theology of fulfillment articulated by a Jewish convert to Christianity, see in the same symposium Ellen T. Charry, "Christian Jews and the Law," *Modern Theology* 11 (1995): 187–93. Wyschogrod criticizes Charry's view on the grounds that it justifies the disappearance of the Jewish people (Wyschogrod, "Response to the Respondents," 235), but it seems to me that Charry is simply distinguishing between "displacement" and "fulfillment." See also Charry's discussion of Judaism and *Dabru Emet*, "The Other Side of the Story," *Princeton Theological Review* 8 (2001): 24–29, with a response in the same issue by the Messianic Jewish theologian Carl Kinbar, "Missing Factors in Jewish-Christian Dialogue," 30–37 and Charry's "Response to Carl Kinbar," 38–39. From the perspective of Messianic Judaism, Kinbar argues against *Dabru Emet*'s thesis that Jews and Christians will not come together until the eschaton.

[67] Kinzer, *Postmissionary Messianic Judaism*, 12.

[68] Ibid., 13. Kinzer states, "This is why I assert that this book is not mainly about Messianic Judaism. While I *am* arguing for the legitimacy and importance of Messianic Judaism, my thesis is that the church's own identity—and not just the identity of Messianic Jews—is at stake in the discussion" (13).

[69] Ibid. (italics removed). Kinzer is responding to the concern expressed by Michael Wyschogrod, who writes, "What I find painful are messianic Jewish congregations which adopt Jewish symbols and practices to attract Jews but are not committed in principle to Torah observance. These groups use Jewish symbols and practices to make the transition of Jews to gentile Christianity easier. Their aim is Jewish integration into a Christianity that does not demand sustained Jewish Torah observance indefinitely" (Wyschogrod, "Response to the Respondents," *Modern Theology* 11 [1995]: 237; quoted in Kinzer, *Postmissionary Messianic Judaism*, 14). Kinzer explains the importance of a new "postmissionary" stance. For Wyschogrod's concerns see also David Berger and Michael Wyschogrod, *Jews and "Jewish Christianity"* (New York: KTAV, 1978).

70 Kinzer, *Postmissionary Messianic Judaism*, 14 (italics removed).
71 Ibid.
72 Ibid., 15.
73 Ibid., 16.
74 Ibid., 15 (italics removed).
75 Ibid., (italics removed).
76 Ibid. Kinzer states, "Postmissionary Messianic Judaism bears witness to the enduring importance of the Jewish people and its way of life for the identity of the Christian church, and likewise bears witness to the enduring importance of Yeshua's mediation for the identity of the Jewish people" (16).
77 Ibid., 16.
78 Ibid. Kinzer comments, "The church of the nations can become an extension of Israel only if its Messianic Jewish partner is deeply rooted in Jewish soil" (16).
79 Ibid.
80 Kinzer quotes Richard John Neuhaus's insightful remark, "The God of Israel is not separable from the people of Israel. It follows that to be in relationship with the God of Israel is to be in relationship with the people of Israel" (Neuhaus, "Salvation Is from the Jews," in *Jews and Christians: People of God*, ed. Carl E. Braaten and Robert W. Jenson, 68; quoted by Kinzer, 15, fn. 8).
81 Kinzer, *Postmissionary Messianic Judaism*, 13.
82 Ibid., 16.
83 Kinzer argues that the answer is yes. He explains, "I am urging that we rethink our presuppositions regarding the relationship between Christianity and Judaism, the church and Israel, Christians and Jews. The terms themselves express an underlying conceptual framework that envisions two separate religions, two separate communities practicing the two separate religions, and the members of those two separate communities" (21). He uses the word "*ekklesia*" because he finds that the words "*Christianity, Christians*, and *church*," as conventionally used, "imply mutual exclusivity" (22) and refer at best to "the developed institutional reality that became overwhelmingly Gentile in composition and character" (22). Likewise he uses the name "Yeshua" rather than Jesus so as "to suggest that Yeshua is still at home with those who are literally his family, and that the church must reckon with the subtle ways it has lost touch with its own identity as a messianic, multinational extension of the Jewish people" (22).
84 Ibid., 25.
85 Ibid. The book is thus "an apologia for the Jewish people as a whole and for Judaism as an ongoing religious tradition" (25)—an apologia that seeks to change both Christian and rabbinic Jewish evaluations of Messianic Judaism's relationship to rabbinic Judaism. In Kinzer's view, the stakes with respect to the reception of his book are very high: "the church's understanding of its own identity stands or falls on how it responds to this apologia. If the ekklesia is truly the earthly body—or part of the earthly body—of a resurrected Jew, it needs finally to come to terms with the people and tradition to which that Jew belongs. This book is intended to help the ekklesia realize and meet that need" (25).
86 Kinzer's book can be divided into two halves. In the first half (comprising four chapters), he argues that the witness of Jesus and the disciples/apostles suggests that they held that Jews (including believers in Jesus as Messiah) were required to

practice Torah observance. The concluding chapter of this first half suggests that the church can and must now redefine itself as the union of a Jewish *ekklesia* and a gentile *ekklesia*. In the second half (comprising five chapters), Kinzer investigates what he views as the Christian and Jewish mistakes that, almost immediately after the writing of the New Testament, produced the division. The Christian mistake was to prohibit Torah observance for believers in Jesus as the Messiah. The fact that many Jews did not believe in Jesus as the Messiah—in itself a sad mistake on the part of those Jews—showed itself to be providentially beneficial when Christians banned Torah observance among Christians. Kinzer then canvasses the emergence and development of Jewish Christianity/Messianic Judaism in the past two centuries, and concludes by turning to contemporary Christianity and offering suggestions for the eventual establishment of a Jewish *ekklesia* that would be parallel with, and united to, the gentile *ekklesia*.

[87] He cites as an example the perspective of Richard B. Hays, *The Moral Vision of the New Testament* (San Francisco, CA: HarperSanFrancisco, 1996) (Kinzer, 29).

[88] Kinzer, 32.

[89] The historical developments that he discusses are the loss of "a visible Jewish nucleus" in the *ekklesia*, the flourishing of rabbinic Judaism, Christian anti-Judaism, the Holocaust, the modern State of Israel, and the emergence of Messianic Judaism. He sees God's providential hand in these developments, guiding the *ekklesia* from its original and disastrous fall toward its eventual renewal (ibid., 42–46).

[90] Ibid., 57.

[91] Ibid., 66.

[92] Ibid., 69. Kinzer goes so far as to say that "Luke-Acts provides the strongest evidence in the New Testament for the validity and importance of Jewish practice for Jews. From the beginning of the Gospel of Luke to the end of the Acts of the Apostles, we find no deviation from this orientation" (71).

[93] Ibid., 74. Compare Francis Watson's interpretation, responding to that of E.P. Sanders, of 1 Cor. 7.19: "Pauline alienation from the Jewish community comes vividly to expression in this transformation of a permission into a signifier of a new difference, the difference between the *ekklēsia* and the synagogue. As such, Paul's declaration of the nullity of circumcision represents an essential moment in the construction of Christian identity" (Watson, *Paul, Judaism, and the Gentiles: Beyond the New Perspective*, 2nd edn. [Grand Rapids, MI: Eerdmans, 2007], 83). Watson goes on to say with regard to 1 Cor. 10.25–26, "Paul's language implies that *all* the characteristically Jewish issues relating to dietary laws are irrelevant to the Corinthians. Equally irrelevant, it seems, is the sabbath. The congregation meets not on the sabbath but on the first day of the week (cf. 1 Cor. 16.2)" (84).

[94] Kinzer, *Postmissionary Messianic Judaism*, 75–82. Kinzer here follows Mark D. Nanos, *The Mystery of Romans: The Jewish Context of Paul's Letter* (Minneapolis, MN: Fortress Press, 1996), 85–165; cf. David Rudolph, "Messianic Jews and Christian Theology," 62–63 (Rudolph draws on Kinzer's *The Nature of Messianic Judaism*), as well as Robert A.J. Gagnon's response to Nanos, "Why the 'Weak' at Rome Cannot Be Non-Christian Jews," *Catholic Biblical Quarterly* 62 (2000): 64–82.

[95] Kinzer, *Postmissionary Messianic Judaism*, 84.

96 Ibid., 87. With regard to Paul, Kinzer concludes, "Paul had a certain amount of halakhic flexibility—but not a complete freedom from halakhah. He varied in his Jewish practice depending on his circumstances, but this text [1 Cor. 9.19–23] gives us no grounds for thinking that he ever actually violated basic Jewish practice (i.e., by eating nonkosher food or by profaning the Sabbath or holidays)."

97 Ibid., 101. The internal quotation comes from Mk 7.27, where Jesus compares the Jews to "the children" and Greeks to "dogs."

98 Ibid., 112.

99 Cf. his reading of Rom. 8–11; ibid., 122–40.

100 Ibid., 149.

101 For discussion of Gal. 2, see ibid., 163–65.

102 Kinzer, *Postmissionary Messianic Judaism*, 73.

103 Ibid. The internal quotation is from James D.G. Dunn, *The Epistle to the Galatians* (Peabody, MA: Hendrickson, 1993), 266–67. Cf. Rudolph, "Messianic Jews and Christian Theology," 64, 67.

104 Kinzer, *Postmissionary Messianic Judaism*, 73.

105 For exegesis of Gal. 5.7–12, with due attention to its complexity and in critical dialogue with Dunn, see Ben Witherington III, *Grace in Galatia: A Commentary on Paul's Letter to the Galatians* (Edinburgh: T & T Clark, 1998), 371–75.

106 For further discussion cf. the *Catechism of the Catholic Church* §§ 580, 613–14, 616–18. As a tentative hypothesis, Kinzer argues that Luke has in view "a new and unwritten third book" having to do with the feast of booths (Kinzer, *Postmissionary Messianic Judaism*, 121).

107 Kinzer cites Luke Timothy Johnson's *The Writings of the New Testament* (Philadelphia, PA: Fortress Press, 1986), 378–79 (Kinzer, *Postmissionary Messianic Judaism*, 170).

108 For Kinzer's reading of Eph. 2, see *Postmissionary Messianic Judaism*, 165–71. Drawing particularly upon Markus Barth, whose position seems more nuanced than Kinzer's, Kinzer argues that "Eph. 2.15 advocates rather than refutes bilateral ecclesiology" (170), since Eph. 2.15 does not call upon Jews to become gentiles or vice versa. What is missing in Kinzer's reading of Eph. 2 is the theology of fulfillment/reconfiguration in the Messiah.

109 Ibid., 52–58.

110 Paul continues, "Eat whatever is sold in the meat market without raising any question on the ground of conscience. For 'the earth is the Lord's, and everything in it.' If one of the unbelievers invites you to dinner and you are disposed to go, eat whatever is set before you without raising any question on the ground of conscience. (But if someone says to you, 'This has been offered in sacrifice,' then out of consideration for the man who informed you, and for conscience' sake—I mean his conscience, not yours—do not eat it.) For why should my liberty be determined by another man's scruples? If I partake with thankfulness, why am I denounced because of that for which I give thanks? So, whatever you eat or drink, or whatever you do, do all to the glory of God. Give no offense to Jews or to Greeks or to the church of God, just as I try to please all men in everything I do, not seeking my own advantage, but that of many, that they may be saved" (1 Cor. 10.25–33). Could Paul eat with unbelievers in this fashion and keep kosher?

[111] For Kinzer's reading of this passage, see Kinzer, *Postmissionary Messianic Judaism*, 145.

[112] Ibid., 136; for discussion of Kinzer's view of Rom. 9–11 see Yocum, "On Kinzer's *Postmissionary Messianic Judaism*," 898–99, 902–3.

[113] Quoted in Kinzer, *Postmissionary Messianic Judaism*, 189, from Ignatius, *To the Magnesians*, in *Apostolic Fathers*, vol. 1, ed. Kirsopp Lake (Cambridge, MA: Harvard University Press, 1912).

[114] See Kinzer, *Postmissionary Messianic Judaism*, 189.

[115] Ibid., 206. Kinzer quotes *Summa theologiae* I–II, q. 103, a. 4. For Augustine's theology of Judaism, see Paula Fredriksen, *Augustine and the Jews: A Christian Defense of Jews and Judaism* (New York: Doubleday, 2008); Lisa A. Unterseher, "The Mark of Cain and the Jews: Augustine's Theology of Jews," *Augustinian Studies* 33 (2002): 99–121.

[116] Wyschogrod, "A Jewish Reading of St. Thomas Aquinas on the Old Law," in *Understanding Scripture*, ed. Clemens Thoma and Michael Wyschogrod (New York: Paulist, 1987), 136; quoted in Kinzer, *Postmissionary Messianic Judaism*, 207. See also Michael Wyschogrod's "Letter to a Friend." Wyschogrod calls upon Christians to enable Jews to observe Torah as Christians, but he does not think that Torah-observant Jewish Christians thereby are good Jews: "it is clear that from the Jewish point of view accepting trinitarian Christianity is not a good thing to do. In fact, it is so bad that a Christian Jew loses all sorts of privileges in the community of Israel, such as being an acceptable witness in a rabbinic court or being counted in a prayer quorum of ten" ("Letter to a Friend," 167).

[117] For a classic work of sacramental theology from this perspective, see Anscar Vonier, O.S.B., *A Key to the Doctrine of the Eucharist* (1925; Bethesda, MD: Zaccheus Press, 2003); see also my *Sacrifice and Community*, especially chapter 5.

[118] Kinzer, *Postmissionary Messianic Judaism*, 208.

[119] Ibid., 209.

[120] Could Christian worship include a "Jewish rite?" Christians already consider the eucharistic rite to be in a real sense "Jewish" as a participation in the sacrificial Body of the Messiah, and the eucharistic rite expresses and embodies the oneness of Jews and gentiles. Ongoing intra-Christian dialogues are considering the question of a "Jewish rite" in light of Messianic Judaism.

[121] Kinzer, *Postmissionary Messianic Judaism*, 210.

[122] Ibid., 211.

[123] Kinzer almost never refers to the Trinity or the Incarnation. The only exception that I noted is found on pp. 231–32. Summarizing an argument made by Bruce Marshall in *Trinity and Truth*, Kinzer states on p. 231, "The doctrine of the Trinity implies that if God is present in Israel, Yeshua is also present there." See Marshall, *Trinity and Truth* (Cambridge: Cambridge University Press, 2000), 178. Kinzer mentions the Incarnation on p. 232 in summarizing an argument made by Robert W. Jenson in "Toward a Christian Theology of Judaism," in *Jews and Christians*, 12–13.

[124] Kinzer, *Postmissionary Messianic Judaism*, 211.

[125] Ibid.

[126] Ibid. Following Kinzer's *The Nature of Messianic Judaism*, David Rudolph puts it this way: "An all-Gentile church is an aberration, a deformity never envisioned by

Jesus and his *shelichim* (apostles). Moreover, a *tertium genus* (third race) *ekklesia* is foreign to the New Testament. For Paul, Jesus-believing Jews and Jesus-believing Gentiles together, in *'echad*-like unity and diversity, form the body of Missiah. Israel's irrevocable calling validates and necessitates this ecclesiological model" (Rudolph, "Messianic Jews and Christian Theology," 83–84).

[127] As *Lumen Gentium* goes on to say, the church is "the assembly of those who look to Jesus in faith" for salvation, unity, and peace (§9). The church is "the visible sacrament of this saving unity," and the Holy Spirit preserves the church so that "it does not fall away from perfect fidelity through weakness of the flesh, but remains the worthy spouse of its Lord" (§9). Cf. Avery Dulles, S.J., *The Catholicity of the Church* (Oxford: Oxford University Press, 1985); Dulles, "Nature, Mission, and Structure of the Church," in *Vatican II: Renewal within Tradition*, ed. Matthew L. Lamb and Matthew Levering (Oxford: Oxford University Press, 2008), 25–36.

[128] Kinzer, *Postmissionary Messianic Judaism*, 211.

[129] Ibid.

[130] Ibid., 210 (Kinzer draws this point from Lindbeck).

[131] Ibid.

[132] Ibid., 310. For an account of Joseph Rabinowitz's contributions, see 273–78. Kinzer notes that while Rabinowitz "takes the initial steps toward the formation of a bilateral ecclesiology" (278), he also "still reflects a missionary orientation" (278). This is so because he "denies the value and validity of rabbinic tradition" and focuses "on Israel entering the (universal) church (without a corresponding emphasis on the church joining Israel" (278).

[133] Ibid., 310.

[134] Ibid., 308.

[135] Novak, "When Jews Are Christians," 227 (see also 219–20).

[136] Kinzer, *Postmissionary Messianic Judaism*, 213, citing John Howard Yoder, *The Jewish-Christian Schism Revisited*, ed. Michael G. Cartwright and Peter Ochs (Grand Rapids, MI: Eerdmans, 2003), 51–61, 76–77.

[137] Kinzer, *Postmissionary Messianic Judaism*, 213 fn. 1, citing Yoder, *The Jewish-Christian Schism Revisited*, 51–61, 76–77. As Kinzer puts it later, "the message about Yeshua that came to Jews in the second century was radically different [from that preached by Peter and Paul]. It spoke of how Israel's covenant and way of life had been annulled in the Messiah, and it claimed that Jewish identity and practice were of no value or even prohibited. Any Jew who was loyal to the covenant would conclude that such a message could not possibly come from the God of Israel. To reject such a purported Messiah would be an act of fidelity to God rather than infidelity!" (224). Here Kinzer refers to Paul M. van Buren, *A Theology of Jewish-Christian Reality*, vol. 2, *A Christian Theology of the People Israel* (San Francisco, CA: Harper & Row, 1983), 34, 276.

[138] Kinzer, *Postmissionary Messianic Judaism*, 215. At this stage of his argument Kinzer cites Bruce D. Marshall's "Christ and the Cultures: The Jewish People and Christian Theology," in *The Cambridge Companion to Christian Doctrine*, ed. Colin E. Gunton (Cambridge: Cambridge University Press, 1997), 91–92 and Robert W. Jenson's "Toward a Christian Theology of Judaism," in *Jews and Christians*, ed. Carl E. Braaten and Robert W. Jenson, 1–13. Marshall, like Michael Wyschogrod,

puts forward the thesis that "[t]he Jewish people cannot be permanently elect unless they can be distinguished at all times from the nations, and the observance of traditional Jewish law seems to be the one mark by which this distinction can be sustained *post Christum*" (Marshall, "Christ and the Cultures," 92). Jenson asks, "Can there be a present body of the risen Jew, Jesus of Nazareth, in which the lineage of Abraham and Sarah so vanishes into a congregation of gentiles as it does in the church? My final—and perhaps most radical—suggestion to Christian theology (*not*, let me say again, to Jewish self-understanding) is that, so long as the time of detour lasts, the embodiment of the risen Christ is whole only in the form of the church *and* an identifiable community of Abraham and Sarah's descendents" (Jenson, "Toward a Christian Theology of Judaism," 13). Both Marshall and Jenson, however, seem to have in view Christianity and Judaism rather than Messianic Judaism, with its conjoined gentile *ekklesia* and a Jewish *ekklesia*.

[139] Kinzer, *Postmissionary Messianic Judaism*, 220. Kinzer cites N.T. Wright's *The New Testament and the People of God* (Minneapolis, MN: Fortress Press, 1992), 400–2, as well as Wright's study of Paul's view of Jesus as the new Adam in Wright's *The Climax of the Covenant* (Minneapolis, MN: Fortress Press, 1991), 18–40. Kinzer notes, however, that "Wright interprets Rom. 11 in a supersessionist manner" (Kinzer, 222). See also Douglas Harink, *Paul among the Postliberals: Pauline Theology beyond Christendom and Modernity* (Grand Rapids, MI: Brazos, 2003). Harink is sympathetic to Messianic Judaism's account of Pauline theology: "Paul nowhere suggests that *Jews* should reject their Torah observance, and in fact seems to assume that they would and should remain committed to it (1 Cor. 7.17–20; cf. Gal. 5.3; Acts 21.17–24)" (219).

[140] R. Kendall Soulen, *The God of Israel and Christian Theology* (Minneapolis, MN: Fortress Press, 1996), 166; quoted in Kinzer, *Postmissionary Messianic Judaism*, 222.

[141] Kinzer here cites Richard Hays, *Echoes of Scripture in the Letters of Paul* (New Haven, CT: Yale University Press, 1989), 61. As Kinzer summarizes Hays's position, Hays "looks at Rom. 11.21 in light of Rom. 8.32 and concludes that, for Paul, Israel's no *to* Yeshua can properly be viewed as a form of participation *in* Yeshua!" (Kinzer, 223). Kinzer recognizes, "This is not the only way that Paul looks at Israel's no. Like other New Testament authors, Paul also believes that the leaders of the Jewish people in his day are culpable for failing to accept Yeshua. However, the more positive appraisal of Israel's no has special significance when seen in the context of later history" (224).

[142] Kinzer, *Postmissionary Messianic Judaism*, 225.

[143] With regard to the connection between the innocent suffering of the Jewish people in the Holocaust and the innocent suffering of Christ on the Cross, Kinzer also cites Richard John Neuhaus, Clemens Thoma, and Thomas Torrance. Kinzer makes clear, however, that he is not suggesting "that the Holocaust was a divinely orchestrated opportunity for Israel to participate in Yeshua's sacrifice. Nor am I suggesting that the Jewish people have lived and suffered blamelessly through the centuries" (230, fn. 42).

[144] Kinzer, *Postmissionary Messianic Judaism*, 233. Kinzer observes, "The Second Vatican Council appears to have had some inkling of these truths. The fourth

paragraph of *Nostra Aetate*, which deals with the Jewish people, begins in this way: 'Sounding the depths of the mystery which is the church, this sacred Council remembers the spiritual ties which link the people of the New Covenant to the stock of Abraham.' Pope John Paul II finds this introduction to be particularly significant: 'The Church of Christ discovers her "bond" with Judaism by "searching into her own mystery." The Jewish religion is not "extrinsic" to us, but in a certain way is "intrinsic" to our own religion'" (Kinzer, 233, quoting John Paul II, *Spiritual Pilgrimage* [New York: Crossroad, 1995], 63).

[145] Novak, "What Does Edith Stein Mean for Jews?," 166.

[146] Ibid., 164.

[147] Novak, "Avoiding Charges of Legalism and Antinomianism in Jewish-Christian Dialogue," 41. As Novak puts it, "If Christianity does not regard itself as going beyond Judaism, why should Christians not become Jews?" (Novak, "What Does Edith Stein Mean for Jews?," 164).

[148] Novak, "What Does Edith Stein Mean for Jews?," 164.

[149] Novak, "Avoiding Charges of Legalism and Antinomianism in Jewish-Christian Dialogue," 41, fn. 36.

[150] Novak, "What Does Edith Stein Mean for Jews?," 160. Most Christians, Novak observes, do not understand the church "as a society into which like-minded persons associate in order to subsequently share in common what they have already experienced as individual believers. In the covenant, one hears the voice of God and responds to it only when already within the community." He goes on to say, "That is why the key Jewish and Christian doctrine of identity is election. . . . God chooses us; we do not choose God, at least originally. That election is either by natural birth or by the rebirth of conversion, which is very much like adoption. We only can confirm or deny the elected community into which, as one former Christian philosopher put it, we have 'been thrown'" (160–61). One's individual response of faith cannot be separated from the community's response: "The communal *where* one hears the voice of God is the necessary condition of *how* one hears it and *what* it concretely says to one" (160).

[151] Novak, "When Jews Are Christians," 220–21.

[152] As noted above, Novak speaks for the great majority of the rabbinic community in saying that accepting Jesus as the Messiah cannot, at this time in history, be separated from the church's doctrinal formulations about the Messiah (e.g., Incarnation and Trinity). Nor can faith in the Messiah be separated from the New Testament's sacramental practices, among them baptism and the Eucharist.

[153] Nicholas Boyle, *Who Are We Now? Christian Humanism and the Global Market from Hegel to Heaney* (Notre Dame, IN: University of Notre Dame Press, 1998), 6.

Chapter 2

[1] Portions of this chapter appeared, in a much earlier form, in my "Reclaiming God's Providence: John Paul II, Maimonides, and Aquinas," in *John Paul II and the Jewish People*, ed. David G. Dalin and Matthew Levering (Lanham, MD: Rowman & Littlefield, 2008), 95–112.

2. David Novak, *Jewish-Christian Dialogue: A Jewish Justification* (Oxford: Oxford University Press, 1989), 141.
3. John Paul II, *Memory and Identity: Conversations at the Dawn of a Millennium* (New York: Rizzoli, 2005), 12. John Paul continues, "I believe that a more careful study of this question could lead us beyond the Cartesian watershed. If we wish to speak rationally about good and evil, we have to return to Saint Thomas Aquinas, that is, to the philosophy of being. With the phenomenological method, for example, we can study experiences of morality, religion, or simply what it is to be human, and draw from them a significant enrichment of our knowledge. Yet we must not forget that all these analyses implicitly presuppose the reality of the Absolute Being and also the reality of being human, that is, being a creature. If we do not set out from such 'realist' presuppositions, we end up in a vacuum" (12). Cf. his remarks at the Yad Vashem Holocaust Memorial in Jerusalem on March 23, 2000: "How could man have such utter contempt for man? Because he had reached the point of contempt for God. Only a godless ideology could plan and carry out the extermination of a whole people" (*John Paul II in the Holy Land: In His Own Words*, eds. Lawrence Boadt, C.S.P. and Kevin di Camillo [New York: Paulist Press, 2005], 99–100).
4. Russell Hittinger, *The First Grace: Rediscovering the Natural Law in a Post-Christian World* (Wilmington, DE: ISI Books, 2003), xi–xii. For further discussion, in dialogue with John Paul II's encyclicals, see Hittinger's brilliant "Human Nature and States of Nature in John Paul II's Theological Anthropology," in *Human Nature in Its Wholeness: A Roman Catholic Perspective*, eds. Daniel N. Robinson, Gladys M. Sweeney, and Richard Gill, L.C. (Washington, D.C.: Catholic University of America Press, 2006), 9–33.
5. Karol Wojtyla, "One Tree," in *The Place Within: The Poetry of Pope John Paul II*, trans. Jerzy Peterkiewicz (New York: Random House, 1982), 116. For further discussion of Wojtyla/John Paul's poetry, as well as a superb exegetical and theological exploration of the meaning of the land of Israel in Scripture, see Gregory Vall, "'Man Is the Land': The Sacramentality of the Land of Israel," in *John Paul II and the Jewish People*, 131–67. Thanks to Piotr Lichacz, O.P., for checking for accuracy the English translations of Wojtyla/John Paul's poetry.
6. Wojtyla, "One Tree," in *The Place Within*, 116.
7. Ibid.
8. Wojtyla, "Identities," in *The Place Within*, 114–115.
9. Ibid., 115.
10. Ibid., 114.
11. Ibid.
12. Ibid., 115.
13. Wojtyla, "The Desert of Judea," in *The Place Within*, 113.
14. Wojtyla, "The Place Within," in *The Place Within*, 118.
15. Wojtyla, "Mount of Olives," in *The Place Within*, 111.
16. John Paul II, "A Hill in the Land of Moriah," in *The Poetry of John Paul II. Roman Triptych: Meditations*, trans. Jerzy Peterkiewicz (Washington, D.C.: United States Conference of Catholic Bishops, 2003), 35.
17. Ibid.
18. Novak, *Talking with Christians: Musings of a Jewish Theologian* (Grand Rapids, MI: Eerdmans, 2005), xii.

[19] Novak, *Jewish-Christian Dialogue*, 15.

[20] Ibid., 21.

[21] Ibid. Novak comments pungently, "Because these exercises are so basically artificial, they are most often nothing more than the endorsement of the political and cultural status quo of those who have come together to participate in them. They are little different from those innocuous invocations and benedictions that have become de rigueur at public functions in America, from the inauguration of presidents to high-school graduations. Because they are so conformist in both substance and tone, these exercises lack the moral dimension found in Judaism and Christianity, namely the awareness of God, who commands his people and judges them. Such services call to mind that the prophetic critique of ancient worship was that it had reduced God to the level of a mere endorser of the people's own values and had ceased to emphasize God's radical demands" (21).

[22] Ibid. Novak remarks elsewhere that "the recognition of commonalities in some ways must be more analogous than identical. These analogies are more in the area of cult and ritual, what the Jewish tradition calls the area 'between humans and God,' that is, those acts like prayer and worship which have God as their direct object. Here Jews and Christians cannot develop a common life together without sliding into capitulation of one side to the other or into syncretism. Nevertheless, we Jews and Christians can still learn a great deal from each other's 'religious' beliefs and practices. That goes far beyond the discovery of 'interesting' similarities and differences between Judaism and Christianity, something that could be the case between any two religions or philosophies. Instead, we can learn much from each other, even up to the point of empathy, because our religious ways of life are both developments of God's covenant with Israel. Worshiping the same God as we do, and reading the same Book (*biblos*) as we do, it is inevitable that our religious ways of life are often parallel. Indeed, throughout our historical interaction, Christians have learned significant things from Jewish piety, and Jews have learned significant things from Christian piety" (Novak, "Avoiding Charges of Legalism and Antinomianism in Jewish-Christian Dialogue," in *Talking with Christians*, 26–45, at 44–45). Novak is well aware that the Old Testament (especially the Catholic Old Testament) and the Hebrew Bible have differences, a point which Jon Levenson emphasizes in "Is Brueggemann Really a Pluralist?," *Harvard Theological Review* 93 (2000): 274–75; for some of the broader issues see Levenson, *The Hebrew Bible, the Old Testament, and Historical Criticism* (Louisville, KY: Westminster/John Knox Press, 1993).

[23] Novak, *Jewish-Christian Dialogue*, 15.

[24] Ibid., 16.

[25] Ibid.

[26] Ibid.

[27] Ibid., 18.

[28] Novak locates Paul and Jesus firmly within Israel: "Paul was not interested in founding a new religion but wanted to broaden the definition of Judaism itself in order to make those who had accepted the Messiahship of Jesus as 'olive shoots grafted on to the tree' of Israel. Finally, as for Jesus wanting to found a religion for the gentiles [the view of Rabbi Jacob Emden, d. 1776], the Gospels report that he was reluctant to deal with them at all" (*Jewish-Christian Dialogue*, 117).

[29] For discussion of Paul's theology of Israel, see J. Ross Wagner, *Heralds of the Good News: Isaiah and Paul in Concert in the Letter to the Romans* (Leiden: Brill, 2003); more controversially Francis Watson, *Paul and the Hermeneutics of Faith* (New York: T & T Clark International, 2004).

[30] Jacob Neusner, *A Rabbi Talks with Jesus: An Intermillennial, Interfaith Exchange* (New York: Doubleday, 1993), xii. Neusner seeks to go beyond Jewish-Christian dialogue that sets the truth question to the side. See also Jacob Neusner and Bruce D. Chilton, *The Intellectual Foundations of Christian and Jewish Discourse: The Philosophy of Religious Argument* (London: Routledge, 1997).

[31] Novak, *Jewish-Christian Dialogue*, 16.

[32] Ibid., 17. As Novak rightly points out, "If . . . all revelations are equally related to the truth, then clearly one cannot take an existential stand on the basis of any one of them to the exclusion of all the others. Rather, one can only stand on the agnosticism common to all. At this point, revelation loses its religious authority" (ibid., 18).

[33] Ibid.

[34] Ibid., 10.

[35] Ibid., 12.

[36] Ibid.

[37] Ibid., 13. See for a contemporary instance of this loathing of monotheism, Regina M. Schwartz, *The Curse of Cain: The Violent Legacy of Monotheism* (Chicago, IL: University of Chicago Press, 1997).

[38] Novak, *Jewish-Christian Dialogue*, 13.

[39] From Wojtyla's poems "Identities," "The Desert of Judea," and "Mount of Olives" translated in *The Place Within*, 115, 113, and 111; from John Paul II's poem "A Hill in the Land of Moriah" translated in *The Poetry of John Paul II. Roman Triptych: Meditations*, 35.

[40] Novak, *Jewish-Christian Dialogue*, 114. Novak remarks, "I use these terms rather than the more usual *universalism* and *particularism* because they are more elemental, and therefore their use entails less philosophical prejudice than the familiar universal-particular dichotomy. In reality, of course, the relationship is between the more-singular and the more-general; no real singularity is without some generality, and no real generality is without some singularity" (115).

[41] Ibid., 115.

[42] Ibid., 118. Novak comments that Philo adopts this approach, and he also places in this group the modern "theology of those Jewish thinkers who were heavily influenced by Kantian universalism, especially Hermann Cohen (d. 1918) and Leo Baeck (d. 1956)" (118).

[43] Ibid., 124.

[44] Ibid., 125. For Maimonides, says Novak, "The very purpose (telos) of Noahide law, then, is to become the complete Torah" (126). Since Christians misinterpreted the Torah, sincere "Christian students of Scripture are potential Jews whose religious actualization is being facilitated by their Jewish teachers" (ibid.). It follows that "Maimonides can be seen as advocating at least covert proselytizing of those Christian scholars interested in the true—which, for him, was the philosophically determined—interpretation of Scripture" (ibid.).

[45] See ibid., 127.

46 Ibid., 129.
47 See also the *Catechism of the Catholic Church*, §§839–40.
48 Novak eschews the topics of "the Incarnation, the Trinity, or Christian ecclesiology" on the grounds that "[s]uch topics are not the business of a Jewish theologian to discuss critically" (Novak, *Talking with Christians*, xii). In Novak's view, the deepest aspects of "the religious life of each faith community" cannot be known to outsiders, since these deepest aspects belong to a lifetime of participation in a set of beliefs and practices. Novak states that "their true presence can be directly understood only within the total context of singular faith" (*Jewish-Christian Dialogue*, 140). Even so, I would note that Christians and Jews can discuss such matters (the Incarnation, the Trinity, Christian ecclesiology) in a manner that generates deeper understanding both of Christianity and of Judaism. Jacob Neusner's *A Rabbi Talks to Jesus*, Neusner's many coauthored books with Bruce D. Chilton, and Michael Wyschogrod's *The Body of Faith* demonstrate the value of such conversations.
49 Novak, *Jewish-Christian Dialogue*, 130.
50 Ibid.
51 Ibid., 133.
52 Ibid., 135.
53 Ibid., 138.
54 Novak, *Jewish-Christian Dialogue*, 138.
55 Ibid., 17.
56 Ibid., 138.
57 Novak, *Jewish-Christian Dialogue*, 141–42.
58 I–II, q. 99, a. 1, ad 2.
59 I–II, q. 98, a. 1.
60 Ibid., 144.
61 Ibid., 146.
62 Ibid., 147.
63 Ibid., 155.
64 Pope John Paul II, *Memory and Identity: Conversations at the Dawn of a Millennium* (New York: Rizzoli, 2005), 12. Unlike John Paul, Novak fears that Aquinas's five ways set the order of creation in opposition to Revelation: see Novak, "Are Philosophical Proofs of the Existence of God Theologically Meaningful?," in *Talking with Christians*, 247–59, at 252. Novak holds that certain proofs of the existence of God "are theologically meaningful statements" (247–48), but only "if one reinterprets them within the context of theology and abandons the hope that they are or can ever be philosophically convincing" (248). As he puts it, "The classical proofs of the existence of God are theologically meaningful if they are understood as statements of the ontological conditions and postulates of revelation" (259). It seems to me that more fully engaging the distinction between natural and supernatural relationship to God would allay Novak's concerns.
65 For discussion of Maimonides's understanding of providence in relation to the Book of Job, see Robert Eisen, *The Book of Job in Medieval Jewish Philosophy* (Oxford: Oxford University Press, 2004), 43–77; David B. Burrell, C.S.C., *Faith and Freedom: An Interfaith Perspective* (Oxford: Blackwell, 2004), chapter 4: "Maimonides, Aquinas, and Gersonides on Providence and Evil"; Martin D. Yaffe, "Providence

in Medieval Aristotelianism: Moses Maimonides and Thomas Aquinas on the Book of Job," *Hebrew Studies* 20–21 (1979–80): 62–74; Idit Dobbs-Weinstein, "Medieval Biblical Commentary and Philosophical Inquiry as Exemplified in the Thought of Moses Maimonides and St. Thomas Aquinas," in *Moses Maimonides and His Time*, ed. Eric L. Ormsby (Washington, D.C.: Catholic University of America Press, 1989), 101–20.

66. See Moses Maimonides, *The Guide of the Perplexed*, trans. Shlomo Pines (Chicago, IL: University of Chicago Press, 1963), 461 (III, ch. 16).

67. Ibid., 462. Novak argues that "the relationship [between God and human beings] Maimonides constitutes is more than anything else a relation *to* a God who seems to closely resemble the God of Aristotle. It is a relation where only God and not man is the object of love. All concern is in one direction: from man to God. Maimonides in no way ever attempts to constitute a truly responsive role for God. There is no real reciprocity here. But the covenant is surely characterized by constant transaction between God and Israel, with that activity being mutual" (Novak, *Natural Law in Judaism* [Cambridge: Cambridge University Press, 1998], 135). At least as regards God's knowledge, Maimonides's God is not the God of Aristotle.

68. Ibid., 466 (III, ch. 17).

69. On the "Ashariyah" see Daniel Gimaret, *La doctrine d'al Ash'ari* (Paris: Cerf, 1990). See also the introduction to the Ash'aris and the Mu'tazilis provided by Marshall G.S. Hodgson's *The Venture of Islam: Conscience and History in a World Civilization*, vol. 2: *The Expansion of Islam in the Middle Periods* (Chicago, IL: University of Chicago Press, 1974), 169–79, 316–25.

70. Maimonides, *The Guide of the Perplexed*, 468 (III, ch. 17).

71. Cf. Lenn E. Goodman, "Maimonides' Responses to Sa'adya Gaon's Theodicy and Their Islamic Backgrounds," in *Studies in Islamic and Judaic Traditions II*, ed. William M. Brinner and Stephen D. Ricks (Atlanta, GA: Scholars Press, 1989), 3–22.

72. Maimonides, *The Guide of the Perplexed*, 471 (III, ch. 17).

73. Regarding God's universal providence over human beings he adduces Ps. 33.15, Jer. 32.19, and Job 32.21 (ibid., 472).

74. Leo Strauss holds that for Maimonides "the doctrine of divine reward and punishment" is an exoteric doctrine that is not true but that is nonetheless politically necessary: see Strauss, "The Place of the Doctrine of Providence according to Maimonides," trans. Gabriel Bartlett and Svetozar Minkov, *Review of Metaphysics* 57 (2004): 537–49, at 545. See also Aviezer Ravitzky, "Samuel Ibn Tibbon and the Esoteric Character of *The Guide of the Perplexed*," *AJS Review* 6 (1981): 87–123; Alvin J. Reines, "Maimonides' Concepts of Providence and Theodicy," *Hebrew Union College Annual* 43 (1972): 169–205. For a reading of Maimonides on providence that ably challenges the esotericist position, see Charles M. Raffel, "Providence as Consequent upon the Intellect: Maimonides' Theory of Providence," *AJS Review* 12 (1987): 25–71.

75. Maimonides, *The Guide of the Perplexed*, 472 (III, ch. 17).

76. Ibid., 475 (III, ch. 18).

77. Ibid., 474 (III, ch. 17). Maimonides states that "when any human individual has obtained, because of the disposition of his matter and his training, a greater portion of this overflow than others, providence will of necessity watch more

carefully over him than over others" (475 [III, ch. 18]). For discussion see Raffel, "Providence as Consequent upon the Intellect," 51–71. See also Harry Blumberg, "The Problem of Immortality in Avicenna, Maimonides and St. Thomas Aquinas," in *Harry Austryn Wolfson: Jubilee Volume on the Occasion of His Seventy-Fifth Birthday*, English Section, vol. 1 (Jerusalem: American Academy for Jewish Research, 1965), 165–85; C. Touati, "Les deux theories de Maïmonide sur la providence," in *Studies in Jewish Religious and Intellectual History*, ed. Siegfried Stein and Raphael Loewe (Tuscaloosa, AL: University of Alabama Press, 1979), 331–43; Jon D. Levenson, *Resurrection and the Restoration of Israel: The Ultimate Victory of the God of Life* (New Haven, CT: Yale University Press, 2006), 18–20.

[78] Maimonides, *The Guide of the Perplexed*, 470 (III, ch. 17).

[79] Maimonides states, "For it is this measure of the overflow of the divine intellect that makes the prophets speak, guides the actions of righteous men, and perfects the knowledge of excellent men with regard to what they know" (ibid., 475 [III, ch. 18]). Davidson notes that Maimonides makes an exception for Moses (Herbert A. Davidson, *Moses Maimonides* [New York, NY: Oxford University Press, 2005], 372).

[80] See Maimonides, *The Guide of the Perplexed*, 475 (III, ch. 18).

[81] Ibid., 476.

[82] Ibid., 475–76.

[83] Cf. Shlomo Pines, "Spinoza's *Tractatus Theologico-Politicus*, Maimonides and Kant," in *Further Studies in Philosophy*, ed. Ora Segal (Jerusalem: The Magnes Press, 1968), 3–54.

[84] Novak, however, elsewhere remarks regarding God's knowledge: "About God's knowledge and concern, 'could you find the limit (*ad takhlit*) of the Self-Sufficient One (*shadday*)' (Job 11.7)? . . . Only God sees the whole" (Novak, *The Election of Israel*, [Cambridge: Cambridge University Press, 1995], 142).

[85] Aquinas criticizes Maimonides's account on these grounds. See I, q. 22, a. 2.

[86] Novak, "Maimonides and Aquinas on Natural Law," in his *Talking with Christians: Musings of a Jewish Theologian* (Grand Rapids, MI: Eerdmans, 2005), 67–88, at 69.

[87] Ibid., 71.

[88] Wojtyla, "Identities," 114.

[89] Wojtyla, "The Desert of Judea," 113.

Chapter 3

[1] A version of this chapter appeared as "The *Imago Dei* in David Novak and Thomas Aquinas: A Jewish-Christian Dialogue," *The Thomist* 72 (2008): 259–311.

[2] See Marc Cardinal Ouellet, *Divine Likeness: Toward a Trinitarian Anthropology of the Family*, trans. Philip Milligan and Linda M. Cicone (Grand Rapids, MI: Eerdmans, 2006). Regarding Gen. 1.26–27 Ouellet observes that "current exegesis is moving beyond two extremes. On the one hand, one finds the purely spiritual interpretation—which is the commonly held opinion of Christian exegesis since Philo—that the notion of image of God concerns only the spiritual dimension of man, allowing him to have dominion over animals and things. On the other hand, there is the purely material interpretation of the image: the fact that the Hebrew term

selem (sculpture, statue) would bring us back to the bodily configuration proper to man, that is, his vertical posture. The majority of exegetes can currently be found between these two opinions" (27). Cf. the biblical scholar Richard Middleton's juxtaposition of "a metaphysical, substantialistic analogy" (the image of God as rooted in human rationality) with "a dynamic, relational notion of the image as ethical conformity or obedient response to God" (the latter being the position of Karl Barth): Middleton, *The Liberating Image: The* Imago Dei *in Genesis 1* (Grand Rapids, MI: Brazos, 2005), 20.

[3] See, for example, Novak, *Natural Law in Judaism* (Cambridge: Cambridge University Press, 1998), chs. 4–5; Novak, *Jewish-Christian Dialogue: A Jewish Justification* (Oxford: Oxford University Press, 1989), 125, 139, 154; Novak, *Covenantal Rights: A Study in Jewish Political Theory* (Cambridge: Cambridge University Press, 2000), 53. As he puts it in *Jewish-Christian Dialogue*, "in Scripture, the Lord God is the creator of this cosmic order, and as creator he transcends its limits. Holiness (*qedushah*) is not part of the cosmic order. Being God's own relational capacity with man, it, too, transcends that order. Those addressed by God's covenant also transcend therein the limits of that order: 'You shall be holy because I the Lord your God am holy' (Lev. 19.2). The relationship, on the human side, only presupposes the cosmic order for its formal structure, but it transcends it in its substantial being-with-God" (154).

[4] Novak, *Jewish-Christian Dialogue*, 139. Novak emphasizes that Maimonides also affirms that "we can be intelligently decent without being oriented to the realm of the transcendent" (139).

[5] Ibid.

[6] Ibid.

[7] Ibid.

[8] Ibid., 141. As Novak shows earlier, Maimonides argues that Christian theology is "polytheistic" and therefore "presupposes a material element in God," in contrast to Islam (60). Yet Maimonides appreciates that Christians, unlike Muslims, have retained the Hebrew Bible. Maimonides teaches, "It is permitted to teach the commandments to Christians [*notzrim*] and to draw them to our religion, but this is not permitted with Muslims because of what is known to you about their belief that this Torah is not divine revelation [*'aynah min ha-Shamayim*] . . . but the uncircumcised ones [Christians] believe that the version [*nosah*] of the Torah has not changed, only they interpret it with their faulty exegesis . . . . But when the Scriptural texts shall be interpreted with correct exegesis [*'al ha-perush ha-nakhon*], it is possible that they shall return to what is best [*'el ha-mutab*] . . . .. There is nothing that they shall find in their Scriptures that differs from ours" (Maimonides, *Teshubot Ha-Rambam*, no. 149, ed. Blau [Jerusalem: 1960], vol. 1, 284–85; quoted in Novak, *Jewish-Christian Dialogue*, 64). For Maimonides on Islam see also Novak, "The Treatment of Islam and Muslims in the Legal Writings of Maimonides," in *Studies in Islamic and Judaic Traditions*, ed. W.M. Brinner and S.D. Ricks (Atlanta, GA: 1986), 233–50.

[9] Novak, *Jewish-Christian Dialogue*, 141.

[10] Novak, *Covenantal Rights*, 39.

[11] Ibid., 40.

[12] Novak, *Natural Law in Judaism*, 43. He cites Prov. 21.30, "There is no wisdom, no understanding, and no counsel that can stand against the Lord." In Novak's view,

Hugo Grotius and other classical liberal theorists have undercut God's sovereignty by positing a "justice" that stands above God.

[13] Novak, *Covenantal Rights*, 39. Novak holds that "fear" displaces "terror" when one experiences being commanded by God. He states, "Whereas the terror we experience in the face of the power of God takes away the ground from under us and thus leaves us no space around us to act, the fear we experience in the observance of the negative commandment of God demarcates the ground under us and a space around us in which to act" (46).

[14] Ibid., 45, 46.

[15] Novak, *Natural Law in Judaism*, 48. Commenting on Gen. 20.11, where Abraham says, "There is no fear of God at all in this place," Novak remarks, "'Fear of God' means the elementary decency that requires human beings to restrain their desires out of fear/respect for the rights of other humans, in this case the right to inviolable marriage, because of the way God has created humans and their dignity. Restraint is called for in the name of a law higher than that of human making when desire leads to unjustified violence of any kind" (48). See also *Covenantal Rights*, 46.

[16] Novak, *Natural Law in Judaism*, 54.

[17] Ibid., 55.

[18] Novak, *Covenantal Rights*, 40. For a Christian appropriation of this view, indebted to Jewish mysticism, see Olivier Clément, *You Are Peter: An Orthodox Theologian's Reflection on the Exercise of Papal Primacy*, trans. M.S. Laird (French 1997; New York: New City Press, 2003), 102–3. Divine action, however, occurs at an entirely different metaphysical level than does human action. If so, then (*pace* Novak and Clément) God does not need to restrain his freedom or power so that human beings might exercise their own.

[19] Novak, *Covenantal Rights*, 40.

[20] Ibid. The image of God, then, is already a covenantal reality. Novak's connection of the image of God with covenant helps to answer Michael Walzer's remark that "after those early verses of Genesis, it [the image of God] is never mentioned or referred to again in the Bible" (Walzer, "Morality and Politics in the Work of Michael Wyschogrod," *Modern Theology* 22 [2006]: 687–92, at 691). Walzer argues that the image of God "does serve to ground much of our common morality. . . . It provides a theological basis for sentiments that we think, independently of theology, we ought to have. It also lends itself to a particular political appropriation—by the liberal left, as in the civil rights speeches of Martin Luther King. It supports an egalitarian politics. I would be inclined to say that this is actually the reason for its power" (691). What Walzer misses is the Bible's consistent point that humans are not autonomous vis-à-vis God: they are his image and owe covenantal obligations to him. For its part, Novak's statement should take into account that God also addresses angels in Scripture.

[21] Novak, *Natural Law in Judaism*, 31. Similarly Jon D. Levenson writes that "it has often been observed, mostly by liberal apologists for Judaism, that the Christian doctrine of original sin finds scant resonance in Jewish tradition. If the point is that Judaism is optimistic about human nature, regarding the impulse to sin as unrooted in our innate constitution, then the observation is altogether in error and fails to reckon not only with the theological anthropology of the Hebrew Bible but also with the pervasive rabbinic idea of the *yetzer ha-ra*',

or 'evil inclination.' This is the inborn force within all of us that requires us to engage in a lifelong struggle if we are to do the right thing." See Levenson, "Did God Forgive Adam? An Exercise in Comparative Midrash," in *Jews and Christians: People of God*, ed. Carl E. Braaten and Robert W. Jenson (Grand Rapids, MI: Eerdmans, 2003), 148–70, at 164. Compare Harold Bloom's comment in his *Jesus and Yahweh: The Names Divine* (New York: Riverhead Books, 2005), 148: "I begin by dismissing St. Paul's and St. Augustine's apologies for God: in Adam's fall, we sinned all. The great Sages of the Talmud held no such barbaric doctrine, a Hellenic importation from the myth of the fire-bringer Prometheus tormented by a sadistic Zeus, and ultimately the Orphic shamanistic story of the revenge of Dionysius upon those who first had torn apart and devoured that infant god."

[22] Novak, *Natural Law in Judaism*, 31–32.

[23] Ibid., 32.

[24] Novak, *Covenantal Rights*, 40. Novak's position is indebted to that of Maimonides: see Avital Wohlman, "La signification de la désobéissance d'Adam selon les trois monothéismes," *Revue Thomiste* 108 (2008): 573–98, at 591.

[25] Novak, *Natural Law in Judaism*, 32.

[26] This does not mean that the first human beings could have avoided death without God upholding them in a unique way, and neither does it mean that human beings become "the exception to creation" and "blur the difference between God and creation" (Novak, *Covenantal Rights*, 38). Novak asks, "Were humans immortal, being born without having to die, could they not even assume that they have succeeded God in the order of things?" (39). The answer, I think, is no. Immortality does not "blur the difference between God and creation," since God's eternity is infinitely distinct from and superior to created immortality. For John Paul II's interpretation of Gen. 2.17, see *Veritatis Splendor* §41. See also Russell Hittinger's discussion of this section of *Veritatis Splendor* in Hittinger's *The First Grace: Rediscovering the Natural Law in a Post-Christian World* (Wilmington, DE: ISI Books, 2003), 40–46.

[27] Novak, *Natural Law in Judaism*, 42, fn. 54.

[28] Ibid.

[29] Ibid., 47.

[30] Ibid., 44. Novak comments, "But is this connection of freedom and justice the same for God as it is for humans? To answer 'yes,' as liberal theology basically does, is to land ourselves in a dead-end . . . . Only when divine freedom is seen as being different from human freedom, can we then see that God is related to justice differently than humans are related to it."

[31] Ibid., 45. He points out in this context that "Kantian autonomy is a substitution of human will for God's will."

[32] Ibid., 47. It would be better to say that in creating the order of finite beings, God orders finite beings to the ultimate end of his goodness, and he owes it to his own goodness that his (free, covenantal, historical) plan not fail in execution.

[33] Ibid., 46.

[34] Ibid., 47.

[35] Ibid., 135. See also Novak, *Covenantal Rights*, 53. As Novak knows, the unity of divine wisdom and divine will characterizes Maimonides's theology. Indeed, Novak himself may not intend to go as far as he does in presenting divine freedom

as unconditioned by the divine wisdom or by the divine ordination for creation. In *Natural Law in Judaism*, after rightly observing that human reason is the precondition of divine revelation, he approvingly cites Maimonides: "For Maimonides, this is so because both the Torah and the world are creations of the same divine wisdom. That is why the science (*madda*) of the Torah and the *scientia* of the world can employ the same methods. Both are the result of a creative word," 30. Novak's views might be interestingly compared with Walter J. Houston, "The Character of YHWH and the Ethics of the Old Testament: Is *Imitatio Dei* Appropriate?" *Journal of Theological Studies* 58 (2007): 1–25. See also Martin Buber, "*Imitatio Dei*," in *Israel and the World* (New York: Schocken, 1948), 66–77.

[36] Novak, *Natural Law in Judaism*, 135.

[37] Ibid. Novak observes that "there is a trend in rabbinic teaching, which is considerably developed in kabbalistic theology, that sees what Israel does *with* God as also being *for* God as well" (135).

[38] Ibid., 43.

[39] Novak, *Covenantal Rights*, 41.

[40] Ibid.

[41] Ibid.

[42] Ibid.

[43] Ibid.

[44] Ibid. Novak is indebted to Hume's way of posing the question of ethics: "In the true order of the created world, human action *for* ('ought') precedes human description *of* ('is')" (41). Yet, when explaining why murder is always wrong, Novak writes, "Here we are not deriving an *ought* from an *is*, at least not in the usual sense. Instead, the very '*is*-ness' or being or presence-in-the-world of that other person is itself an *ought* (which twentieth-century French-Jewish philosopher Emmanuel Levinas described with great phenomenological insight)" (Novak, *The Sanctity of Human Life* [Washington, D.C.: Georgetown University Press, 2007], 38). This insight goes a long way toward overturning the faulty logic of Hume's claim. Moreover, Novak does not think that the created order is devoid of moral weight: "We humans not only owe God everything for having made us, but more directly and positively we owe God everything for enabling us to know how to live according to our own nature and in consistency with the nature of the rest of creation" (Novak, *Covenantal Rights*, 42). In *Natural Law in Judaism*, Novak remarks that "human sociality presupposes a physical order surrounding it, upon which it can depend for its own continuity. But humans discover their own essential order, their own essential law, from their own social experience. Only thereafter do they discover the order of the nonhuman realm by analogy. Both realms are subject to God's law, but humans must freely accept that law upon themselves, unlike the physical realm onto which that order is imposed by determination" (38–39).

[45] Novak, *Covenantal Rights*, 41.

[46] Ibid., 42.

[47] Ibid., 43. Novak explains that "the difference between active subjects and passive objects of these commandments is one of degree rather than one of kind. Even the most active persons need to be passively dependent at times and thus to be the objects of the concern others are commanded (*mitsvah*) to show them in

imitation of God. Even the most passive, dependent persons are often able to show some response to the concern of others for them, some form of thankful (even nonverbal) recognition like the way they are to thank God for any benefit" (43).

48. Ibid., 42.
49. Ibid.
50. Ibid., 41. See also *Natural Law in Judaism*, 30.
51. Novak, *Covenantal Rights*, 42.
52. Ibid., 42–43.
53. Novak, *Natural Law in Judaism*, 35.
54. Ibid., 169.
55. Ibid., 168.
56. As Novak puts it, then, "The issue now is anything but academic, as it once might have been. Maximally, this anthropology must be rejected because it has been invoked as grounds for dehumanizing those at the edges of human life in order to kill them. Minimally, this anthropology must be rejected because even when its adherents avoid drawing immoral conclusions from it in practice, they are still unable to reject with adequate reason such conclusions when they are drawn by others" (ibid., 169).
57. For its part, *Covenantal Rights* aims both to set forth "the insights of the Jewish tradition about rights" and to show the value of these insights for "current political discourse in general," including secular discourse (x). Novak observes, however, that "[s]ince this book brings in as many biblical texts as possible, it should be most readily appropriable by Christians, whose view of polity must come from this primary source of their faith in order to be authentic. And, indeed, it has been in the area of ethics and politics (which cannot be separated one from the other) where Judaism and Christianity have the most in common. In fact, one could say that Christianity consciously appropriated Jewish ethical and political teaching without qualification" (x). Cf. Markus Bockmuehl, *Jewish Law in Gentile Churches: Halakhah and the Beginning of Christian Public Ethics* (Grand Rapids, MI: Baker Academic, 2000).
58. Novak, *Natural Law in Judaism*, 170.
59. Ibid.
60. Ibid.
61. Novak, *Covenantal Rights*, 41.
62. Novak, *Natural Law in Judaism*, 171.
63. Ibid.
64. The emphasis on the impossibility of knowing created realities in themselves is, as Novak recognizes, similar to Kant's philosophy. Novak remarks that his understanding of the shadowy constitution of the human "is quite similar in its logic to the way Kant constitutes the relation of phenomena to the mysterious *Ding an sich*, the 'thing-in-itself' that lies behind them and is never subsumed in them" (ibid., 171).
65. Ibid.
66. Ibid., 168.
67. Hittinger, *The First Grace*, 23, quoting Josef Fuchs, *Moral Demands and Personal Obligations*, trans. Brian McNeil (Washington, D.C.: Georgetown University Press, 1993), 157.

[68] Hittinger, *The First Grace*, 24.
[69] Novak, *Natural Law in Judaism*, 172.
[70] Russell Hittinger, "Human Nature and States of Nature in John Paul II's Theological Anthropology," in *Human Nature in Its Wholeness: A Roman Catholic Perspective*, ed. Daniel N. Robinson, Gladys M. Sweeney, and Richard Gill, L.C. (Washington, D.C.: Catholic University of America Press, 2006), 9–33, at 18.
[71] Ibid., 18–19. Following Karol Wojtyła, Hittinger remarks that "the anthropological premises of Vatican II require at least partial intelligibility of the first Adam. For this Adam is the natural reality, and therefore the natural 'sign' of Christian mysteries. So, while it is true that 'without its creator the creature simply disappears' [*Gaudium et Spes* §36], it is also true that deconstruction of the first Adam will cancel the second" (Hittinger, "Human Nature and States of Nature in John Paul II's Theological Anthropology," 23–24). Without the "at least partial intelligibility of the first Adam," it would follow that "Christian anthropology, and all of the social teachings that flow from it, would be a 'sectarian' construction of the indeterminate *humanum*" (24).
[72] Novak, *Natural Law in Judaism*, 171.
[73] Ibid., 172.
[74] Ibid., 173.
[75] Ibid.
[76] Ibid., 172.
[77] Ibid. Novak argues here for the priority of practical reasoning over theoretical. He continues: "That desire is so powerful, so urgent, that we cannot suppress it to wait for confirmation of the reality of its goal, to wait for the truth of the Subject of that concern to be revealed to us" (172–73).
[78] Hittinger, "Human Nature and States of Nature in John Paul II's Theological Anthropology," 18.
[79] Cf. Novak, "Are Philosophical Proofs of the Existence of God Theologically Meaningful?," in *Talking with Christians: Musings of a Jewish Theologian* (Grand Rapids, MI: Eerdmans, 2005), 247–48.
[80] Novak, *Natural Law in Judaism*, 173.
[81] Ibid. The biblical translation is Novak's own. Earlier, with respect to his argument about human desire for God, he quotes Ps. 38.10, "Towards you (*negdekha*) O' Lord is my whole desire (*kol ta'avati*); let not my cry be hidden from you" (ibid.; for the translation of this verse see *Natural Law in Judaism*, 173, fn. 69).
[82] Ibid., 168.
[83] Hittinger, "Human Nature and States of Nature in John Paul II's Theological Anthropology," 30.
[84] Ibid., 24.
[85] As Hittinger writes with respect to *Veritatis Splendor*, "Relying chiefly on St. Thomas, the Pope contends that practical reason is not, *ab initio*, its own norm. The human agent orders himself (or others) to justice by virtue of participating in a received norm" (*The First Grace*, 48). This participation occurs due to the constitution of human reason, not through the volitional reception of a commandment.
[86] Novak, *Natural Law in Judaism*, 168. This does not mean, however, that Aquinas excludes the body entirely. Since the soul is the form of the body, Aquinas holds that the body participates in the soul's imaging of God: see I, q. 93, a. 3. Arguing

against Osiander, John Calvin makes a similar point: see Calvin, *Institutes of the Christian Religion*, trans. Henry Beveridge (Grand Rapids, MI: Eerdmans, 1989), Book I, ch. xv, §3, 162.

[87] See I, q. 93, a. 2. For further discussion of the image of God according to Augustine and Aquinas, see especially Jean-Pierre Torrell, O.P., *Saint Thomas Aquinas*, vol. 2, *Spiritual Master*, trans. Robert Royal (Washington, D.C.: Catholic University of America Press, 2003), 80–100; Servais Pinckaers, O.P., "Ethics and the Image of God," trans. Mary Thomas Noble, O.P., in *The Pinckaers Reader: Renewing Thomistic Moral Theology*, ed. John Berkman and Craig Steven Titus (Washington, D.C.: Catholic University of America Press, 2005), 130–43; Romanus Cessario, O.P., *Christian Faith and the Theological Life* (Washington, D.C.: Catholic University of America Press, 1996), 38–48; Michael Dauphinais, "Loving the Lord Your God: The *Imago Dei* in Saint Thomas Aquinas," *The Thomist* 63 (1999): 241–67; D. Juvenal Merriell, *To the Image of the Trinity: A Study in the Development of Aquinas' Teaching* (Toronto: Pontifical Institute of Medieval Studies, 1990); John P. O'Callaghan, "*Imago Dei*: A Test Case for St. Thomas's Augustinianism," in *Aquinas the Augustinian*, ed. Michael Dauphinais, Barry David, and Matthew Levering (Washington, D.C.: Catholic University of America Press, 2007), 100–44; Brian J. Shanley, O.P., "Aquinas's Exemplar Ethics," *The Thomist* 72 (2008): 345–69.

[88] I, q. 93, a. 5, obj. 3.

[89] I, q. 93, a. 7.

[90] Ibid. For Aquinas's analogous use of the acts of the soul to describe the Trinitarian processions, see I, q. 27.

[91] I, q. 93, a. 8, *sed contra*, quoting *De Trinitate* book XIV, chapter 12.

[92] I–II, q. 100, a. 10.

[93] Aquinas also notes that in every creature there is an ontological "trace of the Trinity." As we have seen, "in rational creatures, possessing intellect and will, there is found the representation of the Trinity by way of image, inasmuch as there is found in them the word conceived, and the love proceeding" (I, q. 45, a. 7).

[94] I, q. 93, a. 5.

[95] I, q. 93, a. 5, obj. 2, quoting Gregory of Nyssa, *De Homin. Opificio*, xvi and John of Damascus, *De Fid. Orth.*, Book II, chapter 12. Robert Grosseteste made a Latin translation of *The Orthodox Faith* in the mid-thirteenth century, and Aquinas would have had access to a full translation. Using the critical Greek edition in Migne's *Patrologia*, Frederic Chase translates the relevant passage in II.12: "with His own hands He created *man* after His own image and likeness from the visible and invisible natures. From the earth He formed his body and by His own inbreathing gave him a rational and understanding soul, which last we say is the divine image—for 'according to His image' means the intellect and free will, while the 'according to His likeness' means such likeness in virtue as is possible" (St. John of Damascus, *The Orthodox Faith*, in St. John of Damascus, *Writings*, trans. Frederic H. Chase, Jr. [Washington, D.C.: Catholic University of America Press, 1958], 234–35). See also *The Orthodox Faith*, Book III, chapter 14: "if man has been made after the image of the blessed and supersubstantial Godhead, then, since the divine nature is naturally free and volitive, man as its image is also free and volitive by nature. For the Fathers have defined free will as volition" (299).

96 Traces represent "only the causality of the cause, but not its form"; images "represent the cause as regards the similitude of the form, as fire generated represents fire generating" (I, q. 45, a. 7). Human goodness and free will are a likeness not only of God's causality but also, however distant, of God's being.
97 I, q. 5, a. 2, ad 1.
98 I, q. 5, a. 5.
99 I, q. 44, a. 4, ad 3. For further metaphysical precisions, see I, q. 6, a. 4 and I, q. 4, a. 3. In Aquinas's view the very existence of more or less goodness (in the ontological sense) leads to the conclusion that a divine cause of goodness must exist (I, q. 2, a. 3).
100 I, q. 77, a. 2, ad 1.
101 I, q. 19, a. 5.
102 I, q. 19, a. 4.
103 I, q. 19, a. 3.
104 Ibid.
105 Cf. I, q. 19, a. 10. For a discussion of related issues, see Simon Gaine, O.P., *Will There Be Free Will in Heaven? Freedom, Impeccability, and Beatitude* (New York: T & T Clark, 2003).
106 I, q. 82, a. 1, obj. 3.
107 I, q. 82, a. 1, *sed contra*. For Aquinas's extensive treatment of the desire for happiness in relation to human action, see I–II, qq. 1–5.
108 I, q. 82, a. 1.
109 I–II, q. 2, a. 8. For further discussion of the hierarchy of ends constitutive of happiness, see Benedict Ashley, O.P., "Integral Fulfillment According to Germain Grisez," in *The Ashley Reader: Redeeming Reason* (Naples, FL: Sapientia Press, 2006), 225–69.
110 In this communion, divine transcendence serves divine immanence: Pure Act does not need to become less in order to be fully and historically present to human persons. Cf. Thomas Weinandy, O.F.M. Cap., *Does God Suffer?* (Notre Dame, IN: University of Notre Dame Press, 2000), 55–57, 123–27.
111 Cf. I–II, q. 6, a. 1, where Aquinas remarks, "Hence it is that, according to the definitions of Aristotle, Gregory of Nyssa, and Damascene, the voluntary is defined not only as having *a principle within* the agent, but also as implying *knowledge*. Therefore, since man especially knows the end of his work, and moves himself, in his acts especially is the voluntary to be found."
112 See I, q. 6, a. 1, ad 3, and elsewhere.
113 I, q. 93, a. 8.
114 Ibid., *sed contra*. See also I, q. 93, a. 6.
115 Novak, *Natural Law in Judaism*, 169.
116 The Hebrew verb has the sense of "murder," and does not forbid killing in warfare or by the death penalty. For Novak's theological reasoning in favor of the death penalty (with serious qualifications), see Novak, "Can Capital Punishment Ever Be Justified in the Jewish Tradition?" in *Tradition in the Public Square: A David Novak Reader*, 328–44.
117 I, q. 93, a. 7, ad 4.
118 See I–II, q. 54, a. 3.
119 I, q. 77, a. 1.

[120] Ibid.

[121] I, q. 76, a. 1.

[122] I, q. 76, a. 5 (and ad 2); see also I, q. 85, a. 1. Joel B. Green argues that contemporary neuroscience requires a materialist account of the human person—and thus a "relational" or "covenantal" rather than "essentialist" doctrine of the *imago Dei*—because scientists are showing that the brain does what theologians had supposed the spiritual soul to do. See Green, *Body, Soul, and Human Life: The Nature of Humanity in the Bible* (Grand Rapids, MI: Baker Academic, 2008), 63; for his examples of scientific studies see 39–44, 76–87, 115–20.

[123] I, q. 68, a. 12, ad 2.

[124] I, q. 68, a. 12. He observes that if the person has had a lucid interval in which he or she "showed no desire to receive Baptism," then that lack of desire should be respected rather than overruled.

[125] I, q. 68, a. 11, ad 1. As examples, he has in view such persons as Jeremiah and John the Baptist (and, to a different degree, the Virgin Mary).

[126] I–II, q. 110, a. 4.

[127] I–II, q. 49, a. 3, ad 1. Hans S. Reinders, whose position is similar to Novak's on this topic, argues that "Roman Catholic scholars are surely right in their insistence that the potentiality for developing the functions of the human intellect is not to be reduced to their operations. Aristotle entered the debate on the metaphysics of potency with the same view. Even though the existence of a capacity can only be known from its activity, he argued, it does not follow that a capacity only exists when it is used, because prior to the activity there must be a capacity to act. But, despite this ontological differentiation, this capacity to act requires a body that is suitable to its actualization" (Hans S. Reinders, *Receiving the Gift of Friendship: Profound Disability, Theological Anthropology, and Ethics* [Grand Rapids, MI: Eerdmans, 2008], 114). After noting that Catholic doctrine here agrees with Aquinas, Reinders poses what he considers to be an insuperable problem for this anthropology: "some human beings do not have a potential for the activity of reason and will residing in their bodies" (115). But Aquinas does not hinge the presence of a human soul, ordered to union with God, upon the adequate development of the bodily organs. For Reinders, the solution is God's extrinsic claiming of each human being: "Nature cannot provide a firm grounding of what it is that makes our humanity special, nor can reason or history. It follows that, if there is anything significant about our existence, it can only be sustained if it is sustained *extrinsically*—that is, from elsewhere, through the love of God" (39). If the "humanity" of human beings pertains not to something in human beings, but only to the extrinsic claim that God's love makes upon each of us, one wonders whether God's creative gift has become a mere placeholder.

[128] See I–II, q. 51, aa. 1–3.

[129] See I–II, q. 51, a. 4.

[130] For Christian materialist accounts of the human person, see Joel B. Green, *Body, Soul, and Human Life*; Nancey Murphy, *Bodies and Souls, or Spirited Bodies?* (Cambridge: Cambridge University Press, 2006) and Kevin J. Corcoran, *Rethinking Human Nature: A Christian Materialist Alternative to the Soul* (Grand Rapids, MI: Baker Academic, 2006). Green argues that conversion to Christ is "a transformation of conceptual scheme—conceptual, conative, and behavioral (137), but

given this materialist conception one wonders how God draws severely cognitively impaired people into his kingdom. I raise questions for Murphy's position in my review of her book in *National Catholic Bioethics Quarterly* 7 (2007): 635–38. For contemporary accounts of the rational soul, see Robert Sokolowski, "Soul and the Transcendence of the Human Person," in *Christian Faith and Human Understanding: Studies on the Eucharist, Trinity, and the Human Person* (Washington, D.C.: Catholic University of America, 2006), 151–64; Adam G. Cooper, *Life in the Flesh: An Anti-Gnostic Spiritual Philosophy* (Oxford: Oxford University Press, 2008), especially 172–75. For Aquinas's teaching on the human soul, see Gilles Emery, O.P., "The Unity of Man, Body and Soul, in St. Thomas Aquinas," in *Trinity, Church, and the Human Person: Thomistic Essays* (Naples, FL: Sapientia Press, 2007), 209–35. Emery points out that the soul's spiritual nature "does not mean that the soul escapes the creaturely condition, or that it arrogates to itself a divine prerogative, as is sometimes unfortunately thought. If the soul is granted self-subsistence, it is only in virtue of God's creative act, that is, as a gift from the creative wisdom of God" (227).

[131] Novak, *Covenantal Rights*, 41.

[132] Commenting on the relationship between the divine "image" and the divine "likeness" (Gen. 1.26), Aquinas observes that "likeness" can either signify something less than the image or a certain perfection of the image. John Damascene and others understood "likeness" in the latter sense, as a fullness or perfection of the image. See I, q. 93, a. 9.

[133] Novak, *Covenantal Rights*, 41.

[134] Novak, *Natural Law in Judaism*, 168.

[135] Novak, *Covenantal Rights*, 40. Cf. Richard Middleton's "royal-functional interpretation of the image" (Middleton, *The Liberating Image*, 29), to which I will return in the concluding section of this chapter.

[136] Novak, *Covenantal Rights*, 39.

[137] Novak, *Natural Law in Judaism*, 172.

[138] Novak, *Covenantal Rights*, 38–39.

[139] I, q. 93, a. 1.

[140] I, q. 4, a. 3, ad 4. Aquinas comments, "Likeness of creatures to God is not affirmed on account of agreement in form according to the formality of the same genus or species, but solely according to analogy, inasmuch as God is essential being, whereas other things are beings by participation" (I, q. 4, a. 3, ad 3).

[141] I, q. 93, a. 4.

[142] See I, q. 3, a. 1 (especially ad 2), where Aquinas explains why God is not bodily and why the image of God consists in "reason and intelligence."

[143] See A.N. Williams, *The Ground of Union: Deification in Aquinas and Palamas* (Oxford: Oxford University Press, 1999), 96–101.

[144] I, q. 93, a. 4. As Aquinas remarks elsewhere, "The meritorious knowledge and love of God can be in us only by grace. Yet there is a certain natural knowledge and love as seen above (Q. 12, A. 12; Q. 56, A. 3; Q. 60, A. 5). This, too, is natural that the mind, in order to understand God, can make use of reason, in which sense we have already said that the image of God abides ever in the soul; 'whether this image of God be so obsolete,' as it were clouded, 'as almost to amount to nothing,' as in those who have not the use of reason; 'or obscured and disfigured,'

as in sinners; or 'clear and beautiful,' as in the just; as Augustine says (*De Trin.* xiv. 6)" (I, q. 93, a. 8, ad 3).

[145] I, q. 93, a. 4.
[146] Ibid.
[147] Ibid.
[148] Novak, *Covenantal Rights*, 41.
[149] Ibid.
[150] By contrast, Dietrich Bonhoeffer holds that Jesus takes up "the image of man," because the Fall destroys the image of God in human beings. Bonhoeffer states, "Since that day [the Fall], the sons of Adam in their pride have striven to recover the divine image by their own efforts. The more serious and devoted their attempt to regain the lost image and the more proud and convincing their apparent success, the greater their contradiction to God. Their misshapen form, modelled after the god they have invented for themselves, grows more and more like the image of Satan, though they are unaware of it. The divine image, which God in his grace had given to man, is lost for ever on this earth" (Bonhoeffer, *The Cost of Discipleship*, trans. R.H. Fuller, rev. Irmgard Booth [German 1937; New York: Simon & Schuster, 1995], 299). In order to "re-create his image in man," God assumes in Christ "the image and form of fallen man. As man can no longer be like the image of God, God must become like the image of man. But this restoration of the divine image concerns not just a part, but the whole of human nature" (299). Karl Barth takes up and modifies Bonhoeffer's position in Barth's *Church Dogmatics* III/1, pp. 194–97, where he argues that the "image of God" reflects the I-Thou relationship in the Trinity, and thus involves both the capacity to be summoned by God, and the I-Thou relationship in the constitution of human beings as male and female. For discussion see Middleton, *The Liberating Image*, 22–24.
[151] III, q. 3, a. 8.
[152] Ibid., ad 2.
[153] III, q. 3, a. 8.
[154] Ibid.
[155] Ibid.
[156] Ibid.
[157] The further narrative of Scripture confirms the truth of St. Paul's remark: "for although they knew God they did not honor him as God or give thanks to him, but they became futile in their thinking and their senseless minds were darkened. Claiming to be wise, they became fools, and exchanged the glory of the immortal God for images resembling mortal man or birds or animals or reptiles" (Rom. 1.21–23). Cf. Athanasius, *On the Incarnation*, trans. by a Religious of C.S.M.V. (Crestwood, NY: St. Vladimir's Orthodox Theological Seminary, 1993), 37–44 (§§11–15).
[158] III, q. 3, a. 8.
[159] Middleton, *The Liberating Image*, 29.
[160] Novak, *Covenantal Rights*, 39.
[161] Middleton, *The Liberating Image*, 29. Middleton adds that this Renaissance position derived from "[b]lending the volitional emphasis of Augustinian theology with the divinization notion of the Eastern fathers (mediated through the Hermetic literature)" (29).

[162] Ibid., 35.
[163] Ibid., 206.
[164] Ibid., 207.
[165] English translation in *Vatican II*, vol. 1: *The Conciliar and Postconciliar Documents*, ed. Austin Flannery, O.P. (Northport, NY: Costello Publishing Company, 1998), 922. The Latin reads, "Christus, novissimus Adam, in ipsa revelatione mysterii Patris eiusque amoris, hominem ipsi homini plene manifestat eique altissimam eius vocationem patefacit." For the theme of the new Adam, in whom we behold all the virtues, see St. Symeon the New Theologian, *The First Created Man: Seven Homilies*, trans. Seraphim Rose (Platina, CA: St. Herman of Alaska Brotherhood, 2001), 54–58.

Chapter 4

[1] Joseph Cardinal Ratzinger, *Truth and Tolerance: Christian Belief and World Religions*, trans. Henry Taylor (2003; San Francisco, CA: Ignatius Press, 2004), 99.
[2] Novak observes a similarity between Aquinas's approach and that of Maimonides: "Although Aquinas was unaware of Maimonides' constitution of Noahide law as natural law (since Maimonides does not discuss Noahide law in the *Guide*), one could make the following analogy: Maimonides' view of the relation of Noahide law to Mosaic law is logically quite similar to Aquinas's view of the relation of the Old Law to the New Law" (Novak, "Maimonides and Aquinas on Natural Law," in *Thinking with Christians: Musings of a Jewish Theologian* [Grand Rapids, MI: Eerdmans, 2005], 80). Novak comments, "As Maimonides notes with good Aristotelian reasoning, the natural/Noahide law is 'completed' (*ve-nishlamah*) by the Torah of Moses" (80). He explains why Maimonides places natural law within the covenantal framework: "The recognition of natural law, especially as it operates in human nature, is the beginning of a process that could possibly end in prophetic revelation, which grants us vision of the larger created nature of which human nature is a part. But to see natural law apart from its metaphysical ground is to make human reason rather than divine wisdom the measure of all things. That is why Maimonides is reticent to treat natural law apart from the full Law itself.... Natural law can be abstracted from the full Law itself, but it cannot be constituted in any adequate way independent of it" (79–80).
[3] Novak describes his effort to set forth universal natural law from a standpoint of the particularity of Judaism, "Our imagination can tentatively abstract us from our own cultures from time to time, but we cannot transcend them by some nonculturally conceived Archimedean fulcrum.... Instead of an attempt to find some universal phenomenon to ground natural law, it seems more authentic and more useful to see it as the constitution of a universal horizon by a thinker *in* a particular culture *for* his or her own culture." See David Novak, *Natural Law in Judaism* (Cambridge: Cambridge University Press, 1998), 189–90. See also my *Biblical Natural Law: A Theocentric and Teleological Approach* (Oxford: Oxford University Press, 2008).

4. Joseph Cardinal Ratzinger, *Many Religions—One Covenant: Israel, the Church and the World*, trans. Graham Harrison (1998; San Francisco, CA: Ignatius Press, 1999), 50.
5. Novak, *Natural Law in Judaism*, 149. On Noahide law see also, for example, Novak's early essay, originally published in 1979, "Noahide Law: A Foundation for Jewish Philosophy," in *Tradition in the Public Square: A David Novak Reader*, ed. Randi Rashkover and Martin Kavka (Grand Rapids, MI: Eerdmans, 2008), 113–44. For the prohibition of homosexual acts, see Novak's "Religious Communities, Secular Societies, and Sexuality: One Jewish Opinion," in *Tradition in the Public Square*, 283–303.
6. Novak, *Natural Law in Judaism*, 151.
7. Ibid., 151.
8. On this point see Novak's "Philosophy and the Possibility of Revelation: A Theological Response to the Challenge of Leo Strauss," in *Tradition in the Public Square: A David Novak Reader*, 3–20, especially 13.
9. Novak, *Natural Law in Judaism*, 153.
10. Ibid., 157.
11. Ibid. Novak distinguishes between "ontology" and "metaphysics," and ascribes teleology to the latter. He writes, "The ontology that I think best serves Jewish natural law theory is a theology of creation, and one that is not teleological" (158).
12. Ibid., 160. The text appears in *Sifre: Devarim*, ed. Louis Finkelstein (New York: Jewish Theological Seminary, 1969), no. 343, 396f.
13. Ibid., 161.
14. Ibid., 163.
15. Ibid., 158.
16. Ibid., 160.
17. Ibid. Novak remarks that "while there are some rabbinic texts that indicate that the gentiles knew about the Sinai revelation, these same texts also assume that their knowledge of that revelation was after the Torah had already been given to Israel. Thus, in effect, they had to learn it from Israel" (ibid.). As for the other nations' relationship to the Torah once it has been given, Novak observes that "there is no norm that makes conversion to Judaism a requirement, which is a point that well explains the fact that the acceptance of converts does not entail for Jews any legal obligation, or even for most Jews any theological impetus, to proselytize non-Jews" (ibid.).
18. Ibid., 162.
19. Ibid., 163.
20. Ibid., 161.
21. Ibid.
22. Ibid.
23. Ibid., 164.
24. Ibid., 151. He goes on to argue that "an affirmation of natural law can be a coherent guide for making decisions of Jewish law for those in the State of Israel who are dedicated to bringing Jewish law to bear on what others consider to be purely 'secular' matters. The whole movement of *mishpat ivri* (literally, 'Hebrew jurisprudence') is an attempt to do that, but it has been hindered heretofore by the

lack of an adequate philosophical foundation. Since theological agreement is most improbable at this point in Jewish and Israeli history, perhaps philosophical agreement can be more easily reached. In other words, perhaps in the area of political activity, we Jews might have to become (figuratively, that is) the Noahides we had to be before we could accept the covenant at Sinai with rational integrity" (185).

25 Thomas Aquinas, *Summa theologiae*, I–II, q. 98, a. 5, ad 2. Aquinas's understanding of the status of Jews after Christ is disputed. See on this topic Bruce D. Marshall, "*Quasi in Figura*: A Brief Reflection on Jewish Election, after Thomas Aquinas," *Nova et Vetera* 7 (2009): 477–84; Marshall, "Postscript and Prospect," *Nova et Vetera* 7 (2009): 523–28; Trent Pomplun, "*Quasi in figura*: A Cosmological Reading of the Thomistic Phrase," *Nova et Vetera* 7 (2009): 505–22; and Emmanuel Perrier, O.P., "The Election of Israel Today: Supersessionism, Post-supersessionism, and Fulfillment," trans. Matthew Levering, *Nova et Vetera* 7 (2009): 485–503. For further discussion of the issues addressed in this section, see my *Biblical Natural Law: A Theocentric and Teleological Approach* (Oxford: Oxford University Press, 2008) and my *Christ's Fulfillment of Torah and Temple: Salvation according to Thomas Aquinas* (Notre Dame, IN: University of Notre Dame Press, 2002).

26 I–II, q. 98, a. 5.
27 Ibid.
28 Ibid., obj. 3.
29 Ibid., ad 3.
30 I–II, q. 98, a. 5.
31 Quoted by Aquinas in I–II, q. 98, a. 4.
32 I–II, q. 98, a. 4.
33 Novak, *Natural Law in Judaism*, 158.
34 I–II, q. 99, a. 2. Although friendship with God comes through the Paschal mystery, nonetheless the Torah is not extrinsic to this friendship, since the Torah prepares for and points to the Messiah. Aquinas states that "it was possible at the time of the Law, for the minds of the faithful, to be united by faith to Christ incarnate and crucified; so that they were justified by faith in Christ: of which faith the observance of these ceremonies was a sort of profession, inasmuch as they foreshadowed Christ. Hence, in the Old Law, certain sacrifices were offered up for sins, not as though the sacrifices themselves washed sins away, but because they were professions of faith which cleansed from sin. In fact, the Law itself implies this in the terms employed: for it is written (Lev. iv.26, v.16) that in offering the sacrifice for sin *the priest shall pray for him . . . and it shall be forgiven him*, as though the sin were forgiven, not in virtue of the sacrifices, but through the faith and devotion of those who offered them" (I–II, q. 103, a. 2).
35 I–II, q. 99, a. 2.
36 I–II, q. 98, a. 6.
37 Ibid.
38 Ibid., ad 2.
39 I–II, q. 98, a. 6.
40 I–II, q. 102, a. 2. Cf. Maimonides's emphasis on the rationality of the Mosaic law. Maimonides comments, "There is a group of human beings who consider it a

grievous thing that causes should be given for any law; what would please them most is that the intellect would not find a meaning for the commandments and prohibitions. What compels them to feel thus is a sickness that they find in their souls, a sickness to which they are unable to give utterance and of which they cannot furnish a satisfactory account. For they think that if those laws were useful in this existence and had been given to us for this or that reason, it would be as if they derived from the reflection and the understanding of some intelligent being. If, however, there is a thing for which the intellect could not find any meaning at all and that does not lead to something useful, it indubitably derives from God; for the reflection of man would not lead to such a thing. It is as if, according to these people of weak intellects, man were more perfect than his Maker; for man speaks and acts in a manner that leads to some intended end, whereas the deity does not act thus, but commands us to do things that are not useful to us and forbids us to do things that are not harmful to us." Maimonides, *The Guide of the Perplexed*, trans. Shlomo Pines (Chicago, IL: University of Chicago Press, 1963), 524 (III, ch. 31).

[41] I–II, q. 104, a. 1, ad 1.

[42] Regarding the figurative sense of the judicial precepts, Aquinas comments, "The Jewish people were chosen by God that Christ might be born of them. Consequently the entire state of that people had to be prophetic and figurative, as Augustine states (*Contra Faust.* xxii.24). For this reason even the judicial precepts that were given to this people were more figurative than those which were given to other nations. Thus, too, the wars and deeds of this people are expounded in the mystical sense: but not the wars and deeds of the Assyrians or Romans, although the latter are more famous in the eyes of men" (I-II, q. 104, a. 2, ad 2).

[43] I–II, q. 105, a. 1, *sed contra*.

[44] I–II, q. 105, a. 2.

[45] Ibid., ad 1.

[46] I–II, q. 100, a. 1.

[47] For an account of natural law principles, see I–II, q. 94, aa. 2 and 4.

[48] I–II, q. 98, a. 6.

[49] Novak, *Natural Law in Judaism*, 162. See also I–II, q. 94, a. 6: "there belong to the natural law, first, certain most general precepts, that are known to all; and secondly, certain secondary and more detailed precepts, which are, as it were, conclusions following closely from first principles. As to those general principles, the natural law, in the abstract, can nowise be blotted out from men's hearts. But it is blotted out in the case of a particular action, in so far as reason is hindered from applying the general principle to a particular point of practice, on account of concupiscence or some other passion, as stated above (I–II, q. 77, a. 2).—But as to the other, i.e., the secondary precepts, the natural law can be blotted out from the human heart, either by evil persuasions, just as in speculative matters errors occur in respect of necessary conclusions; or by vicious customs and corrupt habits, as among some men, theft, and even unnatural vices, as the Apostle states (Rom. i), were not esteemed sinful."

[50] I–II, q. 99, a. 2, ad 2.

[51] I–II, q. 99, a. 1, ad 2; cf. I–II, q. 94, a. 3. The Torah aims at the perfection of human nature in virtue (holiness).

[52] I–II, q. 99, a. 2, ad 1.
[53] Maimonides, *The Guide of the Perplexed*, 382 (II, ch. 40). Novak concludes from this statement of Maimonides that "[n]atural law, then, can be seen as the precondition for divine grace, the greatest manifestation of which heretofore is the revelation of divine law. The humanly knowable world into which revelation can possibly enter must be a world in which natural law is discernable and respected" (Novak, "Maimonides and Aquinas on Natural Law," in *Talking with Christians: Musings of a Jewish Theologian* [Grand Rapids, MI: Eerdmans, 2005], 71).
[54] Novak, *Natural Law in Judaism*, 134. While agreeing with Maimonides that "both the Torah and the world are creations of the same divine wisdom" (30), Novak argues that Maimonides's thought, with its highly Aristotelian perspective, ultimately falls somewhat into rationalism.
[55] Ibid., 135.
[56] Ibid., 135–36.
[57] Ibid., 144. Earlier Novak sums up his concern: "Jewish theologians who reduce revelation to creation constitute natural law improperly for Judaism" (17).
[58] Ibid., 17–18; cf. 185–86.
[59] Ibid., 18.
[60] Ibid., 20. Novak goes on to observe, "In the deepest sense, there is no 'secular culture.' I know of no historically transmitted culture which when probed deeply enough does not invoke some transcendent reality as its source" (22). See also Novak's discussion of philosophy and theology on 174–78.
[61] Ibid., 20.
[62] Ibid., 25–26. See also Novak's "Is There a Concept of Individual Rights in Jewish Law?" in *Tradition in the Public Square: A David Novak Reader*, 88–110.
[63] Novak, *Natural Law in Judaism*, 145.
[64] Ibid., 146–47. Novak explains that "Created nature is more than just potential for revelation, which would totally subsume it within a particular revelation. Instead, created nature is the sphere of finite human possibilities, some of which are realized in history by revelation and its content. But, and here the comparative dimension of natural law thinking enters the picture, one can see these finite human possibilities being realized in other historical communities as well as in Israel" (147). Later Novak explains further, "What the proposal of natural law should say to its detractors among the theologians is that it is required for the intelligibility of the theological claim (certainly in Judaism) that God's revelation is of immediate normative import. That can only be accepted by the intended recipients of that revelation when they already have an idea of why God is to be obeyed. God is to be obeyed because law is a necessity of human life in community" (176–77).
[65] Novak observes regarding Cain, "So why is he guilty anyway? The only cogent answer is that it is already assumed that he knows murder is a crime. And how if not by his own reason? And what is that reason? Is it not the fact that he and Abel are brothers, that is, minimally, they are equal enough by virtue of ultimately common ancestry so that neither of them has the right to harm the other for his own individual advantage" (ibid., 34–35).
[66] Cf. ibid., 54–55.
[67] Ibid., 158.
[68] Ibid., 60.

[69] Ibid.
[70] Ibid., 61.
[71] Ibid.
[72] Ibid., 77.
[73] This perspective, Novak argues, is what is lacking in liberal Judaism. He points to "a basic similarity in the thought of the three real philosophers among those who might be called modern *liberal* Jewish thinkers: Cohen, Buber, and Levinas. Even though the thought of Buber and that of Levinas are usually seen in contrast to Cohen's Kantian rationalism, all three of them, nonetheless, are very much beholden to Enlightenment notions of universality. One could argue that for all of them, God's only function is to provide some sort of undergirding for ethics, and that is their view of God's function in Judaism as well. And for all of them, both the singularity of revelation and the singularity of the Jewish people as the community elected to receive that revelation in the covenant, sooner or later become subsumed into universal nature" (ibid., 84).
[74] Ibid., 90.
[75] I–II, q. 100, a. 8, ad 3.
[76] Novak, *Natural Law in Judaism*, 90.
[77] I–II, q. 100, a. 8, *sed contra*.
[78] I–II, q. 100, a. 8, ad 2.
[79] I–II, q. 100, a. 8, ad 3.
[80] See my "God and Natural Law: Reflections on Genesis 22," *Modern Theology* 24 (2008): 151–77; also my *Sacrifice and Community: Jewish Offering and Christian Eucharist* (Oxford: Blackwell, 2005).
[81] I–II, q. 100, a. 8.
[82] Ibid.
[83] I–II, q. 100, a. 1.
[84] Ibid.
[85] Ibid.
[86] For the illustration of the Decalogue in the covenantal history of Israel, see David Noel Freedman, *The Nine Commandments: Uncovering the Hidden Pattern of Crime and Punishment in the Hebrew Bible*, with Jeffrey C. Geoghegan and Michael M. Homan, ed. Astrid B. Beck (New York: Doubleday, 2000).
[87] I–II, q. 100, a. 1.
[88] I–II, q. 100, a. 3.
[89] Ibid. Aquinas adds, "Nevertheless both kinds of precepts are contained in the precepts of the decalogue; yet in different ways. For the first general principles are contained in them, as principles in their proximate conclusions; while those which are known through wise men are contained, conversely, as conclusions in their principles" (ibid.). See also I–II, q. 100, a. 11: "the moral precepts derive their efficacy from the very dictate of natural reason, even if they were never included in the Law. Now of these there are three grades: for some are most certain, and so evident as to need no promulgation; such as the commandments of the love of God and our neighbor, and others like those, as stated above (A. 3), which are, as it were, the end of the commandments; wherefore no man can have an erroneous judgment about them. Some precepts are more detailed, the reason of which even an uneducated man can easily grasp; and yet they need to be

promulgated, because human judgment, in a few instances, happens to be led astray concerning them: these are the precepts of the decalogue. Again, there are some precepts the reason of which is not so evident to everyone, but only to the wise; these are moral precepts added to the decalogue, and given to the people by God through Moses and Aaron."

[90] I–II, q. 100, a. 4.
[91] Ibid.
[92] I–II, q. 100, a. 11, ad 2.
[93] I–II, q. 100, a. 5.
[94] I–II, q. 100, a. 3, ad 2.
[95] See I–II, q. 100, a. 11.
[96] II–II, q. 81, a. 1, ad 3. Aquinas goes on to say that "it is a dictate of natural reason in accordance with man's natural inclination that he should tender submission and honor, according to his mode, to that which is above man" (II–II, q. 85, a. 1).
[97] I–II, q. 100, a. 3, ad 2.
[98] I–II, q. 100, a. 5.
[99] Ibid.
[100] I, q. 73, a. 3.
[101] I, q. 73, a. 1.
[102] Ibid. The "completeness of the universe at its first founding" does not require that new creatures or new species do not come into existence later. As Aquinas notes, individual things now being generated can be said to have existed "in their causes" (including their material cause), and new species "existed beforehand in various active powers" (I, q. 73, a. 1, ad 3). Against the view of a number of his contemporaries, Aquinas argues that human beings were created in grace: see I, q. 95, aa. 1 and 3; cf. I, q. 102, a. 4. For discussion see Jean-Pierre Torrell, O.P., "Nature et grâce chez Thomas d'Aquin," *Revue Thomiste* 101 (2001): 167–202, at 168–79; Oliva Blanchette, *The Perfection of the Universe According to Aquinas: A Teleological Cosmology* (University Park, PA: Pennsylvania State University Press, 1992).
[103] I–II, q. 100, a. 5, ad 2.
[104] I–II, q. 100, a. 5.
[105] I–II, q. 100, a. 6.
[106] I–II, q. 91, a. 6. Aquinas here quotes Ps. 48.21 in the Vulgate version, "Homo in honore cum esset non intellexit; conparatus est iumentis insipientibus, et similes factus est illis." Cf. Ps. 49.20 (RSV): "Man cannot abide in his pomp, he is like the beasts that perish."
[107] I–II, q. 94, a. 6; see also I–II, q. 100, a. 11.
[108] Cf. I–II, q. 100, a. 1: "It is therefore evident that since the moral precepts [of the Mosaic law] are about matters which concern good morals; and since good morals are those which are in accord with reason; and since also every judgment of human reason must needs be derived in some way from natural reason; it follows, of necessity, that all the moral precepts belong to the law of nature; but not all in the same way."
[109] I–II, q. 99, a. 2, ad 2.
[110] I–II, q. 100, a. 11.
[111] Ibid.

[112] I–II, q. 100, a. 10. Christ Jesus teaches that these two commandments provide the key to the whole Mosaic law: "On these two commandments depend all the law and the prophets" (Mt. 22.40).

[113] I–II, q. 100, a. 11.

[114] I–II, q. 100, a. 10, ad 3.

[115] Ibid.

[116] II–II, q. 29, a. 3, *sed contra.*

[117] II–II, q. 29, a. 3. Responding to an objection which proposes that peace can be achieved without sanctifying grace, Aquinas observes, "Peace is the *work of justice* indirectly, in so far as justice removes the obstacles to peace: but it is the work of charity directly, since charity, according to its very nature, causes peace. For love is *a unitive force* as Dionysius says (*Div. Nom.* iv): and peace is the union of the appetite's inclinations" (II–II, q. 29, a. 3, ad 3). Peace requires the interior harmony of one's rational and sense appetites, whose disorder is the root cause of conflicts.

[118] II–II, q. 24, a. 2.

[119] I–II, q. 100, a. 11, *sed contra.*

[120] I–II, q. 99, a. 6, ad 3. Qualifying this point (which reflects the witness of such books as Deuteronomy, Judges, 1 and 2 Kings, Ezra, and Nehemiah), he adds, "But certain individuals, although they observed the justice of the Law, met with misfortunes,—either because they had already become spiritual (so that misfortune might withdraw them all the more from attachment to temporal things, and that their virtue might be tried);—or because, while outwardly fulfilling the works of the Law, their heart was altogether fixed on temporal goods, and far removed from God, according to Isa. xxix.13 (Matth. xv.8): *This people honoreth Me with their lips; but their heart is far from Me*" (ibid.). See also Peter Leithart's Introduction to his commentary on 1 and 2 Kings, where he shows why these books should be read among the Former Prophets (as Aquinas read them). Leithart, *1 & 2 Kings* (Grand Rapids, MI: Brazos Press, 2006), 17–19.

[121] Novak, *Natural Law in Judaism*, 90.

[122] I–II, q. 100, a. 12.

[123] Novak, *Natural Law in Judaism*, 31.

[124] See Luther, "How Christians Should Regard Moses," in *Martin Luther's Basic Theological Writings*, ed. Timothy F. Lull (Minneapolis, MN: Fortress Press, 1989), 135–48, at 138. Timothy Lull comments in his Introduction to this section of *Martin Luther's Basic Theological Writings* that "How Christians Should Regard Moses" was published in 1525 as "a reworking of a sermon on the book of Exodus preached on August 27, 1525. It was directed especially against those enthusiastic opponents of Luther who found in the Old Testament, especially in the Law of Moses, a detailed model for society in Luther's time, and one that they thought could be actually realized" (73).

[125] Luther, "How Christians Should Regard Moses," 139.

[126] Ibid.

[127] Ibid.

[128] I–II, q. 103, a. 3, ad 1.

[129] I–II, q. 103, a. 3, ad 4.

[130] For further discussion see most recently my "Christ the Priest: An Exploration of *Sth* III, q. 22," *The Thomist* 71 (2007): 379–417. Cf. III, q. 47, a. 2, a. 1.
[131] See I–II, q. 100, a. 10, obj. 1 and ad 1.
[132] I–II, q. 100, a. 10.
[133] In his commentary on Romans, Aquinas interprets Rom. 2.14–15—"When Gentiles who have not the law do by nature what the law requires, they are a law to themselves. . . . They show that what the law requires is written on their hearts"—to be speaking of gentiles who share in the grace of the Holy Spirit and have faith, hope, and charity. For further discussion, see my "Knowing What Is 'Natural': Thomas Aquinas and Luke Timothy Johnson on Rom. 1–2," *Logos* 12 (2009): 117–142.
[134] II–II, q. 2, a. 7, ad 3. Cf. II–II, q. 2, a. 8, obj. 1 and ad 1.
[135] I–II, q. 90, preface.
[136] Novak, *Natural Law in Judaism*, 90.
[137] I–II, q. 100, a. 10.
[138] I–II, q. 100, a. 12.
[139] Ibid.
[140] Ibid., ad 3.
[141] I–II, q. 100, a. 12, obj. 1 and 2 (and ad 1 and 2).
[142] I–II, q. 100, a. 12.
[143] The opposite position finds its fullest expression in Luther's writings; see also Francis Watson, *Paul and the Hermeneutics of Faith* (New York: T & T Clark International, 2004).
[144] I–II, q. 100, a. 2, ad 1. Aquinas states that "the divine law proposes precepts about all those matters whereby men are well ordered in their relations to God. Now man is united to God by his reason or mind, in which is God's image. Wherefore the divine law proposes precepts about all those matters whereby human reason is well ordered" (I–II, q. 100, a. 2).
[145] Novak, *Natural Law in Judaism*, 31.
[146] I–II, q. 98, a. 2.
[147] I–II, q. 107, a. 1.
[148] I–II, q. 92, a. 1.
[149] This point, however, has at times motivated the rejection of "natural law" entirely, especially among Protestant theologians. On the need for the recovery of the "natural" in Protestant ethics, see Dietrich Bonhoeffer, *Ethics*, ed. Eberhard Bethge, trans. Neville Horton Smith (1949; New York: Macmillan, 1955), 143–49. Bonhoeffer (oddly in my view) distinguishes "natural" from "creaturely." He argues that God preserves the natural for Christ, and that Christ participates in and redeems the natural. See also Stephen J. Grabill, *Rediscovering the Natural Law in Reformed Theological Ethics* (Grand Rapids, MI: 2006). For an insightful critique of the misuse of "nature" by some Catholic moral theologians, see Stanley Hauerwas, *The Peaceable Kingdom: A Primer in Christian Ethics* (Notre Dame, IN: University of Notre Dame Press, 1983), 55–59, although Hauerwas goes to the opposite extreme and refuses to allow that human nature has significant "narrative display" except insofar as "the concepts of both creation and redemption are aids to train us to be creatures of a gracious God who has called us to be citizens in a community of the redeemed" (57).

Chapter 5

[1] See Regina M. Schwartz, *The Curse of Cain: The Violent Legacy of Monotheism* (Chicago, IL: University of Chicago Press, 1997), 2.
[2] Harold Bloom, *Where Shall Wisdom Be Found?* (New York: Riverhead Books, 2004), 1.
[3] Ibid.
[4] Ibid.
[5] Ibid., 2.
[6] Ibid.
[7] Ibid., 3.
[8] Ibid., 4.
[9] Ibid., 5.
[10] Ibid., 6.
[11] Ibid., 7.
[12] Ibid. In *Jesus and Yahweh: The Names Divine* (New York: Riverhead Books, 2005), Bloom distances himself from "trust in the Covenant." He writes, "My own mother *trusted in* the Covenant, despite Yahweh's blatant violation of its terms" (Bloom, *Jesus and Yahweh*, 228). Bloom's view of "Yahweh" is grim: "I cannot recall Yahweh expressing authentic love for anyone" (166; cf. 168). Aware that readers might suppose that his view of Yahweh arises from his own psychology, Bloom observes, "It is an old adage that all of us receive the God we deserve. Whether we deserve a Yahweh so irascible, vengeful, and even murderous is, however, another matter" (148).
[13] Bloom, *Where Shall Wisdom Be Found?*, 7.
[14] Ibid., 283.
[15] Ibid., 284.
[16] Ibid.
[17] Bloom, *Jesus and Yahweh*, 238.
[18] See Leon R. Kass, *The Beginning of Wisdom: Reading Genesis* (New York: Free Press, 2003), 5.
[19] Ibid., 8. Cf. on these topics Kass's *Life, Liberty and the Defense of Dignity: The Challenge for Bioethics* (San Francisco, CA: Encounter Books, 2002) and *The Hungry Soul: Eating and the Perfecting of Our Nature* (Chicago, IL: University of Chicago Press, 1999).
[20] Kass, *The Beginning of Wisdom*, xv.
[21] Ibid.
[22] He states, "The reader may well wonder how these studies have affected my own outlook on life, morals, and religion. I wish I could give a definitive answer, but I am still in the middle of my journey. There are truths that I think I have discovered only with the Bible's help, and I know that my sympathies have shifted toward the biblical pole of the age-old tension between Athens and Jerusalem. I am no longer confident of the sufficiency of unaided human reason. I find congenial the moral sensibilities and demands of the Torah, though I must confess that my practice is still wanting. And I am frankly filled with wonder at the fact that I have been led to this spiritual point, God knows how" (ibid., xiv).
[23] Ibid., 16.
[24] Ibid., 12.

25 Ibid., 13.
26 Ibid.
27 This is not to say that, in interpreting Genesis, Kass neglects the significance of the legal observances that God gives to the people of Israel. On the contrary, he demonstrates an insightful appreciation of them.
28 Ibid., 664.
29 Ibid., 17.
30 Ibid., 15.
31 Ibid.
32 Ibid.
33 Ibid.
34 Ibid., 13. On the impact of belief in God upon the quest for wisdom, cf. Hilary Putnam's *Jewish Philosophy as a Guide to Life: Rosenzweig, Buber, Levinas, Wittgenstein* (Bloomington, IN: Indiana University Press, 2008). For Putnam, largely agreeing with John Dewey, God is "a human projection that embodies our highest ideals" (101).
35 Kass, *The Beginning of Wisdom*, 3.
36 Novak appreciatively reviews Kass's *The Beginning of Wisdom*, along with (much more critically) Norman Podhoretz's *The Prophets: Who They Were, What They Are*, in Novak, "Ideas and Idols," *The New Republic* May 12, 2003 (no. 4608, vol. 228), 29–34.
37 In this respect Novak disagrees with Michael Wyschogrod, *The Body of Faith: God in the People Israel* (1983; Northvale, NJ: Jason Aronson, 1996): see Novak, *The Election of Israel: The Idea of the Chosen People* (Cambridge: Cambridge University Press, 1995), 243.
38 Ibid., 162.
39 Ibid. Novak adds that "our testimony is to belie those who say that the world is redeemed and to insist that the world wait with Israel for her and its redeemer" (ibid.). By contrast, Christians insist that the world is redeemed and yet join in this waiting, a waiting conditioned by the cruciform mode of the world's redemption.
40 Ibid., 253. However, in his *The Sanctity of Human Life* (Washington, D.C.: Georgetown University Press, 2007), Novak holds that the Torah "enables humans to patiently anticipate the final redemption (*ge'ulah*) of Israel, humankind, and the cosmos itself, because through revealed divine law humans have already experienced a small part of that final redemption already" (34). At least in "a small part," then, Israel has "already experienced" the "new divine trajectory into history and nature."
41 Novak, *The Election of Israel*, 253.
42 Ibid., 4.
43 Novak does not lack appreciation for the kabbalists: see, for example, his "Heschel on Revelation," in *Tradition in the Public Square: A David Novak Reader*, ed. Randi Rashkover and Martin Kavka (Grand Rapids, MI: Eerdmans, 2008), 37–45, at 45.
44 Novak, *The Election of Israel*, 7.
45 Ibid., 8.
46 Ibid., 9.

[47] Ibid., 14.
[48] Ibid.
[49] Ibid., 15.
[50] For discussion see ibid., 32ff. Novak makes an interesting connection with Spinoza's background in Amsterdam: "In this new elevation of practices that are essentially moral laws over practices that are more immediately 'religious' laws, Spinoza was following a lead established by his famous heterodox predecessor in Amsterdam, Uriel da Costa. In his rejection of much of Jewish law as morally and religiously cumbersome, da Costa saw the Noahide laws as not only necessary but sufficient for a fulfilled human life" (39). For discussion of Jewish intellectual life in seventeenth-century Amsterdam, see Steven Nadler, *Rembrandt's Jews* (Chicago, IL: University of Chicago Press, 2003). For a detailed account of da Costa's rejection of life after death, see Nadler, *Spinoza's Heresy: Immortality and the Jewish Mind* (Oxford: Oxford University Press, 2001), 165–73.
[51] Novak, *The Election of Israel*, 16. As Novak goes on to remark, "Covenantal election . . . requires an ontology that can constitute possibility, mutual relationship, and purpose" (24). In this regard Novak does not adequately distinguish between Spinoza's ontology and medieval Christian theology of infinite Actuality: "As it was for the medieval Aristotelians, so it was for Spinoza: time is a form of change, and what is eternal cannot by definition change" (25; cf. 109).
[52] Ibid., 111.
[53] As Novak says, "Because Spinoza sees the covenant presented in the Bible as an essentially human device designed by the Jews to relate their society properly to God and to each other, it cannot be eternal" (Ibid., 42). Novak adds, "Spinoza thought that the external event of the founding of the covenant between God and man could presently be better seen as the internal awareness of rational persons" (46).
[54] Ibid., 112.
[55] Novak's perspective here is similar to the viewpoint of my *Participatory Biblical Exegesis: A Theology of Biblical Interpretation* (Notre Dame, IN: University of Notre Dame Press, 2008).
[56] Novak, *The Election of Israel*, 112.
[57] Ibid., 113.
[58] Ibid.
[59] Ibid. Taking as an example "the relation between the Passover event in the past and its celebration in the present," Novak remarks, "A past good can only be appreciated when one is experiencing good in the present. One then wants to relate the past good to the present good, as well as project future good from the present good, so that the present good is not to be taken as peripheral or ephemeral. . . . In other words, the celebration of past redemption is because it has enabled present observance" (150–51).
[60] Ibid., 113. Novak comments in this regard, "Accordingly, the tradition is always the most immediate and evident link between the reading community and the read text" (ibid.).
[61] Ibid., 113–14.
[62] Ibid., 112.
[63] Ibid.

[64] Ibid., 249.
[65] Ibid.
[66] Ibid.
[67] Ibid.
[68] Ibid., 251.
[69] Ibid., 250.
[70] Novak explains the relationship of the *mishpatim* and the *edot*: "The *mishpatim* are the antecedents of the *edot* inasmuch as Israel is part of the universal order of nature (specifically, human nature) before she participates in the singular covenantal order. The covenant presupposes humanity. Since a presupposition is a condition, not a ground, as I have been emphasizing, the *edot*, therefore, transcend the *mishpatim* in intensity and detail. They are not reducible to them as parts of a larger whole, nor are the *mishpatim* simply the means to the *edot* as ends" (ibid., 251).
[71] Ibid., 250.
[72] Ibid., 251.
[73] Ibid.
[74] Ibid., 250.
[75] Ibid.
[76] Ibid., 251–52.
[77] Ibid., 252. For other Jewish theologies of the Aqedah, see my *Sacrifice and Community: Jewish Offering and Christian Eucharist* (Oxford: Blackwell, 2005), 29–49.
[78] Novak, *The Election of Israel*, 252.
[79] Ibid., 253.
[80] Ibid., 252.
[81] Ibid., 253.
[82] Ibid.
[83] Bloom, *Where Shall Wisdom Be Found?*, 7.
[84] Kass, *The Beginning of Wisdom*, 12.
[85] Novak, *The Election of Israel*, 253.
[86] Novak, *The Election of Israel*, 253.

Conclusion

[1] Jacob Neusner, "The Judaeo-Christian Divorce in the First Century and What It Means for the Twenty-First," *New Blackfriars* 87 (2006): 276–81, at 276.
[2] Ibid., 280.
[3] Ibid., 281.
[4] Novak, *Talking with Christians*, 107.
[5] As Joseph Ratzinger observed while still a Cardinal: "The three dimensions of time are thus connected: obedience to God's will bears on an already spoken word that now exists in history and at each new moment has to be made present again in obedience. This obedience, which makes present a bit of God's justice in time, is oriented toward a future when God will gather up the fragments of time and usher them as a whole into his justice." See Joseph Cardinal Ratzinger, "Interreligious Dialogue and Jewish-Christian Relations," trans. Adrian Walker, *Communio* 25 (1998): 29–41, at 37–38.

[6] Novak, *The Sanctity of Human Life* (Washington, D.C.: Georgetown University Press, 2007), xiv.
[7] Novak, *Jewish-Christian Dialogue: A Jewish Justification* (Oxford: Oxford University Press, 1989), 155–56.
[8] Novak, "Is Natural Law a Border Concept between Judaism and Christianity?" in *Tradition in the Public Square: A David Novak Reader*, 213–30, at 216.
[9] Jon D. Levenson, "Is Brueggemann Really a Pluralist?," *Harvard Theological Review* 93 (2000): 265–94, at 284.
[10] Ibid. See also Walter Lowe, "On the Tenacity of Christian Anti-Judaism," *Modern Theology* 22 (2006): 277–94, at 277; cf. 282.
[11] Novak, *The Election of Israel: The Idea of the Chosen People* (Cambridge: Cambridge University Press, 1995), 5.
[12] Novak, "What Does Edith Stein Mean for Jews?," in *Talking with Christians: Musings of a Jewish Theologian* (Grand Rapids, MI: Eerdmans, 2005), 164.
[13] Novak, *Jewish-Christian Dialogue*, 156.

Bibliography

Athanasius, St. *On the Incarnation*. Crestwood, NY: St. Vladimir's Orthodox Seminary, 1993.
Aquinas, Thomas. *Summa theologica*. Trans. The Fathers of the English Dominican Province. Westminster, MD.: Christian Classics, 1981.
Ashley, Benedict, O.P. *The Ashley Reader: Redeeming Reason*. Naples, FL: Sapientia Press, 2006.
Bader-Saye, Scott. *Church and Israel after Christendom: The Politics of Election*. Boulder, CO: Westview Press, 1999.
Batnitzky, Leora. *Idolatry and Representation: The Philosophy of Franz Rosenzweig Reconsidered*. Princeton, NJ: Princeton University Press, 2000.
Berger, David. *The Jewish-Christian Debate in the High Middle Ages: A Critical Edition of the Nizzahon Vetus*. Northvale, NJ: Jacob Aronson, 1996.
—. "Introducing Michael Wyschogrod." *Modern Theology* 22 (2006): 673–75.
Berger, David and Michael Wyschogrod. *Jews and "Jewish Christianity."* New York: KTAV, 1978.
Berry, Wendell. *Life Is a Miracle: An Essay against Modern Superstition*. Washington, D.C.: Counterpoint, 2001.
Blanchette, Oliva. *The Perfection of the Universe according to Aquinas: A Teleological Cosmology*. University Park, PA: Pennsylvania State University Press, 1992.
Bloom, Harold. *Where Shall Wisdom Be Found?* New York: Riverhead Books, 2004.
—. *Jesus and Yahweh: The Names Divine*. New York: Riverhead Books, 2005.
Blumberg, Harry. "The Problem of Immortality in Avicenna, Maimonides and St. Thomas Aquinas." In *Harry Austryn Wolfson: Jubilee Volume on the Occasion of His Seventy-Fifth Birthday*. Ed. Saul Lieberman. English Section. Volume 1. Jerusalem: American Academy for Jewish Research, 1965: 165–85.
Boccaccini, Gabriele. *Middle Judaism: Jewish Thought 300 B.C.E.–200 C.E.* Minneapolis, MN: Fortress Press, 1991.
Bockmuehl, Markus. *Jewish Law in Gentile Churches: Halakhah and the Beginning of Christian Public Ethics*. Grand Rapids, MI: Baker Academic, 2000.
—. *Seeing the Word: Refocusing New Testament Study*. Grand Rapids, MI: Baker Academic, 2006.
Bonhoeffer, Dietrich. *Ethics*. Ed. Eberhard Bethge. Trans. Neville Horton Smith. New York: Macmillan, 1955.
—. *The Cost of Discipleship*. Trans. R.H. Fuller. New York: Simon & Schuster, 1995.
Bourguet, Vincent. "Bioéthique et dualisme ontologique." *Revue Thomiste* 97 (1997): 619–39.
Boyle, Nicholas. *Who Are We Now? Christian Humanism and the Global Market from Hegel to Heaney*. Notre Dame, IN: University of Notre Dame Press, 1998.

Buber, Martin. *Israel and the World.* New York: Schocken, 1948.
—. "Letter to Franz Rosenzweig, July 13, 1924." In *On Jewish Learning* by Franz Rosenzweig. Ed. N.N. Glatzer. Madison, WI: University of Wisconsin Press, 1955: 115.
—. *I and Thou.* Trans. Walter Kaufman. New York: Simon & Schuster, 1996.
—. *Two Types of Faith.* Trans. Norman P. Goldhawk. Syracuse, NY: Syracuse University Press, 2003.
Burrell, David B., C.S.C. *Knowing the Unknowable God: Ibn-Sina, Maimonides, Aquinas.* Notre Dame, IN: University of Notre Dame Press, 1986.
—. *Freedom and Creation in Three Traditions.* Notre Dame, IN: University of Notre Dame Press, 1993.
—. "Response to Michael Wyschogrod's Letter." *Modern Theology* 11 (1995): 181–86.
—. *Friendship and Ways to Truth.* Notre Dame, IN: University of Notre Dame Press, 2000.
—. *Faith and Freedom: An Interfaith Perspective.* Oxford: Blackwell, 2004.
—. "Can We Be Free without a Creator?" In *God, Truth, and Witness: Engaging Stanley Hauerwas.* Ed. L. Gregory Jones, Reinhard Hütter, and C. Rosalee Velloso Ewell. Grand Rapids, MI: Brazos, 2005: 35–52.
—. Review of *Talking with Christians* by David Novak, and *Abraham's Promise* by Michael Wyschogrod. *Modern Theology* 22 (2006): 705–9.
—. "Some Requisites for Interfaith Dialogue." *New Blackfriars* 89 (2008): 300–10.
Calvin, John. *Institutes of the Christian Religion.* Trans. Henry Beveridge. Grand Rapids, MI: Eerdmans, 1989.
Cessario, Romanus, O.P. *Christian Faith and the Theological Life.* Washington, D.C.: Catholic University of America Press, 1996.
Charry, Ellen T. "Christian Jews and the Law." *Modern Theology* 11 (1995): 187–93.
—. "The Other Side of the Story." *Princeton Theological Review* 8 (2001): 24–29.
—. "Response to Carl Kinbar." *Princeton Theological Review* 8 (2001): 38–39.
Clapp, Rodney. *Border Crossings: Christian Trespasses on Popular Culture and Public Affairs.* Grand Rapids, MI: Brazos, 2000.
Clément, Olivier. *You Are Peter: An Orthodox Theologian's Reflection on the Exercise of Papal Primacy.* Trans. M.S. Laird. New York: New City Press, 2003.
Cooper, Adam G. *Life in the Flesh: An Anti-Gnostic Spiritual Philosophy.* Oxford: Oxford University Press, 2008.
Corcoran, Kevin J. *Rethinking Human Nature: A Christian Materialist Alternative to the Soul.* Grand Rapids, MI: Baker Academic, 2006.
Cunningham, Philip A. *A Story of Shalom: The Calling of Christians and Jews by a Covenanting God.* New York: Paulist Press, 2001.
Davidson, Herbert A. *Moses Maimonides.* New York: Oxford University Press, 2005.
Dauphinais, Michael. "Loving the Lord Your God: The *Imago Dei* in Saint Thomas Aquinas." *The Thomist* 63 (1999): 241–67.
Dawkins, Richard. *The God Delusion.* Boston, MA: Houghton Mifflin, 2006.
Dennett, Daniel. *Darwin's Dangerous Idea.* New York: Touchstone, 1995.
Dobbs-Weinstein, Idit. "Medieval Biblical Commentary and Philosophical Inquiry as Exemplified in the Thought of Moses Maimonides and St. Thomas Aquinas."

In *Moses Maimonides and His Time*. Ed. Eric L. Ormsby. Washington, D.C.: Catholic University of America Press, 1989: 101–20.

Dunn, James D.G. *The Epistle to the Galatians*. Peabody, MA: Hendrickson, 1993.

Dulles, Avery, S.J. *The Catholicity of the Church*. Oxford: Oxford University Press, 1985.

Dulles, Avery Cardinal, S.J. "Covenant and Mission." *America* 187, no. 12. October 21, 2002: 8–11.

—. "Nature, Mission, and Structure of the Church." In *Vatican II: Renewal within Tradition*. Ed. Matthew L. Lamb and Matthew Levering. Oxford: Oxford University Press, 2008: 25–36.

Di Noia, J.A., O.P. *The Diversity of Religions: A Christian Perspective*. Washington, D.C.: Catholic University of America Press, 1992.

Eisen, Robert. *The Book of Job in Medieval Jewish Philosophy*. Oxford: Oxford University Press, 2004.

Ellenson, David. "A Jewish View of the Christian God: Some Cautionary and Hopeful Remarks." In *Christianity in Jewish Terms*. Ed. Tikva Frymer-Kensky et al. Boulder, CO: Westview Press, 2000: 69–76.

Emery, Gilles, O.P. *Trinity in Aquinas*. Naples, FL: Sapientia Press, 2006.

—. *Trinity, Church, and the Human Person: Thomistic Essays*. Naples, FL: Sapientia Press, 2007.

Fagenblat, Michael, and Nathan Wolski. "Revelation Here and Beyond: Buber and Levinas on the Bible." In *Levinas and Buber: Dialogue and Difference*. Ed. Peter Atterton, Matthew Calarco, and Maurice Friedman. Pittsburgh, PA: Duquesne University Press, 2004: 157–78.

Fredriksen, Paula. *Augustine and the Jews: A Christian Defense of Jews and Judaism*. New York: Doubleday, 2008.

Freedman, David Noel. *The Nine Commandments: Uncovering the Hidden Pattern of Crime and Punishment in the Hebrew Bible*. With Jeffrey C. Geoghegan and Michael M. Homan. Ed. Astrid B. Beck. New York: Doubleday, 2000.

Fuchs, Joseph. *Moral Demands and Personal Obligations*. Trans. Brian McNeil. Washington, D.C.: Georgetown University Press, 1993.

Gagnon, Robert A.J. "Why the 'Weak' at Rome Cannot Be Non-Christian Jews." *Catholic Biblical Quarterly* 62 (2000): 64–82.

Gaine, Simon, O.P. *Will There Be Free Will in Heaven? Freedom, Impeccability, and Beatitude*. New York: T & T Clark, 2003.

Gimaret, Daniel. *La doctrine d'al Ash'ari*. Paris: Cerf, 1990.

Glatzer, Nahum N., ed. *On Judaism*. New York: Schocken Books, 1996.

Goodman, L.E. "Maimonides' Responses to Sa'adya Gaon's Theodicy and Their Islamic Backgrounds." In *Studies in Islamic and Judaic Traditions II*. Ed. William M. Brinner and Stephen D. Ricks. Atlanta, GA: Scholars Press, 1989: 3–22.

—. *God of Abraham*. Oxford: Oxford University Press, 1996.

Grabill, Stephen J. *Rediscovering the Natural Law in Reformed Theological Ethics*. Grand Rapids, MI: 2006.

Green, Joel B. *Body, Soul, and Human Life: The Nature of Humanity in the Bible*. Grand Rapids, MI: Baker Academic, 2008.

Hadot, Pierre. *Philosophy as a Way of Life*. Ed. Arnold I. Davidson. Trans. Michael Chase. Oxford: Blackwell, 1995.

Harink, Douglas. *Paul among the Postliberals: Pauline Theology beyond Christendom and Modernity*. Grand Rapids, MI: Brazos, 2003.

Hauerwas, Stanley. *The Peaceable Kingdom: A Primer in Christian Ethics*. Notre Dame, IN: University of Notre Dame Press, 1983.

Hays, Richard B. *Echoes of Scripture in the Letters of Paul*. New Haven, CT: Yale University Press, 1989.

—. *The Moral Vision of the New Testament*. San Francisco, CA: Harper SanFrancisco, 1996.

Hittinger, Russell. *The First Grace: Rediscovering the Natural Law in a Post-Christian World*. Wilmington, DE: ISI Books, 2003.

—. "Human Nature and States of Nature in John Paul II's Theological Anthropology." In *Human Nature in Its Wholeness: A Roman Catholic Perspective*. Ed. Daniel N. Robinson, Gladys M. Sweeney, and L.C. Richard Gill. Washington, D.C.: Catholic University of America Press, 2006: 9–33.

Hodgson, Marshall G.S. *The Venture of Islam: Conscience and History in a World Civilization*. Vol. 2: *The Expansion of Islam in the Middle Periods*. Chicago, IL: University of Chicago Press, 1974.

Houston, Walter J. "The Character of YHWH and the Ethics of the Old Testament: Is *Imitatio Dei* Appropriate?" *Journal of Theological Studies* 58 (2007): 1–25.

Hütter, Reinhard. "'In.' Some Incipient Reflections on *The Jewish People and Their Sacred Scriptures in the Christian Bible*." *Pro Ecclesia* 13 (2004): 13–24.

Ignatius of Antioch. *To the Magnesians*. In *Apostolic Fathers*. Vol. 1. Ed. Kirsopp Lake. Cambridge, MA: Harvard University Press, 1912.

Jenson, Robert W. "Toward a Christian Theology of Judaism." In *Jews and Christians, People of God*. Ed. Carl. E. Braaten and Robert W. Jenson. Grand Rapids, MI: Eerdmans, 2003: 1–13.

St. John of Damascus. *The Orthodox Faith*. In St. John of Damascus, *Writings*. Trans. Frederic H. Chase, Jr. Washington, D.C.: Catholic University of America Press, 1958.

Johnson, Luke Timothy. *The Writings of the New Testament*. Philadelphia, PA: Fortress Press, 1986.

Kasper, Walter. "Paths Taken and Enduring Questions in Jewish-Christian Relations Today: Thirty Years of the Commission for Religious Relations with the Jews." In *The Catholic Church and the Jewish People: Recent Reflections from Rome*. Ed. Philip A. Cunningham, Norbert J. Hofmann, S.D.B., and Joseph Sievers. New York: Fordham University Press, 2007: 3–11.

Kass, Leon R. *The Hungry Soul: Eating and the Perfecting of Our Nature*. Chicago, IL: University of Chicago Press, 1999.

—. *Life, Liberty and the Defense of Dignity: The Challenge for Bioethics*. San Francisco, CA: Encounter Books, 2002.

—. *The Beginning of Wisdom: Reading Genesis*. New York: Free Press, 2003.

Kieke-Sciglitano, Anthony C. "Hans Urs von Balthasar and 'The Jewish Critique': Intramural Appropriation and Response." *Toronto Journal of Theology* 14 (1998): 177–96.

Kinbar, Carl. "Missing Factors in Jewish-Christian Dialogue." *Princeton Theological Review* 8 (2001): 30–37.

Kinzer, Mark S. *The Nature of Messianic Judaism: Judaism as Genus, Messianic as Species*. West Hartford, CT: Hashivenu Archives, 2000.

———. *Postmissionary Messianic Judaism: Redefining Christian Engagement with the Jewish People*. Grand Rapids, MI: Brazos, 2005.
Leithart, Peter J. "Marcionism, Postliberalism, and Social Christianity." *Pro Ecclesia* 8 (1999): 85–97.
———. *1 & 2 Kings*. Grand Rapids, MI: Brazos Press, 2006.
Levenson, Jon D. *The Hebrew Bible, the Old Testament, and Historical Criticism*. Louisville, KY: Westminster/John Knox Press, 1993.
———. "Is Brueggemann Really a Pluralist?" *Harvard Theological Review* 93 (2000): 265–94.
———. "How Not to Conduct Jewish-Christian Dialogue." *Commentary* 112, no. 5. December 2001: 31–37.
———. "Did God Forgive Adam? An Exercise in Comparative Midrash." In *Jews and Christians: People of God*. Ed. Carl. E. Braaten and Robert W. Jenson. Grand Rapids, MI: Eerdmans, 2003: 148–70.
———. "The Agenda of *Dabru Emet*." *Review of Rabbinic Judaism* 7 (2004): 1–26.
———. *Resurrection and the Restoration of Israel: The Ultimate Victory of the God of Life*. New Haven, CT: Yale University Press, 2006.
Levering, Matthew. *Christ's Fulfillment of Torah and Temple: Salvation according to Thomas Aquinas*. Notre Dame, IN: University of Notre Dame Press, 2002.
———. *Sacrifice and Community: Jewish Offering and Christian Eucharist*. Oxford: Blackwell, 2005.
———. Review of *Bodies and Souls, or Spirited Bodies?* by Nancey Murphy. *National Catholic Bioethics Quarterly* 7 (2007): 635–38.
———. "Christ the Priest: An Exploration of *Sth* III, q. 22." *The Thomist* 71 (2007): 379–417.
———. "God and Natural Law: Reflections on Genesis 22." *Modern Theology* 24 (2008): 151–77.
———. *Biblical Natural Law: A Theocentric and Teleological Approach*. Oxford: Oxford University Press, 2008.
———. *Participatory Biblical Exegesis: A Theology of Biblical Interpretation*. Notre Dame, IN: University of Notre Dame Press, 2008.
———. "Knowing What Is 'Natural': Thomas Aquinas and Luke Timothy Johnson on Romans 1–2." *Logos* 12 (2009): 117–142.
Lindbeck, George. *The Nature of Doctrine*. Philadelphia, PA: Westminster, 1984.
———. "Response to Michael Wyschogrod's 'Letter to a Friend.'" *Modern Theology* 11 (1995): 205–10.
———. "The Church as Israel: Ecumenism and Ecclesiology." In *Jews and Christians: People of God*. Ed. Carl E. Braaten and Robert W. Jenson. Grand Rapids, MI: Eerdmans, 2003: 78–94.
Longenecker, Bruce W. "Different Answers to Different Questions: Israel, the Gentiles and Salvation History in Romans 9–11." *Journal for the Study of the New Testament* 36 (1989): 95–123.
———. "On Israel's God and God's Israel: Assessing Supersessionism in Paul." *Journal of Theological Studies* 58 (2007): 26–44.
Lowe, Walter. "The Intensification of Time: Michael Wyschogrod and the Task of Christian Theology." *Modern Theology* 22 (2006): 693–99.
———. "On the Tenacity of Christian Anti-Judaism." *Modern Theology* 22 (2006): 277–94.

Luther, Martin. "How Christians Should Regard Moses." In *Martin Luther's Basic Theological Writings*. Ed. Timothy F. Lull. Minneapolis, MN: Augsburg Fortress, 1989: 135–48.

MacIntyre, Alasdair. *Whose Justice? Which Rationality?* Notre Dame, IN: University of Notre Dame Press, 1988.

—. *Three Rival Versions of Moral Enquiry: Encyclopaedia, Genealogy, and Tradition*. Notre Dame, IN: University of Notre Dame Press, 1990.

McDade, John, S.J. "Christians and Jews: Competitive Siblings or the Israel of God?" *New Blackfriars* 89 (2008): 267–79.

McDermott, John M., S.J. "The Jews, Jesus, and the Church." *Josephinum Journal of Theology* 11 (2004): 26–48.

Maimonides, Moses. *The Guide of the Perplexed*. Trans. Shlomo Pines. Chicago, IL: University of Chicago Press, 1963.

Main, Emmanuelle. "Ancienne et Nouvelle Alliances dans le dessein de Dieu. À propos d'un article recent." *Nouvelle revue théologique* 118 (1996): 34–58.

Marquardt, Friedrich-Wilhelm. *Das christliche Bekenntnis zu Jesus, dem Juden. Eine Christologie*. 2 vols. Munich: Kaiser, 1990–1991.

Marshall, Bruce D. "Christ and the Cultures: The Jewish People and Christian Theology." In *The Cambridge Companion to Christian Doctrine*. Ed. Colin E. Gunton. Cambridge: Cambridge University Press, 1997: 81–100.

—. *Trinity and Truth*. Cambridge: Cambridge University Press, 2000.

—. "Elder Brothers: John Paul II's Teaching on the Jewish People as a Question to the Church." In *John Paul II and the Jewish People: A Jewish-Christian Dialogue*. Ed. David G. Dalin and Matthew Levering. Lanham, MD: Rowman and Littlefield, 2008: 113–29.

—. "Postscript and Prospect." *Nova et Vetera* 7 (2009): 523–28.

—. "*Quasi in Figura*: A Brief Reflection on Jewish Election, after Thomas Aquinas." *Nova et Vetera* 7 (2009): 477–84.

Meilaender, Gilbert. *Bioethics: A Primer for Christians*. 2nd edition. Grand Rapids, MI: Eerdmans, 2005.

Merriell, D. Juvenal. *To the Image of the Trinity: A Study in the Development of Aquinas' Teaching*. Toronto: Pontifical Institute of Medieval Studies, 1990.

Middleton, Richard. *The Liberating Image: The* Imago Dei *in Genesis 1*. Grand Rapids, MI: Brazos, 2005.

Murphy, Nancey. *Bodies and Souls, or Spirited Bodies?* Cambridge: Cambridge University Press, 2006.

Nadler, Steven. *Spinoza's Heresy: Immortality and the Jewish Mind*. Oxford: Oxford University Press, 2001.

—. *Rembrandt's Jews*. Chicago, IL: University of Chicago Press, 2003.

Nanos, Mark D. *The Mystery of Romans: The Jewish Context of Paul's Letter*. Minneapolis, MN: Fortress Press, 1996.

National Council of Synagogues and the United States Conference of Catholic Bishops' Committee for Ecumenical and Interreligious Relations. "Reflections on Covenant and Mission." *Origins* 32, no. 13. September 5, 2002: 218–24.

Neuhaus, Richard John. "Salvation Is from the Jews." In *Jews and Christians: People of God*. Ed. Carl E. Braaten and Robert W. Jenson. Grand Rapids, MI: Eerdmans, 2003: 65–77.

Neusner, Jacob. *A Rabbi Talks with Jesus: An Intermillennial, Interfaith Exchange.* New York: Doubleday, 1993.

—. "The Judaeo-Christian Divorce in the First Century and What It Means for the Twenty-First." *New Blackfriars* 87 (2006): 276–81.

Neusner, Jacob, and Bruce D. Chilton. *The Intellectual Foundations of Christian and Jewish Discourse: The Philosophy of Religious Argument.* London: Routledge, 1997.

Noll, Mark A. "Have Christians Done More Harm than Good?" In *Must Christianity Be Violent? Reflections on History, Practice, and Theology.* Ed. Kenneth R. Chase and Alan Jacobs. Grand Rapids, MI: Brazos, 2003: 79–93.

Novak, David. *Suicide and Morality: The Theories of Plato, Aquinas and Kant and Their Relevance for Suicidology.* New York: Scholars Press, 1975.

—. *Law and Theology in Judaism.* 2 vols. New York: KTAV, 1976.

—. *Halakhah in a Theological Dimension.* Chico, CA: Scholars Press, 1985.

—. "The Treatment of Islam and Muslims in the Legal Writings of Maimonides." In *Studies in Islamic and Judaic Traditions.* Ed. W.M. Brinner and S.D. Ricks. Atlanta, GA: Scholars Press, 1986: 233–50.

—. *Jewish-Christian Dialogue: A Jewish Justification.* Oxford: Oxford University Press, 1989.

—. *Jewish Social Ethics.* Oxford: Oxford University Press, 1992.

—. *The Election of Israel.* Cambridge: Cambridge University Press, 1995.

—. "Response to Michael Wyschogrod." *Modern Theology* 11 (1995): 211–18.

—. *Natural Law in Judaism.* Cambridge: Cambridge University Press, 1998.

—. Review of *The God of Israel and Christian Theology* by R. Kendall Soulen. *First Things* 81 (March 1998): 58–60.

—. "Jews and Catholics: Beyond Apologies." *First Things* 89 (January 1999): 20–25.

—. *Covenantal Rights: A Study in Jewish Political Theory.* Cambridge: Cambridge University Press, 2000.

—. "Ideas and Idols." *The New Republic* 228, no. 4608. May 12, 2003: 29–34.

—. *The Jewish Social Contract: An Essay in Political Theology.* Princeton, NJ: Princeton University Press, 2005.

—. *Talking with Christians: Musings of a Jewish Theologian.* Grand Rapids, MI: Eerdmans, 2005.

—. *The Sanctity of Human Life.* Washington, D.C.: Georgetown University Press, 2007.

—. *Tradition in the Public Square: A David Novak Reader.* Ed. Randi Rashkover and Martin Kavka. Grand Rapids, MI: Eerdmans, 2008.

O'Callaghan, John P. "*Imago Dei*: A Test Case for St. Thomas's Augustinianism." In *Aquinas the Augustinian.* Ed. Michael Dauphinais, Barry David, and Matthew Levering. Washington, D.C.: Catholic University of America Press, 2007: 100–44.

Ochs, Peter. "The God of Jews and Christians." In *Christianity in Jewish Terms.* Ed. Tikva Frymer-Kensky et al. Boulder, CO: Westview Press, 2000: 49–69.

Ouellet, Mark Cardinal. *Divine Likeness: Toward a Trinitarian Anthropology of the Family.* Trans. Philip Milligan and Linda M. Cicone. Grand Rapids, MI: Eerdmans, 2006.

Perrier, Emmanuel, O.P. "The Election of Israel Today: Supersessionism, Post-supersessionism, and Fulfillment." *Nova et Vetera* 7 (2009): 485–503.

Pinckaers, Servais, O.P. "Ethics and the Image of God." Trans. Mary Thomas Noble, O.P. In *The Pinckaers Reader: Renewing Thomistic Moral Theology*. Ed. John Berkman and Craig Steven Titus. Washington, D.C.: Catholic University of America Press, 2005: 130–43.

Pines, Shlomo. "Spinoza's *Tractatus Theologico-Politicus*, Maimonides and Kant." In *Further Studies in Philosophy*. Ed. Ora Segal. Jerusalem: The Magnes Press, 1968: 3–54.

Pomplun, Trent. "*Quasi in figura*: A Cosmological Reading of the Thomistic Phrase." *Nova et Vetera* 7 (2009): 505–22.

Pope Benedict XVI/Joseph Ratzinger. *Jesus of Nazareth: From the Baptism in the Jordan to the Transfiguration*. Trans. Adrian J. Walker. New York: Doubleday, 2007.

Pope John Paul II. *The Place Within: The Poetry of Pope John Paul II*. Trans. Jerzy Peterkiewicz. New York: Random House, 1982.

—. *Evangelium Vitae*. Vatican Translation. Boston, MA: Daughters of St. Paul, 1995.

—. *Spiritual Pilgrimage: Texts on Jews and Judaism 1979–1995*. Ed. Eugene J. Fisher and Leon Klenicki. New York: Crossroad, 1995.

—. *The Poetry of John Paul II. Roman Triptych: Meditations*. Trans. Jerzy Peterkiewicz. Washington, D.C.: United States Conference of Catholic Bishops, 2003.

—. *Memory and Identity: Conversations at the Dawn of a Millennium*. New York: Rizzoli, 2005.

—. *John Paul II in the Holy Land: In His Own Words*. Ed. Lawrence Boadt, C.S.P. and Kevin di Camillo. New York: Paulist Press, 2005.

Putnam, Hilary. *Jewish Philosophy as a Guide to Life: Rosenzweig, Buber, Levinas, Wittgenstein*. Bloomington, IN: Indiana University Press, 2008.

Racioner, Leon Menzies. "Hebrew Catholicism: Theology and Politics in Modern Israel." *Heythrop Journal* 45 (2004): 405–15.

Raffel, Charles M. "Providence as Consequent upon the Intellect: Maimonides' Theory of Providence." *AJS Review* 12 (1987): 25–71.

Rashkover, Randi, and Martin Kavka. "Introduction." In *Tradition in the Public Square: A David Novak Reader*. Ed. R. Rashkover and M. Kavka. Grand Rapids, MI: Eerdmans, 2008: xi–xxxiv.

Rashkover, Randi. *Revelation and Theopolitics: Barth, Rosenzweig and the Politics of Praise*. New York: T & T Clark, 2005.

Ratzinger, Joseph. "Interreligious Dialogue and Jewish-Christian Relations." Trans. Adrian Walker. *Communio* 25 (1998): 29–41.

—. *Many Religions—One Covenant: Israel, the Church and the World*. Trans. Graham Harrison. San Francisco, CA: Ignatius Press, 1999.

—. *Truth and Tolerance: Christian Belief and World Religions*. Trans. Henry Taylor. San Francisco, CA: Ignatius Press, 2004.

Ravitzky, Aviezer. "Samuel Ibn Tibbon and the Esoteric Character of *The Guide of the Perplexed*." *AJS Review* 6 (1981): 87–123.

Reinders, Hans S. *Receiving the Gift of Friendship: Profound Disability, Theological Anthropology, and Ethics*. Grand Rapids, MI: Eerdmans, 2008.

Reines, Alvin J. "Maimonides' Concepts of Providence and Theodicy." *Hebrew Union College Annual* 43 (1972): 169–205.

Rosenzweig, Franz. *On Jewish Learning*. Ed. N.N. Glatzer. Madison, WI: University of Wisconsin Press, 1955.

Rudolph, David J. "Messianic Jews and Christian Theology: Restoring an Historical Voice to the Contemporary Discussion." *Pro Ecclesia* 14 (2005): 58–84.
Ruether, Rosemary Radford. *Faith and Fraticide: The Theological Roots of Anti-Semitism.* Eugene, OR: Wipf and Stock, 1996.
Schwartz, Regina M. *The Curse of Cain: The Violent Legacy of Monotheism.* Chicago, IL: University of Chicago Press, 1997.
Shanley, Brian J., O.P. "Aquinas's Exemplar Ethics." *The Thomist* 72 (2008): 345–69.
Sokolowski, Robert. *Christian Faith and Human Understanding: Studies on the Eucharist, Trinity, and the Human Person.* Washington, D.C.: Catholic University of America, 2006.
Soloveitchik, Joseph B. "Confrontation." *Tradition: A Journal of Orthodox Thought* 6 (1964): 5–9.
Soulen, R. Kendall. *The God of Israel and Christian Theology.* Minneapolis, MN: Fortress Press, 1996.
—. "Election, not Selection." *Pro Ecclesia* 15 (2006): 379–86.
—. Review of *Postmissionary Messianic Judaism: Redefining Christian Engagement with the Jewish People* by Mark Kinzer. *Pro Ecclesia* 16 (2007): 105–7.
Steiner, George. *Real Presences.* Chicago, IL: Chicago University Press, 1989.
Strauss, Leo. "The Place of the Doctrine of Providence according to Maimonides." Trans. Gabriel Bartlett and Svetozar Minkov. *Review of Metaphysics* 57 (2004): 537–49.
Symeon the New Theologian. *The First Created Man: Seven Homilies.* Trans. Seraphim Rose. Platina, CA: St. Herman of Alaska Brotherhood, 2001.
Taubes, Jacob. *The Political Theology of Paul.* Trans. Dana Hollander. Stanford, CA: Stanford University Press, 2004.
Torrell, Jean-Pierre, O.P. "Nature et grâce chez Thomas d'Aquin." *Revue Thomiste* 101 (2001): 167–202.
—. *Saint Thomas Aquinas.* Vol. 2: *Spiritual Master.* Trans. Robert Royal. Washington, D.C.: Catholic University of America Press, 2003.
Touati, C. "Les deux theories de Maïmonide sur la providence." In *Studies in Jewish Religious and Intellectual History.* Ed. Siegfried Stein and Raphael Loewe. Tuscaloosa, AL: University of Alabama Press, 1979: 331–43.
Taylor, Charles. *Sources of the Self: The Making of the Modern Identity.* Cambridge, MA: Harvard University Press, 1989.
Unterseher, Lisa A. "The Mark of Cain and the Jews: Augustine's Theology of Jews." *Augustinian Studies* 33 (2002): 99–121.
Van Buren, Paul M. *A Theology of Jewish-Christian Reality.* Vol. 2: *A Christian Theology of the People Israel.* San Francisco, CA: Harper & Row, 1983.
Vanhoye, Albert, S.J. "Salut universel par le Christ et validité de l'Ancienne Alliance." *Nouvelle revue théologique* 116 (1994): 815–35.
Volf, Miroslav. *Exclusion and Embrace: A Theological Exploration of Identity, Otherness, and Reconciliation.* Nashville, TN: Abingdon Press, 1996.
—. *The End of Memory: Remembering Rightly in a Violent World.* Grand Rapids, MI: Eerdmans, 2006.
Von Balthasar, Hans Urs. *Martin Buber and Christianity: A Dialogue between Israel and the Church.* Trans. Alexander Dru. London: Harvill, 1961.
Vonier, Anscar, O.S.B. *A Key to the Doctrine of the Eucharist.* Bethesda, MD: Zaccheus Press, 2003.

Wagner, J. Ross. *Heralds of the Good News: Isaiah and Paul in Concert in the Letter to the Romans.* Leiden: Brill, 2003.
Walzer, Michael. "Morality and Politics in the Work of Michael Wyschogrod." *Modern Theology* 22 (2006): 687–92.
Watson, Francis. *Paul and the Hermeneutics of Faith.* London: T & T Clark International, 2004.
—. *Paul, Judaism, and the Gentiles: Beyond the New Perspective.* 2nd edition. Grand Rapids, MI: Eerdmans, 2007.
Wilson, Edward O. *Consilience.* New York: Vintage, 1999.
Weinandy, Thomas, O.F.M. Cap. *Does God Suffer?* Notre Dame, IN: University of Notre Dame Press, 2000.
Williams, A.N. *The Ground of Union: Deification in Aquinas and Palamas.* Oxford: Oxford University Press, 1999.
Witherington III, Ben. *Grace in Galatia: A Commentary on Paul's Letter to the Galatians.* Edinburgh: T & T Clark, 1998.
Wohlman, Avital. "La signification de la désobéissance d'Adam selon les trois monothéisms." *Revue Thomiste* 108 (2008): 573–98.
Wright, N.T. *The Climax of the Covenant.* Minneapolis, MN: Fortress Press, 1991.
—.*The New Testament and the People of God.* Minneapolis, MN: Fortress Press, 1992.
Wyschogrod, Michael. "A Jewish Reading of St. Thomas Aquinas on the Old Law." In *Understanding Scripture.* Ed. Clemens Thoma and Michael Wyschogrod. New York: Paulist Press, 1987: 125–38.
—. "Letter to a Friend." *Modern Theology* 11 (1995): 165–71.
—. "Response to the Respondents." *Modern Theology* 11 (1995): 235.
—. *The Body of Faith: God in the People Israel.* Northvale, NJ: Jason Aronson, 1996.
—. *Abraham's Promise: Judaism and Jewish-Christian Relations.*Ed. R. Kendall Soulen. Grand Rapids, MI: Eerdmans, 2004.
—. "Franz Rosenzweig's *The Star of Redemption.*" In *Abraham's Promise: Judaism and Jewish-Christian Relations.* Ed. R. Kendall Soulen. Grand Rapids, MI: Eerdmans, 2004: 121–30.
Yaffe, Martin D. "Providence in Medieval Aristotelianism: Moses Maimonides and Thomas Aquinas on the Book of Job." *Hebrew Studies* 20–21 (1979–80): 62–74.
Yocum, John P. "On Mark S. Kinzer's *Postmissionary Messianic Judaism: Redefining Christian Engagement with the Jewish People.*" *Nova et Vetera* 5 (2007): 895–906.
Yoder, John Howard. *The Jewish-Christian Schism Revisited.* Ed. Michael G. Cartwright and Peter Ochs. Grand Rapids, MI: Eerdmans, 2003.

Index

Abel 71, 115
abortion 138n. 42, 138n. 48, 139n. 51
  as a form of eugenics 139n. 58
  Jewish law 7–8
  rabbinic permission 9
  rabbinic prohibition 7–8
Abraham 59, 67, 103, 126
  God's election of 97
  Holy Land and 48, 50
active intellect 60, 61
active mutuality
  image of God and 70–2, 74, 79, 80
Adam 66–7, 75, 165n. 71
  fall of 89
Akiba, Rabbi 116
apostates 23, 25, 140n. 8
Aquinas, Thomas 56, 154n. 3, 157n. 64, 166n. 95, 177n. 106
  on body and soul 165n. 86, 168n. 127
  on Christ's fulfillment of Torah 145n. 58
  on creation 177n. 102
  on goodness 80, 167n. 99
  on image of God 63, 78–89, 90–1, 169n. 132, 169n. 40, 169n. 42, 169n. 44
  on Israel and the nations 96–9, 111
  on Jews 173n. 25, 174n. 42
  Maimonides influences on 61
  on natural law 74, 92, 114, 178n. 133
  on natural law and Sinai 102–13
  on New Testament theology of Christ 39
  on peace 178n. 117
  on percept of Decalogue 176n. 89
  rejection of Torah observance 38
  on sacrifice 173n. 34
  on Trinity 166n. 93
  on voluntary 167n. 111

Aristotle
  on capacity 168n. 127
  God of 68, 158n. 67
  influence on Maimonides 58, 59
  Novak's rejection of 63–4
  on singular and general 54
  voluntary definition of 167n. 111
Ashariyah
  on providence 58–9
Augustine, St. 105, 162n. 21, 174n. 42
  debate over Paul's Torah observance 38
  on image of God 82
  on image of the Trinity 78–9
  natural law of 74
  on New Testament theology of Christ 39
autonomy 57, 64
  image of God and 72–3, 78–82
Avicenna 60, 61
"Avoiding Charges of Legalism and Antinomianism in Jewish-Christian Dialogue" (Novak) 17

Bachrach, Hayyim Yair
  on elective abortion 8, 138n. 48
baptism 14, 35, 84, 153n. 52, 168n. 24
The Beginning of Wisdom: Reading Genesis (Kass) 3, 115, 117
Benedict XVI, Pope 5
  account of Nineveh 92
  on encounter of religions 135n. 27
  on three dimensions of time 183n. 5
Berger, David 143n. 28
biblical interpretation 122–3, 124, 145n. 52
bilateral ecclesiology 2, 30, 40–2, 46, 148n. 86, 149n. 108, 151n. 132, 152n. 138

blasphemy
    prohibition of 93, 137n. 37
Bloom, Harold
    view of "Yahweh" 180n. 12
    on wisdom 3, 115–17, 128
Bockmuehl, Markus 13
Book of Acts 29, 31
Buber, Martin 4, 64, 176n. 73
    contributions to Jewish-Christian
        dialogue 1–2
    God of 1
    nonteleological theory of human
        nature 64
    on Rabbinic Judaism 133n. 4
Burrell, David B. 6, 146n. 66
    on faith in the free Creator 3
    Jewish-Christian friendship 11

Cain 71, 74, 115
    criminal guilt 101, 175n. 65
Carmel, Abraham 15
ceremonial laws 36, 98, 110
chance 58, 60
charity
    supernatural virtue of 108–9
Christian anti-Judaism
    contributing factor to Nazi
        ideology 14–15
Christian anti-supersessionism 3
Christian ecclesiology 40–2, 157n. 48
Christianity
    Buber on 133n. 4
    commonalities between Judaism
        and 51, 61, 144n. 43, 145n. 56,
        150n. 120, 155n. 22
    critical convictions of 27–8
    differences between Judaism and 22,
        51–2, 113, 140n. 6, 155n. 22
    forbiddance of Torah
        observance 148n. 86
    Israel of God and 17–20
    Kinzer on 27, 38–9
    status in Jewish polity 17
    understanding of Judaism qua
        Judaism 25–6
Church
    avoidance of supersessionism 28

Christological and Trinitarian
    doctrine 24
halakhic Christianity and 26
on Jews 141n. 17
multinational extension of people of
    Israel 29, 30
rejection of harsh
    supersessionism 18
relationship between Christ and 35
Second Vatican Council's Dogmatic
    Constitution on 41
circumcision 2, 20, 148n. 93
    Kinzer's reading of Paul's view of 32
    Paul on 33, 34–5
Cohen, Hermann 122, 156n. 42,
    176n. 73
conversion 5, 15, 140n. 8, 168n. 130,
    172n. 17
counter-supersessionism 18–20
covenant 144n. 39
    creation and 63–8, 92
    Kinzer's understanding of fidelity
        to 28, 30
covenantal *Gestalt* 101–2
Covenantal Rights (Novak) 63
Cox, Kenneth, Father *see* Carmel,
    Abraham
creation 87
    covenant and 63–8, 92
    revelation and 99–101, 104

Dabru Emet 142n. 28, 146n. 66
da Costa, Uriel 182n. 50
Dawkins, Richard 10
Decalogue
    covenantal particularity of 104–5
    dispensations of 103–4
    inclusion of Sabbath in 105, 106
    natural law and 107–8
    precepts of 176n. 89
    violations of 102–3
De Trinitate (Augustine) 78
dietary laws 31, 32, 36, 37, 148n. 93,
    149n. 96, 149n. 110
    prohibition of eating pork 38, 100
Di Noia, Joseph Augustine
    understanding of traditions 4

divine freedom 67–9, 78, 81–2, 162n. 30, 162n. 35
divine goodness 79–81, 126, 162n. 32
divine justice 59–60, 67, 103–4, 162n. 30, 183n. 5
divine power
  human nature and 63–8
divine transcendence 68, 91, 122, 167n. 10
  huqqim and 125–6, 127
  image of God and 85–7

economic supersessionism 2
edot 124, 125, 126, 127, 128, 129, 183n. 70
ekklesia 2, 30–1, 39, 40–2, 147n. 83, 147n. 85–6, 148n. 89, 148n. 93, 151n. 126, 152n. 138
election, doctrine of 3, 13, 28, 55, 87, 95, 115, 119, 128–9, 132, 143n. 31, 153n. 150
  life of wisdom and 120–8
  philosophical retrieval of 120–4
  Thomistic gratuitous election 96–7
The Election of Israel: The Idea of the Chosen People (Novak) 115
embryonic life 7–10, 138n. 45, 138n. 47, 139n. 51
Enumah 1
Epicurus
  on providence 58
eucharistic rite 150n. 120
Eve 66–7, 101
  fall of 89

faith
  Kinzer's critique of Paul's notion of 36
fear of God 64–5, 161n. 15
food laws *see* dietary laws
freedom
  God's 67–9, 78, 81–2, 162n. 30, 162n. 35
  human 47, 67, 75, 76, 162n. 30
free will 59–60, 166n. 95–6
  image of God and 79, 80–2, 166n. 95, 167n. 96

"From Supersessionism to Parallelism in Jewish-Christian Dialogue" (Novak) 17, 18
Fuchs, Josef
  position on natural law 74

Genesis
  Kass readings of 118, 180n. 27
  Novak's reading of image of God in 63, 65–7, 90
gentile *ekklesia* 30, 39, 40–2, 148n. 86, 152n. 138
Gnosticism 4–5
God
  fear of 64–5, 161n. 15
  I-Thou relationship with 1
  knowledge 159n. 84
  obedience to voice of 56–7, 61
  omniscience of 58–9
  proofs of existence of 157n. 64
  relationship of human beings with 63–5, 70, 79, 158n. 67
  Torah's friendship with 173n. 34
  see also headings beginning with divine . . ., *e.g.* divine freedom; image of God
Gomorrah 67, 101
goodness 167n. 96
  for ancient philosophers 79–80
  divine 79–81, 126, 162n. 32
Gregory of Nyssa
  on image of God 79, 80
Grotius, Hugo 93, 161n. 12
The Guide of the Perplexed (Maimonides) 99

Habakkuk, Prophet 60
halakhah 93, 134n. 10, 135n. 21, 149n. 96
happiness
  Thomistic view 56, 81–2
Harnack, Adolph von 5
Hegel, Georg Wilhelm Friedrich
  philosophy of religion 144n. 35
Hesychius 105
Hillel, Rabbi 116

Hittinger, Russell 76, 165n. 85
  on Catholic theologians treatment of natural law 74
  on Christian anthropology 165n. 71
  on Enlightenment account of human freedom 75
  on image of God 77
  on natural law 48
Holocaust 14, 148n. 89, 152n. 143, 154n. 3
Holy Land
  as sign of providence 47–51, 53, 61
human beings
  dialogic status of 66–7
  identification as rational animals 74
  as image of God *see* image of God
  providence and 59–60
  relationship between God and 158n. 67
  special status of 65–6, 75, 85–6
human freedom 47, 162n. 30
  compared to God's freedom 67
  Hittinger's account of 75, 76
human nature 48, 171n. 2, 179n. 149, 183n. 70
  critique of image of God as inherent property of 69
  divine power and 63–8
  nonteleological theories of 64
huqqim 124, 125–6, 127, 128, 129
Hütter, Reinhard 6

idolatry 14, 19, 97, 98, 107, 113, 142n. 28
  Adam and Eve's sin of 101
  prohibition of 93
  violence and 71–2
Ignatius of Antioch 38
image of God 10, 63, 159n. 2, 161n. 20, 166n. 95, 169n. 42, 170n. 150
  autonomy and 78–82
  biblical mention 161n. 20
  divine transcendence and 85–7
  Italian humanists interpretation 89
  Novak's position vis-à-vis traditional view 77–8

  as relationship 69–72
  as shadow 72–7
immortality 118, 162n. 26
incarnation 23–5, 157n. 48
  image of God and 87–9
injustice
  providence and 57–61
intellection 83, 122
interhuman relationship laws 124–5
inwardness tradition 5
Isaac 29, 50, 59, 68, 103, 126, 129, 132
Islam
  cognatic with Judaism 144n. 43
  Maimonides on 160n. 8
Israel
  covenantal intimacy with God 97–9
  covenantal privileges 27–9
  edot and 125
  election of *see* election, doctrine of
  eschatological vindication 43
  God's covenantal relationship with 68, 70–1, 108
  national redemption 32
  Noahide law and 94–6
  Novak's location of Paul and Christ within 155n. 28
  particularity of 102
  relationship with YHWH 2–3
I-Thou relationship with God 1

Jacob 29, 59, 68, 104, 119, 132
Jawien, Andrzej 48
  see also John Paul II, Pope
Jerome, St.
  debate over Paul's Torah observance 38
Jerusalem 24, 32, 37, 91, 145n. 53
Jesus Christ 14, 129, 145n. 56, 155n. 28, 177n. 112
  Church and 35–6
  encounter with Samaritan woman 37, 49
  image and form of fallen man 170n. 150
  image of God and 88
  Israel's covenantal privileges and 27–9

Kinzer on 151n. 137
messianic status 16, 23–5, 26, 42–3, 45, 141n. 18, 145n. 53, 145n. 58, 148n. 86, 153n. 152
teleological fulfillment of Israel in 21
Torah and 33
Jewish beliefs and practices 4
Jewish-Christian dialogue 2–3, 10–11, 46, 130–2
   Buber's contributions 1–2
   goals of 4–6
   supersessionism and 16, 18–19
   theological character of 5, 130
   on theonomy/providence 53, 55, 56–7
Jewish-Christian Dialogue (Novak) 47, 53
Jewish-Christianity
   apostolic generation 13
   Messianic Judaism convergence with 22–7
Jewish law 93, 172n. 24, 182n. 50
   on Christians in Jewish polity 17
   on embryonic life 7–8
John of Damascus, St.
   on image of God 79, 80, 82
John Paul II, Pope 6, 57, 91
   address to Synagogue of Rome 6
   on Christianity and Judaism 153n. 144
   on embryonic life 10
   on good and evil 154n. 3
   on Holy Land as sign of providence 47–51, 53, 61
John, St.
   on messianic fulfillment of God's covenant 37
Johnson, Luke Timothy 35
"Journey to the Holy Places" (Jawien) 48
Judaism
   "beliefs and practices" 4
   commonalities between Christianity and 51, 61, 144n. 43, 145n. 56, 150n. 120, 155n. 22
   differences between Christianity and 22, 51–2, 113, 140n. 6, 155n. 22
   incarnation and Trinity and 24–5
   Islam and 144n. 43
   Israel of God and 17–20
   postmissionary Messianic Judaism and 42–4
   saving of Christianity from Gnosticism 4–5
   understanding of Judaism qua 25–6
   view of Messianic Judaism 26–7
Judea desert 49
judicial laws 110
   of Torah 98

Kant, Immanuel 64, 164n. 64
Kass, Leon
   reading of Genesis 120, 180n. 27
   on wisdom 3, 115, 117–19, 128
King, Martin Luther 161n. 20
Kinzer, Mark S. 44, 146n. 68, 147n. 76, 147n. 80, 147n. 86
   on Christ 151n. 137
   on Christianity 27–8
   on Christianity development 38–9
   on "covenant fidelity" 30
   on *ekklesia* 40–2, 147n. 83, 148n. 86
   on Judaism 42, 43–4
   lack of reference to Trinity or incarnation 150n. 123
   Messianic Judaism of 13
   on New Testament 31–2
   on Paul 148n. 96, 152n. 141
   proposal to overcome supersessionism 2, 27–30, 44–5
   on Rabinowitz's contributions 151n. 132
   reading of Paul, critique on 34–8
   understanding of "messianic" in Messianic Judaism 30
knowing and loving
   Thomistic 86–7, 90, 91
Kuyper, Abraham 89

Leithart, Peter 5
Levenson, Jon 132, 142n. 28, 155n. 22, 161n. 21
Levinas, Emmanuel 163n. 44, 176n. 73
Lindbeck, George 4, 12–13, 135n. 21, 139n. 3

Luke, St. 31, 148n. 92
Lumen Gentium 41, 42, 151n. 127
Luther, Martin 178n. 124
  on Mosaic law 110

McCade, John 25
MacIntyre, Alasdair 4, 15
magisterium 145n. 52
Maimonides, Moses 57, 92
  on Islam 160n. 8
  on natural law 99, 171n. 2
  on Noahide law 54
  Novak on Noahide law of 156n. 44
  Novak on teleology of 64, 162n. 35
  Novak's critique of 175n. 54
  on providence 47, 57–61, 158n. 77
  on rationality of Mosaic law
    173n. 40
  on revelation 122
  understanding of human
    relationship to God 68, 158n. 67
Marcionite anti-Judaism 40
Mark, St. 36
Meilaender, Gilbert 9
Memory and Identity: Conversations at the Dawn of a Millennium (John Paul) 47, 154n. 3, 157n. 64
Mendelssohn, Moses 1
messiahhood 15–16, 23–5, 26, 42–3, 45, 141n. 18, 145n. 53, 145n. 58, 148n. 86, 153n. 152
Messianic Judaism 2, 146n. 68–9, 148n. 89
  Christians acceptance of 25–6
  emergence of forms of 23
  Jewish Christianity convergence with 22–7
  Novak's treatment 2
  origin 41
  rabbinic change of view of 26–7
  rabbinic rejection of Judaism of 45–6
  relationship to rabbinic Judaism 147n. 85
  supersessionism and 12–14
  theological difficulty posed for Christianity 26–7

Middleton, Richard 170n. 161
  on image of God 89–90, 160n. 2
miscarriage
  punishment for causing 8–9
  see also abortion
mishpatim 124–5, 127, 128, 129, 183n. 70
Moltmann, Jürgen 90
Moriah, land of 50, 103
Mosaic law 10, 100, 101, 102, 110, 177n. 112, 178n. 124
  adherence to 38
  Maimonides emphasis on rationality of 173n. 40
  Noahide law and 138n. 37, 171n. 2
Moses 54, 101, 102, 104, 105, 108, 110, 138n. 50, 159n. 79, 176n. 89
mother's life
  abortion and 9–10
murder 167n. 116, 175n. 65
  prohibition of 8, 9, 94, 100, 110, 137n. 37, 138n. 50, 163n. 44
Mu'tazila
  on providence 58, 59

Nahmanides 7
natural law 92, 114, 138n. 37, 171n. 2–3, 172n. 21, 174n. 49, 174n. 53, 178n. 133
  Catholic theologians' view 74
  Decalogue and 107–8
  examples from pre-Sinai narratives of the Scripture 101
  justification and 112–13
  Novak on 65
  obedience to 111–12
  Protestant theologians' view 179n. 149
  teleological view 99
  Torah and 97–9
  see also Noahide law
Natural Law in Judaism (Novak) 63, 92, 144n. 39, 160n. 12, 161n. 15
Nazism
  Christian anti-Judaism and 14–15
negative anthropology 75
Neusner, Jacob 52, 130, 156n. 30

New Testament 29, 148n. 86, 148n. 92
  Kinzer's exegesis 39, 42
  Kinzer's reading of Jews and Judaism in 31–2
  Old Testament and 20–1
  sacrament "signs" of 39
Nineveh
  in the book of Jonah 92
Noah
  children of 94
Noahide law 10, 54, 92–4, 114, 137n. 37, 182n. 50
  critique on Maimonides account of 156n. 44
  Jewish theological conception of 7, 8
  Jews relationship to 94–6
  see also natural law
nonhuman creatures
  providence and 59, 61
non-supersessionist ecclesiology 30
Nostra Aetate 6, 137n. 33, 153n. 144
Novak, David 137n. 36, 182n. 51
  on abortion 7–10, 138n. 48
  on Buber-Tillich's dialogue 1–2
  on Cain 175n. 65
  on Christ's messianic status 22–5
  on covenantal election 182n. 51
  on covenantal Gestalt 99–102
  criticism of Marmonides potency-act teleology 55–6
  emphasis on God's absolute power 64–5
  emphasis on obedience to God's voice 56–7, 61
  on God's knowledge 159n. 84
  identity of 136n. 30
  on image of God 69–78, 84, 90–1
  importance of theonomy 56–7
  on Jewish-Christian dialogue 130–1
  location of Paul and Christ within Israel 155n. 28
  on Maimonides and Aquinas's natural law 61
  on Messianic Judaism 43
  on natural law 65, 171n. 3, 174n. 49, 174n. 53, 175n. 64

on Noahide law 92, 93–6, 114, 137n. 37
"open philosophical exegesis of Scripture" 1–2, 130
on priority of covenant 63
reading of Maimonides' account of Noahide law 156n. 44
rejection of rational animal definition 76
rejection of spiritual triumphalism 51–3
on revelations 156n. 32
on singularity 53–5, 156n. 40
on supersessionism 2, 14–22, 45
on Torah 181n. 40
understanding of shadowy constitution of human 164n. 64
on wisdom 120–8

Old Testament 5, 38, 55, 64, 109, 113, 132, 144n. 35, 155n. 22, 178n. 124
  New Testament and 20–1
oral Torah 8, 12, 20–1, 145n. 53
original sin 66–7, 71, 103, 161n. 21

partial-birth abortion 9
Passover 96, 124, 125, 182n. 59
Pauline Christian Judaism 143n. 29
Paul, St. 18, 24, 52, 112, 152n. 141
  on Christ messianic kingship 24
  on circumcision 32, 148n. 93
  on dietary laws 148n. 93, 149n. 110
  ekklesia 151n. 126
  image of Church as "olive tree" 17
  Kinzer's critique on Jewish practices of 149n. 96
  on original sin 66
  purification of 31–2
  on supersessionism 142n. 24
  on Torah observance 32–4
  on Torah observance, critique of Kinzer 34–8
peace 6, 53, 109, 131, 132, 178n. 117
Pelagius 109
personal freedom
  compatibility of theonomy with 56–7

Peter, St. 24, 50, 151n. 137
  on dietary laws 32
  living "like a Gentile" 33
Pico della Mirandola, Giovanni 89
pilgrimage
  to Holy Land 48–9, 50–1, 53, 56
  theonomy and 57–8
pork
  prohibition of eating 38, 100
postmissionary Messianic Judaism
    27–30, 147n. 76
  Judaism and 42–4
  problems 30–1
pre-Sinai narratives 102–4
  examples from 101
providence 47
  Holy Land as sign of 47–51
  Maimonides on 158n. 77
  suffering of the just and 57–61
punitive supersessionism 2

rabbi(s)
  authority on Jewish beliefs and
    practices 45
  guidelines for sojourners in Israel
    (*ger toshav*) 17
  Noahide law and 93
rabbinic Judaism 2–3, 12–13, 25, 130,
    148n. 89
  Buber on 133n. 4
  Christians' understanding of 26
  view on Messianic Judaism 26–7,
    147n. 85
Rabinowitz, Joseph 41
  Kinzer on contributions of 151n. 132
radical/harsh supersessionism
  Christian rejection of 18, 19, 20
  Novak's rejection of 40, 46
  theological deficiency 20–1
Rashi
  on embryonic life 7, 9, 138n. 42
rationality 166n. 93, 166n. 95
  image of God and 71–4, 78–9, 82–4,
    87, 90–1
  Novak's rejection of definition of
    rational animal 76
Ratzinger, Joseph *see* Benedict XVI, Pope

revelation 52, 53, 55–6, 175n. 64
  creation and 99–101, 104
  of religious authority 156n. 32
right to life 7–10, 138n. 42, 139n. 51
robbery 102–3, 174n. 49
  prohibition of 93, 94
Rosenzweig, Franz 122, 133n. 4,
    144n. 39
  emphasis on Jewish learning 1
  on Judaism, Christianity and Gnostic
    elements 4–5

Saadiah 57, 89
  Novak's critique of 144n. 39
Sabbath 104–7, 108, 110, 114, 148n. 93,
    149n. 96
  violation of 7
Saul 19
Schleiermacher, Friedrich 5, 143n. 31,
    144n. 35
Schwartz, Regina 115
self-defense, principle of 9
self-movement
  image of God and 79, 80–2
sexual immorality 8
  Joseph's refusal to commit
    adultery 101
  prohibition of 93, 110, 137n. 37
Shoah 6, 14, 136n. 31, 141n. 17
sin(s)
  consequences of 107–8, 128
  conversion and 148n. 8
  God's promise to judge 59, 60
  mortal sin 38
  natural law and 98–9
  original sin 66–7, 71, 103, 161n. 21
  sacrifices and 173n. 34
singularity 53–4, 125, 128, 156n. 40,
    176n. 73
  relationship to the general 54–5,
    121–2, 156n. 40
Sodom 67, 101
sojourners in Israel (*ger toshav*) 17
Soloveitchik, Joseph B., Rabbi 143n. 34
soul
  body and 99, 165n. 86, 168n. 127
  image of the Trinity and 78–9

powers of 83
spiritual nature of 83–4, 169n. 130
Soulen, Kendall R. 142n. 27
　on risen Jesus 43
　on supersessionism kinds 2
　view of abortion 9, 139n. 58
Spinoza, Baruch 143n. 31, 181n. 50, 182n. 53
　Novak's critique of election doctrine of 120–2
　rejection of rabbinic readings of Bible 122–3
spiritual triumphalism 51–3
Stein, Edith 15, 43, 140n. 8, 141n. 21
Stephen, St. 24
Strauss, Eduard 1
structural supersessionism 2
sufferings 60, 116, 129
　Jewish 143–4, 152n. 143
　of the just 57–9
Summa theologiae (Aquinas) 92, 173n. 25
supersessionism 2, 12, 142n. 24
　emergence of forms of Messianic Judaism and 23
　Jewish counter supersessionists *vs.* 18–20
　Kinzer's proposal to overcome 2, 27–30, 44–5
　Messianic Judaism and 12–14
　Novak's kinds of 17–18
　Soulen's kinds of 2
Sykes, Stephen 5

Talmud 93, 144n. 38
　Jews conception of relationship between Torah and 20
　view of embryonic life 7, 8–9
Tarphon, Rabbi 116
teleology 20–2, 55, 172n. 11
　Novak on Maimonides' 64
　Novak on Saadiah's 144n. 39
theological liberalism
　key ingredients of 5
theology
　speculative and practical 6–11
　teleology 20–2

theonomous morality 47, 56–7
theonomy 3, 10, 47, 61–2
　John Paul on 47–51
　Novak on 56–7
Tillich, Paul 1–2
Torah 2, 137n. 37, 138n. 50, 156n. 44, 160n. 8, 163n. 35, 172n. 17, 175n. 54, 180n. 22, 181n. 40
　choosing secularity over observance of 122
　correlation of election with 124
　friendship with God and 173n. 34
　Israel's acceptance of 94, 95
　Israel's election and 120
　Jews conception of relationship between Talmud and 20
　observance of 28, 29, 30, 32–8, 70–1, 139n. 3, 143n. 29, 145n. 58, 146n. 69, 148n. 86, 150n. 116, 152n. 139
　Paul's observance of 38
　simultaneous positive and negative pedagogy of 97–9
　wisdom and 121
traditions 4
　coherence and comprehensiveness of 5
transcendence
　divine 68, 78, 85–7, 122, 125, 167n. 110
　human 75–6, 116
　wisdom and 117
the Trinity 19, 23–5, 150n. 116, 157n. 48
　Augustine on 78–9
　Kinzer's lack of reference to 150n. 123

unborn children
　grace of sanctification 83

Veritatis Splendor (John Paul encyclical) 47, 165n. 85
violence
　idolatry and 71
Volf, Miroslav 4, 5
Von Balthasar, Hans Urs 1

Watson, Francis 140n. 26, 143n. 29, 148n. 93
"When Jews Are Christians" (Novak) 23, 27, 42, 145n. 52
Where Shall Wisdom Be Found? (Bloom) 3, 115, 117
wisdom 3, 128–9, 131–2, 160n. 12
   approaches to 115
   election and 120–8
   esoteric/aesthetic view 115–17
   philosophic and ethical view 117–19

Wojtyla, Karol *see* John Paul II, Pope
Word incarnate 87–9
Wright, N. T. 24
Wyschogrod, Michael 140n. 3, 143n. 28, 146n. 66, 146n. 69, 150n. 116, 151n. 138
   on Torah observance 38–9

Yoder, John Howard 42

Zunz, Leopold 1